Palgrave Macmillan Memory Studies

The nascent field of Memory Studies emerges from contemporary trends that include a shift from concern with historical knowledge of events to that of memory, from 'what we know' to 'how we remember it'; changes in generational memory; the rapid advance of technologies of memory; panics over declining powers of memory, which mirror our fascination with the possibilities of memory enhancement; and the development of trauma narratives in reshaping the past. These factors have contributed to an intensification of public discourses on our past over the last thirty years. Technological, political, interpersonal, social and cultural shifts affect what, how and why people and societies remember and forget. This groundbreaking series tackles questions such as: What is 'memory' under these conditions? What are its prospects, and also the prospects for its interdisciplinary and systematic study? What are the conceptual, theoretical and methodological tools for its investigation and illumination?

Stefan Berger · Thomas Fetzer
Editors

Collective Memory of Economic Crises and Transformations

palgrave
macmillan

Editors
Stefan Berger
Ruhr University Bochum
Bochum, Nordrhein-Westfalen, Germany

Thomas Fetzer
Central European University
Vienna, Austria

ISSN 2634-6257 ISSN 2634-6265 (electronic)
Palgrave Macmillan Memory Studies
ISBN 978-3-032-09093-5 ISBN 978-3-032-09094-2 (eBook)
https://doi.org/10.1007/978-3-032-09094-2

This work was supported by Tohoku University.

Cover credit: Front cover image by Erzsébet Rácz

This Palgrave Macmillan imprint is published by the registered company Springer Nature Switzerland AG
The registered company address is: Gewerbestrasse 11, 6330 Cham, Switzerland

Contents

Notes on Contributors

Stefan Berger is Professor of Social History and Director of the Institute for Social Movements at Ruhr University Bochum. He is also executive chair of the Foundation History of the Ruhr and honorary professor at Cardiff University in the UK. He has published widely on the comparative history of social movements, on histories of de-industrialisation and industrial heritage, on the history of nationalism and national identity, on British-German relations, and on the cultural heritage of war. His most recent publications include, e.g., *Industrial Heritage and Regional Identity*, edited with Christian Wicke and Jana Golombek, London: Routledge, 2018.

Youssef Cassis is Professor at the Robert Schuman Centre for Advanced Studies, European University Institute, Florence, and Director of the European Research Council funded project MERCATOR—'The Memory of Financial Crises: Financial Actors and Global Risk'. His work focuses mainly on banking and financial history, as well as business history more generally. His most recent books include, e.g., *Capitals of Capital. A History of International Financial Centres, 1780–2005*, Cambridge: CUP, 2006. He has edited several books in economic and financial history, including, with Catherine Schenk, *Remembering and Learning from Financial Crises*, Oxford: OUP, 2021.

Marguérite Corporaal, is Full Professor of Irish Literature in Transnational Contexts at Radboud University, the Netherlands. She was PI of

Relocated Remembrance: The Great Famine in Irish (Diaspora) Fiction, 1847–1921. Corporaal was awarded an NWO-VICI grant for her project *Redefining the Region.* Furthermore, Corporaal is the PI of *Heritages of Hunger*, funded as part of the Dutch research council NWO's NWA programme. She is the author of *Relocated Memories of the Great Famine in Irish and Diaspora Fiction, 1847–70*, Syracuse: SUP, 2017, and co-editor of, amongst others, *Famines and the Making of Heritage*, London: Routledge, 2024.

Linara Dovydaitytė is Associate Professor of Art History at the Faculty of Arts, and a senior researcher at V. Kavolis Transdisciplinary Research Institute at Vytautas Magnus University in Kaunas, Lithuania. Her research focuses on Soviet art and heritage, visual culture, and museum studies. Recently, her writings attended to the cultural representations of modern industry, including nuclear one, as in her co-authored book *Learning the Nuclear: Educational Tourism in (Post)Industrial Sites*, Berlin: Peter Lang, 2021. Currently, she is co-editing a book to be published by UCL Press introducing nuclear cultural heritage as a novel area of interdisciplinary research and practice.

Thomas Fetzer is Associate Professor at Central European University Vienna, Department of International Relations. His research deals with the role of ideas in the international political economy, with a specific focus on (economic) nationalism, as well as with the social dimension of the international political economy. In recent years, he has also been involved in projects addressing the significance of history and memory politics for International Relations, with particular emphasis on the recent transformations unleashed by Russia's war of aggression against Ukraine.

Oliver Kühschelm is co-director of the Institute of Rural History in St. Pölten, Austria. He also teaches history at the University of Vienna, where in 2017 he gained his habilitation in economic and social history. He has published about history of the middle classes, business, and consumption, the construction of national imaginaries and national economies, as well as on the history of migration. His current research focusses on industrial heritage in rural areas and the social and cultural history of Austrian direct investments in the former socialist countries. His publications include, e.g., *Geflohen und Geblieben*, Wien: Böhlau, 2024.

Naoki Odanaka is Professor of Socio-Intellectual History at the School of Economics, Tohoku University (Sendai, Japan). He has published on the socio-economic history of France and on the history-related sciences (historical theory, methodology of history, historiography, history education, and so on). His most recent publication includes, e.g., La Pergola: Un grand ensemble résidentiel à Montpellier (1960–2010), in *Etudes Héraultaises*, Vol. 54, 2020, and Continuity and Change in the Historiography of Contemporary Japan (1945-present): Nation-State and Progressivism, in *Routledge Companion to East Asian Historiography*, edited by Q. Edward Wang, London: Routledge, forthcoming.

Giuseppe Telesca is Tutor in Contemporary Economic History at the University of Glasgow. From 2021 to 2025, he was research fellow at the Robert Schuman Centre for Advanced Studies, European University Institute, Florence, where he worked on the ERC-funded project: 'MERCATOR. The Memory of Financial Crises: Financial Actors and Global Risk'. He has published on the memory of financial crises, the evolution of financial elites, the history of the Italian banking system, and the relationship between sport and business. His publications include, e.g., *History, Memory, and the Return of Financial Crises After Bretton Woods,* co-edited with Youssef Cassis, Oxford: OUP, forthcoming.

Ruzanna Tsaturyan is a researcher at the Institute of Archaeology and Ethnography, National Academy of Sciences of Armenia. She also teaches at the Faculty of History at Yerevan State University, Armenia. Her research focuses on cultural heritage, social resilience, gender, and memory. Her recent publications include *Charents Memorial Hall in Charentsavan: Ideology and Urbanism in a Soviet Town*, *Proceedings of the History Museum of Armenia*, No. 11, 2023; and Curating Mnemonic Security: Museum Responses to War in Armenia and Poland (with Joanna Wawrzyniak), in *Pathways to Agonism: Disputed Territories and Memory*, *Mobilizing Memories* series, Volume 6, Brill, 2025.

Tetiana Vodotyka is the Academic Director of the M.A. in Urban Studies and Post War Reconstruction at the Kyiv School of Economics. Born in Kherson and educated at Taras Shevchenko National University of Kyiv and the Institute of History of Ukraine (Ph.D., 2014), she has a distinguished record in urban and economic history. Her research spans the history of entrepreneurship and urban culture in nineteenth to early twentieth-century Ukraine. Vodotyka leads the ejournal *City:*

History, Culture, Society and is the author and co-author of several nonfiction works, e.g., *2023 Challenge. Opportunity. Change. The History of Ukrainian Entrepreneurship.*

Joanna Wawrzyniak is an associate professor of sociology and the founding director of the Center for Research on Social Memory at the University of Warsaw. Her research focuses on the memory of socialism, neoliberal transformation, deindustrialization, and the decolonization of heritage. Her recent books include the co-edited volume *Remembering the Neoliberal Turn*, London: Routledge, 2023, as well as the co-authored Cuts: An Oral History of Transformation (in Polish), *Krytyka Polityczna*, 2020. She currently serves as President of the Memory Studies Association (2024–2025) and as Vice-Chair of the COST Action Slow Memory: Transformative Practices for Times of Uneven and Accelerating Change.

List of Figures

List of Tables

Introduction: Collective Memory in the Context of Economic Crises and Transformations

Stefan Berger and Thomas Fetzer

Memory narratives of economic crises and transformations often leave powerful long-term legacies that not only feed into subsequent political debate but are also drawn upon as purported lessons in addressing contemporary challenges and crises. Such dynamics could be observed during the 2007/8 global financial crisis (Cassis and Schenk 2021), as much as during the European state debt crisis of the early 2010s (Verovšek 2014; O'Callaghan 2012). Still more dramatically, in Russia, narratives of the economic and social dislocations of the 'lost 1990s' have arguably contributed to the rise of imperialist revanchism over the last decades (Malinova 2024), while 'Trumpist' economic nationalist agendas in the United States have continuously harked back to imagined past 'Golden Ages' of power and prosperity ever since the mid-2010s.

S. Berger (✉)
Ruhr University Bochum, Bochum, Germany
e-mail: stefan.berger@rub.de

T. Fetzer
Central European University, Vienna, Austria

S. Berger and T. Fetzer (eds.), *Collective Memory of Economic Crises and Transformations*, Palgrave Macmillan Memory Studies,
https://doi.org/10.1007/978-3-032-09094-2_1

1 The Economy/Memory Nexus—A Story of Relative Neglect

These prominent examples notwithstanding, little attention has so far been paid to the economy in the discipline of memory studies—witness, for example, the marginal consideration given to economic themes in the numerous 'realms of memory' volumes that have been published since Nora's pioneering work (Nora 1996). Thirty years later, memory studies has developed into its own thriving discipline with a flagship journal, *Memory Studies*, and a hugely successful professional association which holds annual conferences attended by thousands of scholars from around the world. Much of this scholarship is dedicated to traumatic impact events, including war, genocide, and ethnic cleansing. Other work, in the wake of the phenomenal success of Nora's volumes and conceptual work, has focused on national memory, so much so that one is inclined to ask whether there are nations left in the world who have not written their 'realms of memory' (Berger and Seiffert 2014). Other institutions, from churches to political parties and from trade unions to social movements have also been turning their gaze to memory. Ancient historians have written the realms of memory of the ancient world (Stein-Hölkeskamp and Hölkeskamp 2020), medieval historians have followed suit (Schwedler 2021). And yet, all those processes that were not necessarily related to an institution and that were often slow in developing, tended to escape the attention of memory studies scholars. More recently Jenny Wüstenberg has developed the concept of 'slow memory' in order to redirect their attention to precisely those longer-term processes and developments (Wüstenberg 2023). The COST-project that is directed by her has developed a number of working groups which deal with different aspects of slow memory one of which, is concerned with the memory of work (Berger and Wawrzyniak, forthcoming). Work is at the heart of many economic processes, but 'the economy' is a much wider field than that of work. It involves business history, the history of marketing, the history of economic cycles, diverse forms of economic crises and economic nationalism, and many other facets which all generated forms of memory. Some of these themes have begun to be researched (see below), yet, as a discipline, memory studies has overall rather neglected the economic realm.

This overall pattern is particularly discernible in the growing scholarship on transnational and global memory, which has emerged in recent decades, closely associated with the 'connective turn' and the rise of digital memory studies (Hoskins 2017). While bringing together a great range of conceptual and methodological approaches, transnational memory scholarship has mostly been concerned with political and cultural dynamics, whether from a top-down perspective addressing the emergence of the global spread of a 'politics of regret' related to the memory of genocides, and associated with human rights promotion through international organizations (Levi and Sznajder 2002; Olick 2013), or from a bottom-up perspective dedicated to the hybrid 'in-between' memory cultures of migrant communities (Radstone and Wilson 2021). In the most widely cited programmatic work on transnational and global memory (Assmann and Conrad 2010; de Cesari and Rigney 2014; Wüstenberg 2019), economic themes are largely absent. Moreover, where scholars do consider the economy as a transnational realm, it is conceptualized as 'external' to memory. Studies concerned with the impact of global tourism on sites associated with the memory of mass violence, for example, accord significance to such commercial tourism flows in terms of how they 'feed' local memory into transnational mnemonic discourses on crimes against humanity. Yet, while cross-border economic flows can thus help create transnational 'spaces of memory', they have little bearing on mnemonic 'content', except that they tend to flatten and homogenize local memory to facilitate its transnational 'consumption' (e.g. Björkdahl and Kappler 2019).

In economic history, economics, and political economy scholarship, conversely, memory narratives have hardly been systematically explored, despite the fact that the last two decades have witnessed the emergence of multiple new approaches to address the relationship between culture and the economy. Yet, neither 'cultural economic history' (Berghahn 2010), nor 'cultural economics' (Fernandez 2016), 'cultural economy' (du Gay and Pryke 2002), or 'cultural political economy' (Best and Paterson 2010) scholarship has demonstrated much interest in questions of historical memory. Political economy scholars working from within constructivist or discursive institutionalist approaches have programmatically highlighted the significance of memory narratives alongside other discursive repertoires (see Schmidt 2008). However, their empirical work rarely foregrounds memory and remembrance.

2 The Economy/Memory Nexus: An Emerging Theme

While a systematic encounter between the disciplines of memory studies and economics/political economy has thus not yet developed, a range of so far rather isolated literatures, from different disciplines, clearly point to the importance of economic events and processes for collective memory (and vice versa).

Drawing on work on the nexus between nationalism and economy (Crane 1998; Berger and Fetzer 2019; Pickel 2022; Reinert 2023), for example, the significance of past economic achievements for national identity narratives is easy to discern. Indeed, as the popular trope about the 'economic miracles' in post-1945 Germany and Japan indicates, rapid and unexpected economic success may be remembered in quasi-religious terms of salvation and redemption (Müller 2005). Conversely, economic crises or catastrophes also leave their traces—witness the prominence of the Great Famine for Irish collective memory (Mark-Fitzgerald 2013; Corporaal 2017) or the important role of nineteenth century imperialist exploitation for memory narratives both in the imperialist states and the colonized ones (Geppert and Müller 2015; Thampi 2005).

From a very different, transnational perspective, recent work has highlighted the significance of past financial crises for the current governance of the global economy (Cassis and Schenk 2021). Brigitte Granville has described the attempt by economists and policymakers to control inflation as an exercise involving the memory of past inflationary pressures on the economy (Granville 2013). Maria Tamboukou has examined how the memory of work has been gendered in the transatlantic garment industry (Tamboukou 2016). Addressing the corporate level, researchers have highlighted organizational cultures of remembrance (Mai 2015), while others have pointed to the ways in which specific firms and products can acquire symbolic meaning for broader narratives about the past (Kühschelm 2019), a question that is also addressed in the literature on the use of memory in marketing and advertising. Moreover, closely associated with this latter theme, scholars have highlighted the pervasiveness of heritage tourism and practices of 'place branding' (Aronczyk 2013).

Systemic economic transformations have likewise been demonstrated to be important vectors of collective memory constructions (Wawrzyniak 2021), as have industrial heritage, and associated distinct regional cultures (Berger 2019). Regarding post-1945 Europe, economy-related memory of large-scale transformations has been explored in the context of postwar reconstruction (Holm 2016; Treber 2014) and of the systemic transformation in Central and Eastern Europe during the 1990s (Pehe and Wawrzyniak 2024).

A particularly dynamic field of research has been dealing with the relationship between collective memory and economic redress for past injustice, originating in attempts to deal with crimes against humanity during World War Two (Filipkowski and Wawrzaniak 2023). Following West Germany's commitment to payments to Israel and individual Holocaust survivors in the early 1950s (Bachleitner 2021), economic redress claims were subsequently extended to cover Nazi Germany's forced labour system; in the process, the memory of the victims acquired public prominence, while financial compensation measures, even if inadequate in their implicit 'monetization' of historical injustice, came to be considered as an important element of transitional justice agendas. Recent debates about requests for German war reparations in Greece and Poland testify to the continued political salience of these mnemonic dynamics (Kilian 2016; Sopinski 2022).

Other scholars have explored how, partly building on the memory activism related to compensation for victims of Nazi crimes, economic redress debates have since spread to many other contexts (see Moffett 2017). Apart from Latin America with its longer-established transitional justice systems (Skaar et al. 2016), economic redress debates have been examined in relation to post-Apartheid South Africa, post-communist Central and Eastern Europe (Kuti 2009), former Yugoslav countries in the wake of the wars of the 1990s (Barton-Hronesova 2021), as well as in the context of reconciliation processes vis-à-vis indigenous populations across the globe (Lenzerini 2008). In recent years, a particularly important debate has revolved around the memory of slavery and colonialism as systems of economic exploitation (Araujo 2020).

Diametrically opposite to memories of injustice and exploitation, other research has emphasized that economy-related mnemonic narratives of 'old regimes' may also take various forms of nostalgia. The salience of such narratives has been particularly demonstrated in the context of the transition from planned to market economies in Eastern Europe during the 1990s and 2000s. Sociologists unearthed different concepts underlying nostalgia—one reading highlighted a 'retrospective utopia' that contrasted socialist ideals of solidarity with the often harsh realities of transition economies (Velikonja 2009), while an alternative narrative focused on notions of a 'people's economy' centred on a lost world of informal barter deals, which had helped in coping with the vicissitudes of centrally planned economies (see Buzalka 2018). A great deal of research was also dedicated to the question how post-socialist nostalgia was expressed in consumer culture (Bach 2002; Volcic 2007). In most instances, this mirrored what Svetlana Boym has called 'reflective nostalgia', characterized by irony and humour (exemplified in 'ostalgic' films like *Good Bye Lenin*—see Cook 2007), while lacking the strong ideological beliefs associated with 'restorative nostalgia' (Boym 2007). However, the case of Russia reminds us of the importance of the latter category—here, banal nostalgia for the economic security of the late Soviet Union successively merged with wider narratives about the loss of great power status and thus came to be linked to the political descent into autocracy under Putin (Mazur 2015).

3 Our Volume and its Contributions

While this brief review has highlighted a variety of research strands and themes, these are all embedded in very specific sub-fields of inquiry, which are scattered across different literature contexts and academic disciplines, thus lacking visibility as a field of study. Our book seeks to bring some of these diverse perspectives together and, going further, to advance a more systematic analysis of the relationship between collective memory narratives and the economy. Given the early stage of research on this theme, the book has an exploratory character, whose main aim is to provide a broad 'mapping' of the different ways in which analyses of the economy/memory nexus can be approached. We include different concepts of 'collective memory' (political, social, cultural), different methodologies, and a variety of specific empirical aspects, brought together under the broad theme of economic crises and transformations in the nineteenth and twentieth centuries. Moreover, the book employs a wide analytical scope, paying attention to a variety of economic 'carriers' of memory narratives (e.g. products, economic culture discourses, cross-border investment flows), with an equal focus on the role of collective memory narratives for the political management of economic transformations, as well as on its significance for longer-term social and cultural change. In sum, we conceptualize our book as an agenda-setting exercise for a new and distinct sub-field of studies—'collective memory and the economy'—demonstrating its conceptual and empirical potential to inspire more in-depth research in the future. We submit that the study of the economy/memory nexus should be taken more seriously by economic historians and (political) economists, as well as by memory studies scholars.

Our analyses will be guided by a twofold set of questions. On the one hand, we explore the genesis of economy-focused memory narratives: How, and under what conditions do economic crises and transformations shape the construction of such narratives? Who are the key actors and institutions in such processes? Which power relations underpin them? How are economy-focused narratives reflected at different levels of memory narratives, i.e. 'political/canon' vs. 'cultural/archive' (Assmann 2006)? On the other hand, we also investigate how such memory narratives acquire political salience in subsequent periods of time. To what extent and how are narratives about earlier economic crises and transformations later invoked as 'lessons' to be drawn/learnt from the past? How does the impact of memory narratives change over time? How, and why, does this impact vary across countries?

The volume is structured into four parts. Each part features two chapters, which address different types of economic crises and transformations, namely cyclical economic crises (Chapters 2 and 3), the transformation of industrial economies (Chapters 4 and 5), systemic economic transformations (Chapters 6 and 7), and the transformation of national economies through international economic integration (Chapters 8 and 9).

Financial crises resulting in stock exchange crashes were often followed by deep recessions. None so far was bigger than the 1929 Wall Street Crash and the ensuing banking crisis and Great Depression. When analyzing such cyclical economic crises as memory (Chapter 2), it is striking how much more 'impact events' (Fuchs 2012) such as the Wall Street crash or the Black Monday of 19 October 1987, register in memory than the often drawn-out economic crises that follow those 'spectacular events' (Nora 1989, 20). Cassis and Telesca show how important contemporary political contexts are for the prominence of collective memory. Thus, the crash of 1929 received much more attention on the occasion of its 50th anniversary in 1979 than in 2004, when it was 75 years since the occurrence of this most famous world-wide economic crisis. In 1979 the discussion of possible analogies triggered a memory boom in the context of the neoliberal turn which challenged Keynesianism that had held sway in economics from the 1940s to the 1970s. The competition between different economic theories and their impact on politics turned the memory of 1929 into hot memory that impacted on contemporary political debates (Lorenz 2014). In 2004, by contrast, there was no strong contemporary sounding board for the actualization of memory, which had, in effect, been archived. However, the financial and economic crisis of 2007/8 also underlined how memory can return powerfully from the archive (Assmann 2012).

A completely different form of economic crisis is discussed in Chapter 3, where Corporaal discusses hunger crises in Ireland, Finland, post-1945 Germany and the Netherlands in 1944/5, among others. Again, we can see how the memory discourses on hunger are connected to contemporary concerns and debates. Thus, they have been used to critique nineteenth century liberal concepts of political economy, in particular the laissez-faire ideology assigned to that century, but also allegedly immoral market principles in general. The memory of hunger could also be actualized in connection with attempts of charity organizations to raise support for victims of contemporary hunger and other crises. The Quakers are a good example of a religious group who used memory in precisely this way. Finally, hunger crises were also mobilized in the context of national memory, in particular in the context of what Jie-Hyun Lim has termed 'victimhood nationalism', i.e. a nationalism that seeks to build the nation on the basis of collective victimhood of those belonging to the nation (Lim 2025). It was often connected to a search for justice and recognition but also frequently stressed the agency of victim groups.

Victim groups and their experiences are also prominently foregrounded in memories of the transformation of industrial economies. Although deindustrialization at best partially describes what has been involved in such transformations, an emphasis on deindustrialization and its consequences for working-class communities was often the focus of studies carried out within the field of 'deindustrialization studies' (Strangleman et al. 2025). Chapter 4 attempts to provide a global perspective on memories of deindustrialization by drawing up a global typology of regimes of deindustrialization and their associated memoryscapes. It is in line with recent attempts to scale up the history of deindustrialization from hitherto intense research into local memory landscapes (High and Berger 2025). Berger argues that market-radical forms of deindustrialization produced silences as well as vivid counter-memories from those opposed to neoliberal transformations. Statist and corporatist forms of deindustrialization, in contrast, produced significant memoryscapes, both of industrialization and deindustrialization, which attempt to relate past, present and future in a way in which local and regional self-understandings can be scripted into the future. Post-communist variants of deindustrialization after 1945 tended to be market radical at first but also changed their approach over time. In any case, Berger stresses the importance of asynchronic interpretations of the memoryscapes of deindustrialization, as diverse places could be part of different types of memoryscapes over time. Furthermore he highlights the cases in the global south, where the post- and decolonial discourses impact heavily on deindustrial memory.

The post-communist memory of deindustrialization is the exclusive focus of Chapter 5 in this volume, which compares developments in Poland, Armenia, and Lithuania. Wawrzyniak, Dovydaitytė, and Tsaturyan emphasize the different contexts in which deindustrial memory developed: in Poland, under conditions of relative economic autonomy, in Armenia, in the planned cities that had been part of its Soviet history of deindustrialization, and in Lithuania, in a region of the Soviet Union that had been completely integrated into the Soviet planned economy. They thus underline the internal stratification of what Berger in his chapter described as one possible type of deindustrial memory. Overall, the chapter shows how much this memory was veering back and forth between erasure, preservation, and re-imagination. By and large, memories of the inefficiency of state-controlled industries justified market-radical reforms, in which workers' memories were marginalized while their former worksites were demolished. Some forms of working-class heritage, such as Solidarity in Poland with its key site Gdańsk became contested national heritage. Attempts in East-Central Europe to re-enter the memory space of Europe in the 1990s did lead to the prominence of narratives of (European) modernization which led, among other things, to Poland also entering networks such as the European Route of Industrial Heritage. This upgraded deindustrial memory and allowed it, in a limited way, to step out of the oblivion of neoliberal forms of deindustrialization. In Lithuania, by contrast, the widespread perception of industry as a colonial Soviet imposition meant that no one claimed the social ownership of the country's industrial past, not even workers or trade unions. If anything, a technological (positive) and environmental (negative) memory of the industrial past remained. In Armenia, industrial memory is also not widely recognized—apart from isolated enclaves. The renationalization of the country post-independence meant a strong focus on national traditions in its memory landscape from which industrialization as a Soviet imposition was excluded.

Approaching the relationship between collective memory and economy through the lens of systemic political transformations entails an analytical focus on instances of political regime change after periods of violent upheaval (wars, civil wars, revolutions), as well as on cases of the transformation of political systems (e.g. transition from authoritarian to democratic rule) and of radical changes of territorial control. Research questions may relate to the memory of the old system in operation prior to systemic transformations and/or to the memory of the transformation processes themselves. As outlined above, significant work has already been done on this theme, especially in connection with the post-1990 transformation in Central and Eastern Europe.

Two chapters of our volume contribute to this scholarly field of inquiry, highlighting so far rather little explored aspects and country case studies. Chapter 6, by Tetiana Vodotyka, explores the little-known case of Ukraine, through a focus on the collective memory of entrepreneurs since the late nineteenth century, covering the two systemic transitions of the Bolshevik takeover in 1917 and the collapse of the Soviet Union in 1991, as well as the impact of Russian military invasions since 2014. Drawing eclectically on memory politics scholarship and postcolonial approaches, Vodotyka first explores the locally driven commemoration of entrepreneurs prior to World War One, focused on urban toponomy and the erection of monuments for philanthropic business leaders, as well as their subsequent erasure after 1917; special emphasis is dedicated to the analysis of the Bolshevik rewriting of the role of foreign entrepreneurs, which came to be portrayed as imperialist exploiters. The analysis of the post-1991 period depicts the return to the memory of pre-1914 entrepreneurs, highlighting the key role played by instrumental interests of the new economic elites, as well as the fact that a new prominence for the memory of business was facilitated by the absence of mnemonic contestation—in contrast to clashes over the legacy of earlier political figures fighting for Ukrainian independence. Moreover, the reappropriation of the memory of foreign entrepreneurs from Belgium and UK, particularly in the Donbas region, fed into the wider narratives of Ukraine's 'European turn' away from the Russian and Soviet empires.

Chapter 7, by Oliver Kühschelm, also deals with the memory of entrepreneurs in the post-1991 transition period, but focuses less on their overall place in political mnemonic shifts, but on the significance of memory narratives for corporate decision-making at the micro level, illustrated with the case of a local Austrian savings bank's forays into the neighbouring Czech market in the early 1990s. Drawing on the notion of 'fictional expectations' (Beckert 2016) to explain investments in finance, Kühschelm conceptualizes memory as a crucial way to construct narratives around such decisions, and then explores this dynamic through his case study; he demonstrates that nostalgic representations of the common economic space of the Habsburg empire were as important as the more problematic interwar legacies in motivating cross-border investment. Moreover, he also emphasizes how such memories were mobilized in opposition to competing financial institutions in the capital Vienna. The chapter highlights that the importance of systemic political transformations for economic memory is not confined to transition societies themselves but can spread more widely through their association with (nostalgic) memories from eras preceding the existence of the overturned political regime.

Finally, we include consideration of the significance of the international economy for the creation and reproduction of memory-infused national identity narratives, a theme that connects our research to the broader literature on the relationship between nationalism and the economy (Berger and Fetzer 2019). Notions of economic memory have for some time been explored in this literature, not only with regard to the national symbolism associated with everyday consumer culture (Kühschelm et al. 2012) and practices of 'nation branding' (Aronczyk 2013), but also in a wider political perspective: National success in international markets has been associated with notions of national economic traditions, most evidently in Britain's nineteenth century concept of the 'free trade nation' (Trentmann 2008), while, conversely, memories of internationally induced economic crises also often acquire salience for national identity—witness, for example, the emphasis on economic exploitation in how the legacies of nineteenth century Western imperialism are remembered in India and China (Miller 2013) or, more recently, how the Euro debt crisis has rekindled memories of World War Two and colonialism in Greece and Ireland (Hourigan 2014; Fouka and Voth 2023).

Chapters 8 and 9 of our volume, by Naoki Odanaka and Thomas Fetzer, contribute to these debates, respectively addressing the first economic globalization period of the late nineteenth century (Odanaka) and the more recent second post-1970s 'wave' (Fetzer). Odanaka's chapter deals with the mnemonic impact of Western free trade imperialism on Japan, which, similarly to China, brought the forced opening of the country to the international economy and left powerful traces in collective memory, quintessentially illustrated in the evocative narratives and depictions of the *kurofune* ('Black ships') of Commodore Matthew Perry that had landed to request the opening of Japanese ports in 1853. While scholars have already addressed the longer-term political salience of this *kurofune* symbolism in the context of debates about economic reform in post-1945 Japan (e.g. Hall 2005), Odanaka focuses on the more immediate impact of this forced opening on Meiji era economic policy, closely examining debates among the economic and state elite, as well as key policy documents reflecting shifts in the country's industrial strategy against the backdrop of standard Ricardian comparative advantage trade models. The chapter argues that the memory of forced opening entailed a push to accelerate economic modernization along Western lines, with special emphasis on the development of heavy industry and transportation-related sectors that were considered key to hasten the mobility of goods, information and people—and thus to forestall a future of an economically weak and colonized Japanese nation.

Fetzer's chapter addresses the more recent post-1945 internationalization period through an analysis of German economic memory. Building on scholarship highlighting the salience of the country's postwar 'economic miracle' as a key source of its collective identity (Müller 2005), the chapter conceptualizes this memory as a 'golden age' narrative, which became particularly influential in the context of heightened economic Europeanization and globalization since the 1990s when key pillars of the country's economic model became the object of a controversial debate. The chapter depicts three different versions of such golden age narratives—respectively focusing on currency, the social market economy principle, and notions of 'productive capital'—outlines their associated diagnoses of how a golden age had been lost, and highlights the corresponding forward-looking political agendas, pointing to the significance of these agendas for contemporary German politics. In the last part, the chapter briefly compares German patterns to the British case, which, while highlighting crucial differences in terms of chronology and themes, also points to the wider significance of economic golden age narratives in the context of international economic integration.

Overall, our book attempts a broad mapping of the economy/memory nexus underlining how fruitful further explorations of this nexus will be.

In the conclusion we will highlight some of the red lines of investigation that emerge from the eight substantive chapters of this volume, and we will suggest avenues for future research in this field.

References

Araujo, L. 2020. *Slavery in the age of Memory: Engaging the past*. London: Bloomsbury.

Aronczyk, M. 2013. *Branding the nation: The global business of National Identity*. Oxford: Oxford University Press.

Assmann, A. 2006. Memory, individual and collective. In *The Oxford handbook of contextual political analysis*, ed. Robert E. Goodin and Charles Tilly, 210–224. Oxford: Oxford University Press.

Assmann, Aleida. 2012. Function and storage: Two modes of Memory. In *Functions, media, archives*, ed. Cultural Memory and Western Civilization, 119–136. Cambridge: Cambridge University Press.

Assmann, Aleida, and Sebastian Conrad, eds. 2010. *Memory in a global age discourses*. Practices and Trajectories: Palgrave Macmillan.

Bach, Jonathan. 2002. The taste remains: Consumption, (N)ostalgia, and the production of East Germany. *Public Culture* 14 (3): 545–556.

Bachleitner, Kathrin. 2021. *Collective Memory in international relations*. Oxford: Oxford University Press.

Barton-Hronesova, Jessie. 2021. *The struggle for redress victim Capital in Bosnia and Herzegovina*. Palgrave.

Beckert, Jens. 2016. *Imagined futures: Fictional expectations and capitalist dynamics*. Cambridge, Mass.: Harvard University Press.

Berger, S., ed. 2019. *Constructing industrial pasts: Heritage, historical culture and identity in regions undergoingstructural economic transformation*. Berghahn Books.

Berger, S., and T. Fetzer, eds. 2019. *Nationalism and the economy: Explorations into a neglected relationship*. Budapest: Central European University Press.

Berger, S., and J. Seiffert, eds. 2014. *Erinnerungsorte: Chancen, Grenzen und Perspektiven eines Erfolgskonzeptes in den Kulturwissenschaften*. Essen: Klartext.

Berger Stefan and Joanna Wawrzyniak. 2026. Remembering Industrial Pasts: A Slow Memory Approach, in Slowing Down Memory Studies: Theory and Practice of Remembering for Transformative Change, Edited by Joanna Wawrzyniak and Jenny Wüstenberg, Bloomsbury, forthcoming.

Berghahn, V. 2010. The debate on Americanization among economic and cultural historians. *Cold War History* 10 (1): 107–130.

Best, J., and M. Paterson. 2010. *Cultural Political Economy*. London/New York: Routledge.

Björkdahl, Annika, and Stefanie Kappler. 2019. The creation of transnational Memory spaces: Professionalization and commercialization. *International Journal of Politics, Culture, and Society* 32:383–401.
Boym, Svetlana. 2007. Nostalgia and its discontents. *Hedgehog Review* 9 (2):
Buzalka, Juraj. 2018. Post-peasant memories: Populist or communist nostalgia. *East European Politics and Societies* 32 (4): 988–1006.
Cassis, Y., and C. Schenk. 2021. *Remembering and learning from financial crises*. Oxford University Press.
Cook, Roger. 2007. Good bye, Lenin!: Free-market nostalgia for socialist consumerism. *Seminar: A Journal of Germanic Studies* 43 (2): 206–219.
Corporaal, M. 2017. *Relocated memories of the great famine in Irish and diaspora fiction, 1847–70*. Syracuse University Press.
Crane, G. T. 1998. Economic nationalism: Bringing the nation Back. *Millenium* 27 (1): 55–75.
De Cesari, Chiara, and Ann Rigney, eds. 2014. *Transnational Memory: Circulation, articulation, scales*. New York: De Gruyter.
Du Gay, P., and M. Pryke. 2002. *Cultural economy: Cultural analysis and commercial life*. London/New York: Sage.
Fernandez, R. 2016. *Culture and economics. In the new Palgrave dictionary of economics*. London: Palgrave.
Filipkovski, Piotr, and Joanna Wawrzyniak. 2023. Redress Economies. In *The Routledge handbook on Memory activism*, ed. Yifat Gutman and Jenny Wüstenberg. New York: Routledge.
Fouka, Vasiliki, and Hans-Joachim Voth. 2023. Collective remembrance and private choice: German–Greek conflict and behavior in times of crisis. *American Political Science Review* 117 (3): 851–870.
Fuchs, Anne. 2012. *After the Dresden bombing. Pathways to Memory, 1945 to the present*. Basingstoke: Palgrave Macmillan.
Geppert, Dominik, and Frank Lorenz Müller, eds. 2015. *Sites of Imperial Memory. Commemorating colonial rule in the nineteenth and twentieth centuries*. Manchester: Manchester University Press.
Granville, B. 2013. *Remembering inflation*. Princeton: Princeton University Press.
Hall, D. 2005. The continuing salience of economic nationalism in Japan. In *Economic nationalism in a globalizing world*, ed. E. Helleiner and A. Pickel, 118–138. Ithaca: Cornell University Press.
High, S., and S. Berger, eds. 2025. *The politics of industrial closure: Transnational patterns and cross-National Comparisons*. Toronto: University of Toronto Press.
Holm, Michael. 2016. The Marshall plan and Memory. In *The Marshall plan: A new Deal for Europe*. New York: Routledge.

Hoskins, Andrew, ed. 2017. *Digital Memory studies: Media pasts in transition.* New York: Routledge.

Hourigan, Niamh. 2014. Reversed Memory, collective action and the Irish economic crisis 2010-2013. *Irish Journal of Anthropology* 17 (1): 21–27.

Kilian, Jürgen. 2016. The Greek 'forced loan' during the second world war. Demand for reparations or restitution? *Comparative Southeast European Studies* 94 (1): 96–108.

Kühschelm, O. et. al. (eds.). 2012. Konsum und Nation. Zur Geschichte nationalisierender Inszenierungen in der Produktkommunikation. Bielefeld: transcript.

Kühschelm, O. 2019. Nationalizing consumption: Products, brands and nations. In *Nationalism and the economy: Explorations into a neglected relationship*, ed. S. Berger and T. Fetzer, 163–187. Budapest: Central European University Press.

Kuti, Csongor. 2009. *Post-communist restitution and the rule of law.* Budapest: Central European University Press.

Lenzerini, Federico. 2008. *Reparations for indigenous peoples: International and comparative perspectives.* Oxford: Oxford University Press.

Levy, Daniel, and Natan Sznaider. 2002. Memory unbound the holocaust and the formation of cosmopolitan Memory. *European Journal of Social Theory* 5 (1): 87–106.

Lim, Jie-Hyun. 2025. *Victimhood nationalism: History and Memory in a global age.* New York: Columbia University Press.

Lorenz, C. 2014. Blurred lines. History, Memory and the experience of time. In *Erinnerungsorte: Chancen, Grenzen und Perspektiven eines Erfolgskonzeptes in den Kulturwissenschaften*, ed. S. Berger and J. Seiffert, 73–90. Essen: Klartext.

Mai, D. 2015. *Organizational cultures of remembrance: Exploring the relationships between Memory, identity and image in an automobile company.* Berlin: De Gruyter.

Malinova, Olga. 2024. Political uses of memory of the early period of the post-Soviet transformations in contemporary Russia. In *Remembering the neoliberal turn: Economic change and collective memory in Eastern Europe after 1989*, eds. Pehe, Veronika and Joanna Wawrzyniak, New York: Routledge.

Mark-Fitzgerald, E. 2013. *Commemorating the Irish famine.* Liverpool: Liverpool University Press.

Mazur, Liudmila. 2015. Golden age mythology and the nostalgia of catastrophes in post-soviet Russia. *Canadian Slavonic Papers* 57 (3–4): 213–238.

Miller, Manjari Chatterjee, 2013. *Wronged by empire: Post-imperial ideology and foreign policy in India and China.* Wronged by Empire. Stanford University Press.

Moffett, Luke. 2017. Transitional justice and reparations: Remedying the past? In *Research handbook on transitional justice*, ed. Cheryl Lawther and Luke Moffett, 2nd ed., 377–400. Cheltenham: Edward Elgar.

Müller, K. 2005. Nationalist undercurrents in German economic liberalism. In *Economic nationalism in a globalizing world*, ed. E. Helleiner and A. Pickel, 141–163. Ithaca: Cornell University Press.

Nora, P. 1989. Between memory and history. *Representations* 26 (Special Issue): 7–24.

Nora, P. 1996. *Realms of Memory: Rethinking the French past*. Clumbia University Press.

Olick, Jeffrey. 2013. *The politics of regret*. On Collective Memory and Historical Responsibility: Routledge.

O'Callaghan, Patrick. 2012. Collective memory in law and policy: The problem of the sovereign debt crisis. *Legal Studies* 32 (4): 642–660.

Pehe, Veronika, and Joanna Wawrzyniak. 2024. *Remembering the neoliberal turn: Economic change and collective memory in Eastern Europe after 1989*. New York: Routledge.

Pickel, Andreas, ed. 2022. *Handbook of economic nationalism*. Cheltenham: Edward Elgar.

Radstone, Susannah, and Rita Wilson, eds. 2021. *Translating worlds: Migration, Memory and culture*. Oxford/New York: Routledge.

Reinert, Kenneth A. 2023. *The lure of economic nationalism. Beyond zero sum*. London: Anthem.

Schmidt, V. 2008. Discursive institutionalism: The explanatory power of ideas and discourse. *Annual Review of Political Science* 11:303–326.

Schwedler, G. 2021. *A cultural history of Memory in the middle ages*. London: Bloomsbury.

Skaar, Elin et. al. (eds.). 2016. Transitional justice in Latin America: The uneven road from impunity towards accountability. New York: Routledge.

Sopinski, Michal. 2022. Legal and political aspects of war reparations from Germany. *International Law Quarterly* 3 (3): 59–79.

Stein-Hölkeskamp, E. and K. J. Hölkeskamp (eds.). 2020. *Erinnerungsorte der Antike*, 2nd vol., 2nd edn. Munich: C.H. Beck.

Strangleman, T., S. Lee Linkon, S. High, J. Clarke, and S. Berger, eds. 2025. *The Routledge international handbook of deindustrialization studies*. London: Routledge.

Tamboukou, M. 2016. *Gendering the Memory of work. Women workers' narratives*. London: Routledge.

Thampi, Madhavi, ed. 2005. *China and India in the colonial world*. New Delhi: Social Science Press.

Treber, Leonie. 2014. *Mythos Trümmerfrauen: Von der Trümmerbeseitigung in der Kriegs- und Nachkriegszeit und der Entstehung eines deutschen Erinnerungsortes*. Essen: Klartext.

Trentmann, F. 2008. *Free trade nation. Commerce, consumption, and civil Society in Modern Britain*. Oxford: Oxford University Press.

Velikonja, Mitja. 2009. Lost in transition nostalgia for socialism in post-socialist countries. *East European Politics and Societies* 23 (4): 535–551.

Verovšek, Peter J. 2014. Memory and the Euro-crisis of leadership: The effects of generational change in Germany and the EU. *Constellations* 21 (2): 239–248.

Volcic, Zala. 2007. Yugo-nostalgia: Cultural Memory andMedia in the former Yugoslavia. *Critical Studies in Media Communication* 24 (1): 21–38.

Wawrzyniak, J. 2021. 'Hard times but our own'. Post-socialist nostalgia and the transformation of industrial life in Poland. *Zeithistorische Forschungen/Studies in Contemporary History* 18 (1): 73–92.

Wüstenberg, Jenny. 2019. Locating transnational Memory. *International Journal of Politics, Culture and Society* 32:371–382.

Wüstenberg, Jenny. 2023. Towards a slow Memory studies. In *Critical Memory studies: New approaches*, ed. Brett A. Kaplan, 87–109. London: Bloomsbury.

Cyclical Economic Crises

Battles of Narratives, Battles of Memory: Making Sense of the Ebbs and Flows of the Memory of the Great Depression

Giuseppe Telesca and Youssef Cassis

1 Introduction

It has often been claimed that financial markets have short memory, but the (alleged) tendency to forget financial crises has surprisingly escaped any tests, until recently. The issue is not irrelevant if one believes that the memory of financial crises—or its absence—could play a role in shaping economic narratives that, in turn, influence the behaviour of economic agents, hence producing consequences.

We define narratives as cultural and social phenomena that help us to make sense of the world by framing it through ordering reality, assigning causality, constructing meaning (Hansen 2012). There is a clear link between narratives and memory, because whereas narratives help us to make sense of unfolding events, they also provide templates to recount

G. Telesca (✉)
University of Glasgow, Glasgow, UK
e-mail: Giuseppe.Telesca@glasgow.ac.uk

Y. Cassis
European University Institute, Fiesole, Italy

S. Berger and T. Fetzer (eds.), *Collective Memory of Economic Crises and Transformations*, Palgrave Macmillan Memory Studies,
https://doi.org/10.1007/978-3-032-09094-2_2

the past. As Jerome Bruner put it: 'the typical form of framing experience (and our memory of it) is in narrative form [...] what does not get structured narratively suffers loss in memory'. Unlike constructions based on scientific procedures, narratives cannot be subjected to empirical falsification; they are acceptable on the basis of their 'verisimilitude' (Bruner 1990, 56), or on the basis of their 'virality' (Shiller 2017). This implies the existence of competing narratives at work to make sense of the reality, even though each historical period is associated with master-narratives that are more or less successfully challenged by counter-narratives.[1] As narrative, memory also operates under the pressure of challenges and alternatives: there are counter-memories which are shaped by and, in turn, reinforce counter-narratives.

Having underlined the connection between narratives and memory, it has to be said that there is a link between narratives and economics as well. Narratives' influence on the perception of the events that they describe renders them performative and, as a result, enables them to produce economic consequences (MacKenzie 2006; Hansen 2012, 697). Many scholars have argued that narratives such as the 'new era' (1920s), the 'new economy' (1990s), or the 'great moderation' (2000s), contributed to the creation of bubbles destined to burst dramatically when financial markets eventually realised that also this time—to use Reinhart's and Rogoff's formula (2009)—was (not) different (Eichengreen 2015, 3 and 21). Following this line of reasoning, we can preliminary claim that the absence of memory of past financial crises can bring about complacency and loss of awareness of the financial system instability.

Memory studies, however, have gone beyond the idea that the construction of memory is a binary struggle between forgetting and recollecting. First of all, memory is assembled through a non-spontaneous process of framing and selecting, in which forgetting plays a crucial, and not necessarily harmful role (Connerton 2008). What is more, remembering and forgetting can be seen, rather than as two distinct entities, as two inextricably intertwined faces of the same medal (Brockmeier 2002). In the light of these considerations, remembering seems to be less a matter of accurate recall of isolated pieces of information and more an

[1] The theorisation of master-narratives has been influenced by François Lyotard's work on grand narratives associated with the Enlightenment and Marxism (1979). For a discussion of the implications of Lyotard's research and related literature see Meretoja (2020).

exercise in arranging fragments of information into a general scheme—a process that does not exclude distortion or obliteration of 'incongruous' facts (Wertsch 2002, 4–9). If this is true, not only sheer amnesia, but also a certain interpretation of previous financial crises can be both influenced by, and contribute to, the success of certain narratives rather than others.

In this chapter we test this claim by focusing on the way in which some of the most distributed, read and authoritative American, British, French, and German newspapers and magazines have remembered the crises of the Great Depression in the long term. The Great Depression has been the unescapable reference, the crisis with which all financial panics and economic downturns have been compared. This was true in the mid-1970s, in 1987 and, especially, during the Global Financial Crisis of 2008, which has been repeatedly described as the most severe crisis since the Great Depression, hence our decision to analyse its long-term memory.

It must be said, preliminarily, that the journalism-memory link is not an obvious one. Journalism is more interested in the *here-and-now* than in the *there-and-then*; it is hungry for breaking news and has no space for yesterday's stories. Yet, this link is unavoidable: memory is possible if shared orally, or through texts and artefacts that mediate between individuals, bridging space and time. Here 'mediation' acquires a double meaning: on the one hand it permits the sharing and transmission of memory, on the other hand it allows the re-configuration and re-definition of memory through time (Erll and Rigney 2009). With regard to journalists, references to the past help them to find connections, elaborate inferences, find short-hand explanations, establish a yardstick to measure the magnitude of the events they are recounting. Because they are not historians, and because they have neither the time nor the space for context, nuances, and/or the exploration of grey areas, journalists' use of history is necessarily kept to the essential (Zelizer 2008a). If journalists are believed to write the first draft of history when reporting on current affairs, they tend to provide a very concise summary of the final drafts written by historians when making use of the past. This is exactly what makes their writing interesting from the point of view of memory studies.

In the selection of our sample, we aimed at covering a large spectrum of focuses and political orientations. Our choice fell on 16 papers: the Financial Times, The Economist, The Guardian and The Times for Britain; L'Express, Le Figaro, Le Monde, and Libération for France; Der Spiegel, Die Zeit, the Frankfurter Allgemeine Zeitung, and the

Süddeutsche Zeitung for Germany; the New York Times, Time Magazine, the Wall Street Journal, and the Washington Post for the United States. As for the list of the financial crises of the Great Depression, this included the Wall Street crash of October 1929, the banking crises of 1931 in Europe (Credit-Anstalt in May, the German banking crisis in July) and the American banking crisis that culminated in the bank holiday of March 1933.[2] We decided to look at the way in which financial crises were remembered in two circumstances: significant anniversaries of the financial crises of the Great Depression (the 10th, the 20th, the 25th, the 50th,[th] and the 75th anniversary); and other financial turbulences.[3] For the anniversaries we checked all the issues of the month preceding and the one following the crisis; for the crises we looked at the papers' issues of the month following the triggering event.

On anniversaries—which represent the focus of this chapter— it was the memory of the crisis evoked, rather than the news story that triggered the engagement with the past. On other financial turbulences, it was the news story that triggered the evocation of the past. The memory of previous crises provided an element of comparison that, depending on the circumstances, was declined in two directions. On the one hand, looking at the present through the lens of the past could represent an opportunity to confirm or dismiss potential analogies between now and then. In this case the main question raised in the article was: *could it happen again*? On the other hand, looking at the past through the lens of the present could represent an occasion to reassess the crisis that was remembered. In this case the main question raised in the article was: *what did really happen then*?

[2] The memory of the 1931 sterling crisis has been dealt with separately: see Telesca (2021, 2024).

[3] We focussed on four major financial crises: the 1973–4 bank failures in Britain, Germany and the US, which were a consequence of the financial instability of the early 1970s; the 1982 International Debt Crisis, which spread across the Global South and threatened with collapse the international financial system; 1987 'Black Monday' and the 2007–8 Global Financial Crisis.

2 An Uneven Memory of the Great Depression

As Table 1 makes it clear, a first finding of this survey is that crises, more than anniversaries, provide the trigger for remembering the Great Depression: 568 articles (79.2 per cent of the total) mentioning the Great Depression were written on the occasion of other crises, while only 149 (20.8 per cent of the total) were written at times of anniversaries. A second finding is that whereas the whole experience of the Great Depression has never been completely forgotten, the financial crises of the period 1929–1933 have been remembered unevenly. The 1929 Wall Street crash gets the lion share of recollection (74.6 per cent of the total), while the banking crises of the early 1930s in Europe (18.3 per cent) and the United States (7.1 per cent)[4] are less remembered and, on some occasions, completely forgotten (Cassis and Knaps 2021). On the one hand this conclusion is striking, considering the consensus reached among economic historians and economists that the 1930s banking crises played a bigger role than the 1929 'Great Crash' in determining the severity and length of the Great Depression.[5] On the other hand, this discrepancy seems to confirm that there is a divide between history, which in this case has played down the 1929 stock market crisis' contribution to the Great Depression, and memory, which concentrates exactly on that episode.[6]

Robert Shiller argues that the persistence of the 1929 memory is due to the fact that the 'Great Crash' represents an irresistible, and timeless, morality tale: a deserved punishment after the excesses of the 'roaring 1920s'—a formula that, not by chance, starts to be used only from the 1930s onwards (Shiller 2017, 990–991). Reflecting on historical events as potential *lieux de mémoire*, Pierre Nora distinguishes between two types

[4] The memory discrepancy between European banking crises and US banking crises of the early 1930s is probably related to the fact that our sample included twelve European and only four American papers.

[5] Maury Klein's survey (2001, 326) on the scholarship dedicated to the 1929 Wall Street crash concluded that 'one of the most surprising aspects of the literature covering an event that ranks so high on the roster of national traumas is its paucity'.

[6] History and memory share the same ground, the past, and up until the Enlightenment were not clearly separated. During the nineteenth century, history emerged as a distinct and superior discipline: academic, objective, nuanced, determined to keep the past in the past unlike memory. This dichotomy, a central tenet of the historical discipline for most of the twentieth century, has been challenged from the 1990s onwards, when 'the idea that history's value lies in its ability to insulate itself from memory has receded' (Cubitt 2019, 131). See also Erll and Nünning (2008).

Table 1 Total number of articles mentioning the 'Great Crash' (1929), the European banking crises (1931) or the American banking crisis (1933) during their anniversaries or other financial turbulences

	1929	*1931*	*1933*
Anniversaries	123	20	6
Crises	412	111	45
Total	535	131	51

Source Database of American, British, French, and German newspapers and magazines

of events that can aspire to this status: the *founding* event, which could seem of little importance when it happens, but, retrospectively, acquires the standing of inaugural rupture; and the *spectacular* event, which is immediately invested of symbolic meaning. The 'Great Crash' is the *spectacular* event of the Great Depression, an event that can be forgotten as such, but will be revived in the future. To the question whether the essence of the *lieu de mémoire* lies in the original event, or in its return in the cycles of memory, Nora's answer is that it lies in both, because 'all *lieux de mémoire* are objects *mise-en-abîme*' (Nora 1989, 20).

Other major financial crises have been forgotten, at any rate by the wider public, and unlike 1929, have not been revived. This is especially the case with the periodical crises of the nineteenth century, which occurred at regular intervals, every seven to ten years: in 1866, 1873, 1882, 1890, 1900, 1907. They took place at the peak of a phase of expansion and were followed by a phase of recession, each lasting three to five years and marked by falling prices and profits, waves of business failures, fall of industrial and agricultural output, and rise of unemployment. These crises were most often triggered by a financial shock, such as the collapse of a bank or a stock market crash, leading to a full-blown financial crisis: the failure of Overend Gurney in London in 1866, the stock market crash in Vienna in 1873, the collapse of the Union Générale in Lyon in 1882, the near bankruptcy of Baring Brothers in London in 1890, the suspension of Knickerbocker Trust in New York in 1907—all highly 'spectacular' events (Cassis 2016). These events and the crises that followed were personally remembered by financial actors, reported in the press and talked about by contemporaries, who had a direct memory of at least one previous crisis, usually more. A 'communicative memory', as defined by Jan Assmann, was clearly at play and would make for a fascinating study.

However, the transmission of such memory does not go beyond three or four generations, unlike the more formalised and mediated 'cultural memory', which can go back several centuries and sometimes turn into myth (Assmann 2008a, 2008b).

It is important to add that the 'Great Crash', with the passing of time, seems to work as a memory trigger for the overall experience of the Great Depression. This becomes evident in the Anglo-American papers, even semantically, when the tendency to accompany the recollection of the 'Great Crash' with expressions such as '1929 and all that' or similar formulas takes hold (The Economist 1979, Bartley 1987, The Economist 2008). At the same time, the 'Great Crash' and, by extension, the Great Depression, become far less remembered than 'referred to'—a tendency starting to emerge in the mid-to late 1970s, with the increased temporal distance from the event, the advent of a new generation of financial actors and commentators, and the return of financial crises. It was referred to in order to assess the likelihood of the outbreak of a major crisis, or to condemn or approve changes taking place in the financial markets, and became increasingly politicised, especially regarding the Thatcher and Reagan policies (Cassis and Knaps 2021, 23). This tendency would be in full display by the 2008 Global Financial Crisis. The history rather than the memory of the Great Depression was used to discuss state intervention, the future of capitalism, and the many other concerns of the day. And in the same way as memory moved to history, this latter moved to economics, especially as far as the 'lessons' of the Great Depression are concerned: Keynesianism might have been shaped by the Great Depression, but it is above all an advance in economic theory (Cassis and Knaps 2021, 34–35).

3 The Ebbs and Flows of the Memory of 1929

If the analysis concentrates only on the 123 articles dedicated to the 1929 anniversaries—with the important *caveat* that, often, the 'Great Crash' evokes the entire experience of the Great Depression—another crucial finding of the survey consists in the fact that the memory of the financial crises of the Great Depression does not fade away over time, as the consensus recalled at the beginning of this chapter seems to imply. The memory of financial crises is instead subjected to ebbs and flows.

As Table 2 makes it clear, in contrast to the little attention devoted to the Wall Street crash on its 10th, 20th, and 25th anniversaries, a 'boom' of the memory of 1929 occurs on its 50th anniversary, in 1979. The intensity of this revival is corroborated by a qualitative assessment that goes beyond the mere number of articles.

Not only was 1929 more remembered on its 50th anniversary but, as Table 3 demonstrates, its recollection occupies more space in the papers of the sample than in the past. This clearly emerges when taking into account the position of the articles commemorating 1929 (total front pages, business front pages, opinion pieces), their length (number of articles longer than 800 words), and the type of engagement with the memory. With respect to this aspect, we distinguish articles that *necessitate* memory, which directly and exclusively engage with 1929; articles that *invite* memory, where the reference to the 'Great Crash' is used as a term of comparison with the present; and articles that *indulge* memory, where 1929 is just an afterthought of the news story (Zelizer 2008b).

Table 2 Total number of articles mentioning the 1929 Wall Street crash on its anniversaries

10th Anniversary	*20th Anniversary*	*25th Anniversary*	*50th Anniversary*	*75th Anniversary*
9	9	14	70	21

Source Database of American, British, French and German newspapers and magazines

Table 3 Details of the anniversary articles devoted to the Wall Street crash

	10th Ann.	*20th Ann.*	*25th Ann.*	*50th Ann.*	*75th Ann.*
Total n. articles	9	9	14	70	21
Tot front pages	–	1	4	9	3
Business front p.	1	–	1	13	–
Opinion pieces	1	–	–	5	–
% long articles	44.4	33.3	15.4	51.4	28.6
Necessitate	3	2	3	28	8
Invite	2	3	7	24	4
Indulge	4	4	4	17	9

Source Database of American, British, French and German newspapers and magazines

The rediscovery of the 'Great Crash' can be explained by developments in the media industry (availability of more space in newspapers and magazines, increased interest in financial phenomena) and by the return of financial instability. In 1979, and for the first time since the Great Depression, when looking at the current situation the question *could it happen again*? seemed to be—at least potentially—justified. This had not been the case in previous anniversaries. On the 25th anniversary, for instance, The Guardian reported that American statisticians had put the 1954 trend of industrial stock prices on the same chart than 1929, but added, immediately: 'all comments agree, of course, that the parallel [between 1929 and 1954] exists only on the chart' (The Guardian 1954).

The economic context of 1979 was conducive to a debate on the stock exchange crash. Time Magazine, for instance, identified three 'frightening similarities' between 1929 and 1979: the Fed's decision to increase interest rates, a move already experienced on the eve of the 'Great Crash'; the exposure of American banks to unreliable international debtors both in 1929 and in 1979; the American credit boom, connected to the instalment plans in the 1920s and to the explosion of 'plastic money' (credit cards) in the 1970s. The article argued that these analogies did not necessarily mean that the world was about to witness another Crash (Time 1979). While many articles of the sample conceded that the willingness to cooperate internationally and the levels of regulation, liquidity, and sophistication of the stock market in 1979 were all reasons to be confident that a repeat of 1929 was unlikely (Bremmer 1979, Financial Times 1979, Duroselle 1979, Rowen 1979), not everyone shared the same optimism. We will come back to this point in the next section.

If we go back to Table 2, we observe a low level of recollection of, and engagement with the 'Great Crash' on its 75th anniversary, confirmed by the qualitative assessment of Table 3. Had it not been for the 13 articles that the Frankfurter Allgemeine Zeitung (nine) and the Süddeutsche Zeitung (four) dedicated to the Wall Street crash, the numbers of 2004 would have been in line with the ones of the first two anniversaries. It is worth noticing that the decreasing interest in the 'Great Crash' recorded in 2004 was happening on the bedrock of increasing availability of space in the newspapers, due to the online revolution, and growing financial instability.[7]

[7] A non-exhaustive list of the financial turbulences of the period would start with the East Asia currency crisis in 1997 and the Japanese banking crisis in 1997–8, and continue

The data emerging from the microcosm of our sample seem to confirm the commonly held view that bankers, financial traders and, more generally, public opinion, had, in the two to three decades preceding the global financial crisis of 2007–8, shown indifference towards history, forgetting that the financial system was vulnerable and 'feeding their models with historical data that went only a few years back, with predictable consequences for the quality of the models that offered very limited historical significance' (Tett 2007).

4 The 1979 Battle over the Memory of '1929 and All That'

The analysis of our database reveals that the financial crises of the period 1929–1933 have been remembered unevenly, with the 1929 Wall Street crash being by far more remembered than the banking crises in Europe and the United States of the 1930s. If we zoom into the anniversaries, our database tells us that the memory of the financial crises of the Great Depression, rather than fading away with the passing of time, has been subjected to ebbs and flows. We have seen that similar circumstances render the recollection of past crises likelier, as they justify the question *could it happen again*? Yet, remembrance doesn't happen automatically: it occured in 1979, for instance, but not in 2004. To understand why, it is time to deal with the category of 'crisis', whose etymology combines notions of (objective) crisis and (subjective) critique, a blend that highlights the link between crisis and human perception (Koselleck and Richter 2006). To have a crisis you need observers who 'proclaim' it and call for critical decisions to be taken in the present to overcome it. As historians, then, we need to reflect on who is 'calling' the crisis and which critical decisions are deemed necessary to surmount it (Graf 2010).

The end of Bretton Woods, two oil crises and stagflation had opened up the space in the marketplace in economic ideas and policies. This process was particularly advanced in the United States where, at the end of the 1970s, the consensus around the institutional framework promoted

with the hedge fund Long-Term Capital Management's near failure, in relation with Russia's debt default in 1998, and the stock market boom-and-bust cycle linked to the dot.com bubble of the early 2000s (Cassis 2011, 42–47).

after the Great Depression was being increasingly questioned by a multitude of social, political and economic actors.[8] At stakes, after the events of the 1970s, was the Keynesian narrative which had held sway for half-a-century and posited that markets cannot be left to their own devices. When this had happened and finance had acquired too dominant a position in society, so the narrative went, instability had followed in the form of financial bubbles and crises. A counter-narrative, which postulated that markets should be left to their own devices in order to liberate the 'animal spirits' of the economy and maintain financial stability, had always existed (Hall 1993; Hansen 2014). It reinforced its appeal during the 1970s also thanks to the generalised use of the notion of crisis. This is not to deny that stagflation was a serious economic malaise, but simply to highlight that the way in which the events were recounted and bound together contributed to shape the responses to the crisis, hence determining the way in which this latter unfolded (Hay 2010).

Seen in this light, the 50th anniversary of the 'Great Crash' acquires a significance that it is time to explore looking at the other direction of the analogy between past and present mentioned in the introduction of this chapter: the anniversary articles that, in 1979, analysed the current situation as a vantage point to reassess the 'Great Crash' and re-evaluate *what did really happen* half-a-century earlier. Here, we need to keep in mind Natalie Davis's and Randolph Stern's consideration that 'whenever memory is invoked, we should be asking ourselves: by whom, where, in which context, against what' (Davis and Stern 1989, 2).

The Wall Street Journal dedicated a series of politically charged articles to the 'Great Crash' and the Great Depression. The opening salvo was fired by Jude Wanniski, a former member of the newspaper's board of contributors. The journalist had already played a role in the popularisation of the Laffer Curve writing for the National Affair, in 1978, a colourful piece about a 1974 dinner in a Washington restaurant during which economist Arthur Laffer had drawn his curve on a napkin to explain his theory to Dick Cheney and Donald Rumsfeld, two heavyweights of the then Republican administration (Shiller 2017, 981). In his 1979 anniversary piece, Wanniski argued that the crisis of the 1970s, and the

[8] As the Washington Post observed in October 1979, what Franklin Delano Roosevelt had created in the aftermath of the 1929 collapse was 'both taken for granted and dismissed as inadequate to the demands of the new period of economic tension America appear[ed] to be entering' (Johnson 1979).

inability of Keynesianism to explain stagflation, indicated that the time was ripe for a change of direction in the economic theory and a revival of the classic economic theory. This latter, according to the journalist, had been doomed by its incapacity to explain the oversupply provoked by the Great Depression. Wanniski provided an alternative explanation of the 'Great Crash', arguing that the Wall Street's collapse had been the result of the 'rational expectation' of the stock market once it had learned, in the last week of October 1929, that a majority in favour of the Smoot-Hawley Tariff had been reached in the Congress of the United States. In the journalist's reading of the events the Smoot-Hawley Act—a political interference in the working of the markets—was the crucial factor that explained the Great Depression (Wanniski 1979). Wanniski's interpretation was hardly a novelty in the historiographical debate. New, in 1979, was this interpretation being used in a larger arena to advocate the dismissal of Keynesianism: a different perspective on 1929 put at the service of the emerging neoliberal counter-narrative. Three days later, a Wall Street Journal's leader reiterated this operation by warning that a repeat of 1929 could indeed happen again as a consequence of a government's mistakes in the form of profligacy, 'heavy attack on profits', or willingness to impose 'regulatory costs' to the economy (Wall Street Journal 1979a). Another Wall Street Journal's editorial, published on the very anniversary of 'Black Tuesday', repeated the warning, indicating two risks: on the one hand a 'massive policy blunder in the order of the Smoot-Hawley Tariff', with the 'impending windfall profits tax' being the most likely candidate in this case; on the other hand political pressure of the Congress over the Fed for fear of recession, followed by the weakening of Paul Volker's determination to fight inflation and monetary growth, which would in turn trigger hyperinflation, a flight from the dollar and the international trading system's collapse (Wall Street Journal 1979b).

A Keynesian reading of the 1970s challenges, and how they compared with 50 years earlier, came from another piece hosted in the Wall Street Journal, and written by Arthur Schlesinger Jr., a former John F. Kennedy's advisor, and a New York University history professor at the time of writing. In his piece, Schlesinger recalled the first chaotic steps of the New Deal, the original contradictions of the project and its limits, underlining that the entire operation had been 'a process of trial and error'. In spite of the different circumstances, the same pragmatism that Roosevelt had demonstrated in 1929 was needed in 1979. Schlesinger wrote that:

> [economic] orthodoxy is as impotent in the face of rising prices today as it was half a century ago in face of declining output. Our masters know no more how to end inflation in 1979 than they knew how to end depression in 1933. And, now as then, orthodox policies are only going to make things worse [...] In view of the bankruptcy of orthodoxy, it may be no more prudent now than it was fifty years ago to sell the heretics short. This is perhaps one lesson to be drawn from the Wall Street Crash (Schlesinger 1979).

The interest around 1929 in 1979 is not only related to the importance of the anniversary (the 50th), but also to the moment in which it occurs. Anniversary journalism generally recount stories of the past as a closed chapter. On some occasion, though, and given certain circumstances, commemorative stories provide an opportunity for media to look critically at, and debate the meaning of, the past (Edy 1999). As this section has shown, at the end of the 1970s this process of renegotiation of the memory of the 'Great Crash' was mainly investing the United States. It will take the biggest single-day stock market debacle in history, recorded worldwide on 19 October 1987, 'Black Monday', to activate a similarly politically charged debate in Europe—particularly in the British press confronted, since 1979, with Margaret Thatcher's attempt at 'rolling back the state'. This dispute acquired more strength in the aftermath of the *Big Bang*, a reform of the London Stock Exchange modelled on the mid-1970s reform of the New York Stock Exchange, and on the eve of the launch of a big sale of British Petroleum shares—the symbol of a society in which shareholders, whose number had increased from 2 to 9 million in the previous four years, were outnumbering people affiliated to trade unions (The Economist 1987). In these circumstances, while The Guardian interpreted the collapse of the stock exchanges around the world as a sign of crisis for the Anglo-Saxon conservative political project (Aitken 1987), The Times sympathised with 'the unknown yuppie', disgraced and accused of greed after 'Black Monday', but celebrated in the paper as 'the advanced Guard of Britain's overdue capitalist revolution' (The Times 1987).

5 Conclusion

Delving into the 1979 debate on '1929 and all that' has demonstrated that the battle over economic ideas, policies and narratives, and the battle over memory were coeval and, we argue, strictly intertwined. Aleida Assmann's distinction between active and passive remembering can be helpful here to explain this link. Assmann (2008a, 2008b) argues that, as forgetting, also remembering presents an active and a passive dimension. She distinguishes the actively circulated memory that keeps the past in the present (*canon*) from the passively stored memory that preserves the past as past (*archive*). The *archive* can be seen as a sort of no man's land in which past events are located on the frontier between forgetting and remembering, where they are 'no longer' and 'not yet'. For the past to become relevant for the present the work of gatekeepers of memory, agents who try to move the 'memory files' from the *archive* to the *canon*, is needed. Newspapers and news outlets are crucial gatekeepers of memory; they certainly are not the only ones, possibly not the most powerful, but they contribute to the choice of whether to keep the past into the past or to move the past into the present.

It is far from certain that the move from the *archive* to the *canon* will be successful. In the case under scrutiny, for instance, articles that engaged with the memory of 1929 in order to criticise the post-Great Depression consensus had already been published before the 50th anniversary of 1929, or on the anniversaries of the other financial crises of the Great Depression.[9] Yet, what has been described in the previous section as the battle over the memory of '1929 and all that' happens only in 1979, because the crisis of the 1970s raises the attention to new ideas and policies and, at the same time, brings to the foreground new narrative representations of the reality (Lipartito 1995, 8–11). The memory of 1929, in this context, becomes part and parcel of this struggle. The gatekeepers of memory's attempt to make past crises relevant for the present

[9] A New York Times piece written on the twentieth anniversary of 1929, published an interview with an economist of the Brookings Institution who was critical of the Glass-Steagall Act (New York Times 1949). On the 25th anniversary of the 1931 banking crisis in Germany, the Frankfurter Allgemeine Zeitung complained about the excesses of state regulation, considered a legacy of that crisis (Welter 1956). A piece published in the wake of the 1973–74 bank failures, looked with suspicion at the idea to tightening financial regulation arguing that the Great Depression was also brought about by stern controls on banks (The Economist 1974).

is an important battleground in the war on narratives and signification. It goes without saying that even though we are talking about second-order narrative representations of the reality, the struggle to control the process of signification is a power struggle heavily charged in political terms (Hansen 2015).

The 75th anniversary of 1929 falls in circumstances that are equal and opposite to its 50th anniversary. In 2004 there were a few polemic pieces against the new consensus and the neoliberal narrative, which had emerged from the battle of ideas—and memory—that had started in the late 1970s. In these articles, the memory of 1929 was used as a warning tale and a repeat of the crash was seen as an actual threat.[10] By 2004, however, the neoliberal narrative had taken over the memory, and this in spite of growing signals of financial instability. These signals were not ignored. However, even when financial instability was taken into account, the 'lessons of 1929' were generally dismissed as irrelevant.

In this sense, it is worth looking again at the Wall Street Journal, which in 2004 published two articles that evoked 1929 while reflecting on Alan Greenspan's years at the helm of the Fed. In the first, Greenspan's successes in 'pushing the government out of the economy' and 'making a strong case for the Glass-Steagall Act repeal'—arguably the strongest regulatory legacy of the Great Depression—were celebrated (Ip 2004a). In the second article, a 2001 Greenspan's speech was quoted in which the Fed Chairman had argued that, after the Great Depression, 'a kind of vicious circle of government replacement of market oversight' had been set in motion (Ip 2004b). This vicious circle had, according to Greenspan, reduced the incentive for bankers and businessmen to act prudently, because of the Fed acting as lender of last resort, and made depositors less concerned about the reputation of the banks to which they entrusted their money, because of the creation of a federal deposit insurance in 1933 (Greenspan 2001).

[10] The Financial Times hosted the article of a Yale professor of mathematics who had just published a book concerned with how little was known about the volatility of the financial markets 75 years after 1929 (Mandelbrot 2004). The Süddeutsche Zeitung published an interview with Robert Shiller, already known for his warnings about the housing bubble (Süddeutsche Zeitung 2004).

We can conclude that, by 2004, the memory of '1929 and all that', which in 1979 had been moved from the *archive* to the active remembering in order to support the emerging neoliberal counter-narrative—had been successfully put back into the *archive* folder by the gatekeepers of memory, who considered the lessons of 1929 to be either irrelevant or counterproductive to tackle the challenges of the Twentieth-First century financial reality.

References

Aitken, Ian. 1987. A hollow laugh on the way to the bank. *The Guardian* (October 26).

Assmann, Aleida. 2008a. Canon and archive. In *Cultural memory studies: An international and interdisciplinary handbook*, ed. A. Erll and A. Nünning, 97–107. Berlin and New York: Walter de Gruyter.

Assmann, Jan. 2008b. Communicative and cultural memory. In *Cultural memory studies: An international and interdisciplinary handbook*, ed. A. Erll and A. Nünning, 109–118. Berlin and New York: Walter de Gruyter.

Bartley, Robert L. 1987. 1929 and all that. *Wall Street Journal*, November 24.

Bremmer, Alex. 1979. Shades of 1929 in panic wall street share trading. *The Guardian*, October 11.

Brockmeier, Jens. 2002. Remembering and forgetting: Narrative as cultural memory. *Culture and Psychology* 8:15–43.

Bruner, Jerome S. 1990. *Acts of meaning: Four lectures on mind and culture*. Cambridge and London: Harvard University Press.

Cassis, Youssef. 2011. *Crises and opportunities: The shaping of modern finance*. Oxford: Oxford University Press.

Cassis, Youssef. 2016. Economic and financial crises. In *Capitalism: The reemergence of a historical concept*, ed. J. Kocka and M. van der Linden, 13–31. London and New York: Bloomsbury Academic.

Cassis, Youssef, and Anna M. Knaps. 2021. The memory of financial crises: The great depression and the global financial crisis of 2008. In *Remembering and learning from financial crises*, ed. Y. Cassis and C. Schenk, 18–38. Oxford: Oxford University Press.

Connerton, Paul. 2008. Seven types of forgetting. *Memory Studies* 1:59–71.

Cubitt, Geoffrey. 2019. History of memory. In *Debating new approaches to history*, ed. M. Tamm and P. Burke, 127–158. London: Bloomsbury Academic.

Davis, Natalie Z., and Randolph Stern. 1989. Introduction. *Representations* 26 (Special Issue): 1–6.

Duroselle, Jean-Baptiste. 1979. 24 octobre 1929: le jeudi noir de Wall Street. *Le Figaro*, October 24.

Edy, Jill A. 1999. Journalistic uses of collective memory. *Journal of Communication* 49:71–85.

Eichengreen, Barry. 2015. *Hall of mirrors: The great depression, the great recession, and the uses—And misuses—Of history*. New York: Oxford University Press.

Erll, Astrid, and Ansgar Nünning. 2008. Introduction. In *Cultural memory studies: An international and interdisciplinary handbook*, ed. A. Erll and A. Nünning, 1–15. Berlin and New York: Walter de Gruyter.

Erll, Astrid, and Ann Rigney. 2009. *Mediation, remediation and the dynamics of cultural memory*. Berlin: Walter de Gruyter.

Financial Times. 1979. Ripples from the wall street storm. October 13.

Graf, Rüdiger. 2010. Either-or: The narrative of "crisis" in Weimar Germany and in historiography. *Central European History* 43:592–615.

Greenspan, Alan. 2001. The financial safety net. 37th Annual Conference on Bank Structure and Competition of the Federal Reserve Bank of Chicago, Chicago, IL, May 10. https://www.federalreserve.gov/boarddocs/speeches/2001/20010510/default.htm. Accessed on 3 March 2024.

Hall, Peter A. 1993. Policy paradigms, social learning, and the state: The case of economic policymaking in Britain. *Comparative Politics* 25:275–296.

Hansen, Per. 2012. Business history: A cultural and narrative approach. *Business History Review* 86:693–717.

Hansen, Per. 2014. From finance capitalism to financialization: A cultural and narrative perspective of 150 years of financial history. *Enterprise and Society* 15:605–641.

Hansen, Per. 2015. Review essay of *Hall of mirrors: The great depression, the great recession, and the uses—And misuses—Of history*, by B. *Eichengreen*. *Business History Review* 89:557–569.

Hay, Colin. 2010. Chronicles of a death foretold: The winter of discontent and construction of the crisis of British Keynesianism. *Parliamentary Affairs* 63:446–470.

Ip, Greg. 2004a. Greenspan's legacy. The navigator. *Wall Street Journal*, November 18.

Ip, Greg. 2004b. Greenspan's legacy. The deregulator. *Wall Street Journal*, November 19.

Johnson, Haynes. 1979. 50 years after the depression: Saving the government that saves us. *Washington Post*, October 14.

Klein, Maury. 2001. The stock market crash of 1929: A review article. *Business History Review* 75:325–351.

Koselleck, Reinhart, and Michaela W. Richter. 2006. Crisis. *Journal of the History of Ideas* 67:357–400.

Lipartito, Kenneth. 1995. Culture and the practice of business history. *Business and Economic History* 24:1–41.

Lyotard, François. 1979. *La condition Postmoderne*. Paris: Les Éditions de Minuit.

MacKenzie, Donald. 2006. *An engine, not a camera: How financial models shape markets*. London and Cambridge, MA: MIT Press.

Mandelbrot, Benoit. 2004. Great confusion since the great crash. *Financial Times*, October 22.

Meretoja, Hanna. 2020. A dialogics of counter-narratives. In *Routledge handbook of counter-narratives*, ed. K. Lueg and M. W. Lundholt, 30–42. London: Routledge.

New York Times. 1949. Banks are urged for smaller firms, October 29.

Nora, Pierre. 1989. Between memory and history. *Representations* 26 (Special Issue): 7–24.

Reinhart, Carmen, and Kenneth Rogoff. 2009. *This time is different: Eight centuries of financial folly*. Princeton: Princeton University Press.

Rowen, Hobart. 1979. Today is not 1929. *Washington Post*, October 28.

Schlesinger, Arthur Jr. 1979. The revolution that never was. *Wall Street Journal*, October 24.

Shiller, Robert. 2017. Narrative economics. *American Economic Review* 107:967–1004.

Süddeutsche Zeitung. 2004. Parallelen sind unverkennbar. October 22.

Telesca, Giuseppe. 2021. Myths and memory: The crisis of the pound and the political use of the memory of 1931 in the United Kingdom. In *Remembering and learning from financial crises*, ed. Y. Cassis and C. Schenk, 57–81. Oxford: Oxford University Press.

Telesca, Giuseppe. 2024. Exorcising dysfunctional myths. Betrayal, economic incompetence, and the memory of the 1931 second Labour government's crisis. *Labour History Review*, 89: 229–251.

Tett, Gillian. 2007. Doomed to repeat it? *Financial Times*, August 27.

The Economist. 1974. A world banking crisis? August 3.

The Economist. 1979. 1929 and all this. October 13.

The Economist. 1987. Tell Sid it's a risky business. October 24.

The Economist. 2008. 1929 and all that. October 4.

The Guardian. 1954. Wall street anniversary. November 2.

The Times. 1987. The pedlars of certainty. October 26.

Time. 1979. Could the great crash of '29 recur?. October 22.

Wall Street Journal. 1979a. 1929's unlearned lessons. October 29.

Wall Street Journal. 1979b. The crash of '79? October 29.

Wanniski, Jude. 1979. The crash and classical economics. *Wall Street Journal*, October 26.

Welter, Erich. 1956. Der 13. *Juli: Von der Devisenzuteilung zur Kommandowirtschaft. Frankfurter Allgemeine Zeitung*, July 14.
Wertsch, James V. 2002. *Voices of collective remembering*. Cambridge and New York: Cambridge University Press.
Zelizer, Barbie. 2008a. Journalism's memory work. In *Cultural memory studies: An international and interdisciplinary handbook*, ed. A. Erll and A. Nünning, 379–388. Berlin and New York: Walter de Gruyter.
Zelizer, Barbie. 2008b. Why memory's work on journalism does not reflect journalism's work on memory. *Memory Studies* 1:79–87.

Collective Famine Memories and the Economies of Catastrophe

Marguérite Corporaal

1 Introduction

As, amongst others, Astrid Erll has argued, memory is inherently fluid, as it can travel through time and space, "across [...] and also beyond cultures", and in that process, attain new meanings which serve present agendas and future ambitions (Erll 2014, 29). Erll's claim certainly applies to the collective memories of economic crises caused by catastrophes, such as famines which took place across Europe between 1845 and 1947. Indeed, in the case of the rich legacies of European famines, we clearly see how past eras of mass starvation are often utilised and reframed as economic crises in the context of present societal issues, especially other hunger crises. Thus, a tweet by Taoiseach Micheál Martín, posted on 6 July 2022, about his visit to the Holodomor Memorial in Kyiv, related the Ukrainian famine of 1932–33 to Russia's war politics, stating "Russia must not be allowed to use food as a weapon in this immoral and unjustified war". Furthermore, by stating that "[b]oth Ukraine and Ireland know the suffering and pain of famine", Martín also explicitly drew

M. Corporaal (✉)
Radboud University, Nijmegen, Netherlands
e-mail: marguerite.corporaal@ru.nl

S. Berger and T. Fetzer (eds.), *Collective Memory of Economic Crises and Transformations*, Palgrave Macmillan Memory Studies,
https://doi.org/10.1007/978-3-032-09094-2_3

analogies between the ongoing Russian aggression, including its food blockades, and collective recollections of the Holodomor and Ireland's Great Famine (1845–50), probably as a way to elicit further attention for the threat of hunger in Ukraine and the Global South resulting from Russia's Black Sea blockade. Even more recently, Azril Mohd Amin called the acute malnutrition in Northern Gaza "another form of Holodomor", comparing the "deliberate strategy of starvation employed by the Israeli regime" with the "man-made famine imposed by the Soviet regime in Ukraine during the early 1930s" (Amin 2024). In a similar vein, during the annual commemoration of the Great Famine on 19 May 2024, present Taoiseach Simon Harris declared that "the unfolding famine in Gaza" is "repellent to the Irish psyche" (Mannion 2024).

These examples reveal the politicisation of famine pasts till today; a phenomenon that can be explained by the fact that famines are recurrent and cyclical, despite the fact that, as Amartya Sen has famously argued, often sufficient food is available. As Sen observes, it is people's entitlement relations in a society that determine their access to sufficient food (1981, 49); a claim repeated by Stephen Devereux (2006, 4–5) and Alex de Waal (2018, Chapter 2), who have moreover emphasised the accountability of those in power regarding the causation or prevention of famines. Famine legacies are not only mobilised as strategies to comment on the occurrence or threats of renewed hunger crises, but also to critique present economic policies and conditions, as is exemplified by Greek Prime Minister Tsipras's statement in a 2015 speech to parliament that Germany, instead of demanding further financial cut-backs in Greece, should actually make reparations for its pillage of the country during WWII, which, in his view, had caused the 1941–42 famine (Coleman 2015; Corporaal and de Zwarte 2021, 11). Additionally, the collective memories of European famines also reflect on the economies surrounding such calamities; an underexplored issue, which this chapter will focus on.

James V. Wertsch states that societies organise memory into recurring narrative "templates" or schemata, as ways to give meaning to the past (Wertsch 2002, 57), and this also holds for famine remembrance. Famines are remembered very differently in various national contexts, and in a few cases, one can even speak of a scarcity rather than plenitude of collective famine memory. Nonetheless, cultural memories regarding various European famines are often structured according to similar, recurrent plots that are rooted in interrelated conceptualisations of political and economic responsibility, relief and agency. The present study will discuss three of such repetitive narrative templates regarding economies of hunger which inform past and present European memories, and which are all interrelated by their concern with aid and resilience.

One important script that informs past and present famine legacies is centred around severe criticism of the nineteenth-century concept of political economy, a socio-economic doctrine inspired by Adam Smith and Thomas Malthus, that was rooted in the concepts of limited government intervention, self-reliance and a self-regulating market (Kells Ingram 1888, 64; de Quincey 1844, 117), and that was embraced by neoliberal cabinets in, amongst others, the United Kingdom and Finland. This template holds governments and the upper classes accountable for aggravating the suffering of the starving, poorer classes. As will be demonstrated, in the collective memory of Ireland's Great Famine, the government's adherence to philosophies of political economy plays a significant role: the London administration's laissez-faire policies are generally criticised, and are even interpreted as politics to strengthen England's sway over Ireland as well as to deliberately exterminate its population. Similar critiques on the Helsinki government's policies of self-reliance and self-regulation can also be found in the legacies of the Finnish famine.

A second recurring transnational template in European hunger legacies concerns a celebration of charity, in the form of donations or relief programmes, as a way to alleviate famine distress and help regenerate stricken communities. Regional famine heritage in Finland, Ireland and the Netherlands, often in the form of monuments or museum collections, critically remembers relief work, initiated by local authorities, national or imperial governments, which proved unsuccessful in alleviating distress. By contrast, there is a growing emergence of famine legacies which recollect transnational solidarity. The third recurring template that will be addressed is economic agency by famine victims. There are many long forgotten stories of how, for example, famine-stricken women showed resilience by playing an active role in (illegal) food distribution and through black markets in, for example, Francoist Spain (1939–52), Germany during and following World War I (1914–24), occupied Greece (1941–42) and the occupied Netherlands (Anderson 2020; Arco Blanco et al. 2021; Cox 2019; Hionidou 2006; Tönsmeyer et al. 2021; de Zwarte 2020). As this chapter will demonstrate, such narratives have become increasingly visible in current memory practices.

2 Famine Memory and Political Economy

The narrative template which denounces neoliberal policies in remedying the effects of famine is strongly present in the past and present cultural legacies of Ireland's Great Famine. This is by no means remarkable, as these laissez-faire politics were frequently endorsed by government representatives. Whilst British Prime Minister Robert Peel had repealed the Corn Laws, imported Indian meal and set up relief schemes at the onset of Ireland's Great Famine, his successor in 1846, Whig Lord John Russell, resorted to relief policies of non-interference. As Peter Gray argues, Russell and his ministry believed that Ireland "lacked not capital, but the will to create wealth" (1999, 48), and phased out Peel's relief measures in order to encourage social and economic reforms on the colonised sister isle (Ó Gradá 1999, 78; Boyland and Foley 1992, 8). The London government's laissez-faire policies were particularly endorsed by colonial administrator and assistant to the Treasury Sir Charles Trevelyan, a former student of Malthus at Haileybury, who in *The Irish Crisis* (1848) had viewed the Famine and subsequent emigration schemes as natural mechanisms by which the "fearful surplus population" of Ireland would be checked (1848, 78). Trevelyan considered the Famine "a direct stroke of an all-wise and all-merciful Providence", in that it would prompt a reformation of Irish character, causing "morbid habits to give place to a more healthy action" (Trevelyan 1848, 201). These ideas, which merged philosophies of political economy with imperial bias, were more widespread regarding famines occurring under British imperial rule at large. Thus, William Pulteney Allison in *Observations on the Famine of 1846–7, in the Highlands of Scotland and in Ireland* (1847) claimed that the potato blight that affected the Scottish Highlands and Ireland and that entailed mass starvation and emigration was "one of the positive checks" of nature in areas with a redundancy of population that cannot possibly be fed (1847, 6).

In the collective cultural memory of Ireland's Great Famine, the government's adherence to philosophies of political economy is generally criticised as a political failure to alleviate the catastrophe, and even interpreted as a scheme to strengthen England's sway over Ireland, as well as to deliberately exterminate its population. *The Adventures of Doctor Brady* (1869), a novel by the Tallaght-born reporter of *The Times,* William Howard Russell, parodies the Malthusian rhetoric utilised by, amongst others, Trevelyan in relation to famine-stricken Ireland: the necessity to prove its validity depends on sacrificing the Irish population. Maurice Prendergast's inflammatory nationalist treatise implies that England has deliberately abandoned the starving Irish to uphold the doctrines of political economists who are delighted by the "sudden and violent augmentation and public exhibition before the world of a normal process" (1869, 208). The narrator's account of Maurice's argument subsequently ridicules these political economists who "revel in famines" mainly to see their theory "beautifully [...] proved", and whose logical fallacies makes the easily persuaded government believe that "[i]t is quite certain that if the people can pay for it, food will go to them: if it does not go, and they die in consequence, it only proves that they did not want food, or ought not to get it, and that they deserve to die!" (Russell 1869, 208–9). In a similar vein, Mildred Darby's *The Hunger* (1910) represents the rhetoric of laissez-faire as a form of political violence towards the peasant class. She critiques the inefficiency of "the doctrines of political economy", showing that its insistence on not disturbing the "labour market" rather than offering "[r]eproductive work", whereby the starving Irish "might earn food" leads to high mortality rates which could have been avoided: "Food could not be *given* them by the Government, for fear of pauperising a nation! [...] If the Government sold them the meal of which they stood in such sore need, it could not be for sums below the market price—or more truly, the inflated famine prices—lest any underselling should ruin the shopkeepers and the meal mongers" (Merry [Darby] 1910, 3; see also Corporaal 2020, 82).

The idea that plans to eliminate the Catholic Irish are behind the government's unwavering endorsement of political economy features most prominently in Irish-American famine legacies, often in ways that resonate with the rhetoric used by Young Irelander John Mitchel. For example, in Dillon O'Brien's Irish-American novel *The Dalys of Dalystown* (1866), emigrant Henry Daly condemns Lord John Russell's strident support for political economy. Henry suggests that the Prime Minister's "spouting in the British House of Commons about political economy" serves his ulterior ambition to "uproot the Celtic race from Ireland" (O'Brien 1866, 499); a passage which resonates with Irish radical nationalist and exile in America John Mitchel's assertion in *Jail Journal: Or Five Years in British Prisons* (1854) that "four years of British policy, with the Famine to aid" resulted in "killing fully two millions", as Parliamentary politics encouraged "the extermination, that is, the slaughter" of the tenantry (Mitchel 1854, 7–8).

Interestingly, this script that equates neoliberal economic policies with deliberate eradication features very strongly in more recent legacies of the Great Irish Famine. The haunting legacy of Trevelyan's neglect to provide adequate relief features in Michael Farrell's painting "Black '47" (1997–98), created on the occasion of the sesquicentenary of the bleakest famine year. The artwork portrays Assistant Secretary Charles Trevelyan justifying why he withholds food and money from the Irish in their plight. He points to a few potatoes on the table, suggesting that the Irish's reliance on them as their staple food, a sign of an unhealthy economy, is the root of all misery. Meanwhile, at the other end of the table, one can see a group of skeletons emerging from a grave, symbolising the Famine victims who claim retribution for the way in which they were abandoned by the London government. Beneath the skeletons, one can see shoes, as tangible reminders of these people's lives, but also as hints of the roads they helped create on the relief works: these were infamous for offering those who worked on digging the roads too little payment to afford the expensive food in times of scarcity (Ó Gradá 1999, 64). Farrell's painting can be read as an accusation of the British government turning its back on the suffering Irish, making the people's access to food subordinate to its market principles.

Two recent Famine novels likewise criticise the British government's economic policies towards hunger-stricken Ireland. In Marita Conlon McKenna's *The Hungry Road* (2020), which is set in Famine-stricken Skibbereen, Father Fitzpatrick is infuriated at the market principles to which the London government adheres despite the wide-scale disaster: "the British authorities, who did so little to sustain the living as the country starved, still permitted food, grain and livestock to be exported to English cities and made absolutely no provision for the inevitable – the internment of the dead" (McKenna 2020, 185). Kalyan Ray's 2014 novel, *No Country*, includes chapters set in, amongst others, Bengal during the 1910s, Calcutta during the 1940s and New York during the 1980s. A very prominent part of this novel, by a writer whose family settled in the United States after having been uprooted from Bangladesh, is, however, set in Ireland prior to and during the Great Famine. In a letter which character Robert Aherne writes to his grandson Neal in September 1987, he reflects upon the Great Famine which his Irish grandfather Padraig had witnessed in 1847, and directly compares it to the 1942–43 Bengal famine that he was testimony to: "My grandfather Padraig had come from an Ireland racked by famine—the kind of famine that I myself saw in

Calcutta and the surrounding countryside in 1942-43". As Robert states, "All the grains were taken from Bengal's fine harvests for the war effort in Burma, leaving the Bengalis starving", a situation reminiscent of the disastrous laissez-faire governmental policies during Ireland's Great Famine: "What has the Empire learnt from the 1840s to the 1940s? Or perhaps, they learn too well" (Ray 2014, 493). Interestingly, this passage suggests how famine memories may overlap and intersect, even if they took place in different times and countries. Stating that "[m]emories are not owned by groups", and therefore do not run parallel with group boundaries, Michael Rothberg suggests that different sets of cultural memory exist "in dynamic transfers", as "multidirectional memory" (Rothberg 2009, 5). Ray's novel stages such "multidirectional" memories of starvation which condemn past colonial policies of political economy.

This plot of political economy that structures legacies of famines happening under British imperial rule is also present in heritages of hunger elsewhere in Europe, most notably Finland. In fact, it is a significant "transnational" template in past and present collective famine memories: it appears to be a script that gives shape and meaning to famine pasts that transcend national borders (Rigney and de Cesari 2014, 7, 4). Johan Vilhelm Snellman, Minister of Finance in the devolved government of Finland when it was a Grand Duchy integrated in Russia's empire, was a staunch adherent of political economy. Snellman promoted "self-sufficiency and frugality", and was critical of people's belief that "the crown would help them when in need", feeling that the population should learn to "help themselves through hard work and saving", and should "take better care of their personal economy" instead of relying on state support (Reese 2017, 91, 94). Snellman's propagation of the principles of political economy, which dominated the Finnish Senate's famine policies, came at a time when Finland's countryside, especially in the northern regions, was severely afflicted by famine after periods of fierce frost had destroyed the crops (Newby 2014; Häakinen and Forsberg 2018). The Finnish Hunger years (1866–68) cost the lives of 8.5 per cent of Finland's population, whilst Snellman was reluctant to borrow money abroad to relieve the crisis, in order to protect the newly introduced currency (Newby 2023, 60, 181, 270; Häakinen and Forsberg 2015).

The damage caused by the Helsinki government's policies of self-reliance and self-regulation left its traces on cultural memories of the

Finnish famine. This becomes, for instance, clear from Juho Reijonen's story "Nälkävuonna: Karjalainen Kertomus", translated by Andrew Newby as "During The Year of Hunger (A Karelian Tale)", which was published in the literary magazine *Nuori Suomi* on 16 December 1893. The story centres on Perttu and his large family, who have nothing to eat after the severe winter cold has badly affected cultivation and restricted agricultural labour. Facing distress and starvation, there is no remedy at hand, for "at mid-winter the master of Kohiseva House came to inform Perttu that there was no longer any surplus in the charity coffers to give to anyone in Kuohatti. The guardian of the poor-law board had announced at church that the state could not afford to spend money on just nothing, and that the people of Kuohatti had better work" (Reijonen 1893, 2018b, II). The government is portrayed as unwilling to supply relief for the sake of alleviating destitution and famine, sticking to market principles of labour and a self-regulating economy. Reijonen's narrative retrospectively exposes the inefficiencies of Snellman's laissez-faire policies, which are moreover rooted in Malthusian concerns about overpopulation. Perttu has many mouths to feed, but is simply told by the master that "the one who bears children shall also carry their woes" (Reijonen 1893, 2018a, I).

A more covert critique of the domestic government's failure to offer adequate relief is expressed by a series of monuments that can be found along the railway track between Riihimäki and St. Petersburg, which is also known as the "'Hunger Track' [*nälkärata*] or 'Skeleton Track' [*luurata*]" (Boerman 2024, 183). Whilst supposed to function as a public relief work during Finland's worst famine years, in reality, they intensified the crisis, as many people flocked to the site of the works to find employment. Furthermore, the "harsh working conditions and spread of epidemic diseases at the railway construction sites led to a spike in local mortality rates" (Boerman 2024, 183), to which mass graves alongside the track testify. Nearly a century after the famine years, the burial sites became marked with plaques and memorials (Newby 2023, 48). Examples of these include a fenced railway builders' grave in Hausjärvi, "with cross motif" and an inscription to the memory of those who died on this relief project in 1867 (Newby 2017, 187).

As Boerman points out, the fact that these mass graves became designated as memory sites through later "heritage interventions" (Boerman 2024, 184) is significant. They create a counternarrative to the dominant template of "character traits such as self-sufficiency, forbearance, and sedulity" that became integral to the Finnish Fennoman movement's construction of an independent, Finnish national identity (Boerman 2024, 185; see also Newby 2023, 215); an identity that was to a great extent formulated by Snellman himself, through essays published in his own nationalist Swedish-language newspaper *Saima* (suppressed in 1846; Meinander 2011, 125–27). In fact, Boerman states, the famine sites "scattered along the Finnish part of the railway" are peripheral *lieux de mémoire* that critique the national narrative of progress and modernity that Snellman's policies are often believed to have embodied (Boerman 2024, 191). The centenary of the hunger years also saw other sites of unsuccessful relief works, in terms of high death tolls, marked by memorials, which have been identified by Andrew Newby: one is an erected stone with a (1967) which pays tribute to the many casualties amongst the builders of the Tokerotie road in Jalasjärvi, Southern Ostrobothnia (Newby 2017, 189). These memorial sites also convey critiques on the Helsinki government's inadequate relief policies, showing that economic policies, which sought to boost the modernisation of national infrastructures, came with a considerable human sacrifice.

Such memorial sites to Finland's famine years which contest national narratives of self-sufficiency and stamina are overall rare, however; and the national narrative of self-reliance and stoic persistence that lies at the heart of Finland's nation formation, and that was promoted by Snellman's writings, such as *Taytaessa Seitseemankymmntaviisi Vuotta* ("Self-Reliance and Other Essays", 1881), appears to have informed Finnish famine heritage. As Andrew Newby and Eliza Krataari claim, after the Civil War and Finnish independence, the famine years had to be framed as "the inevitable economic birth pains of a new nation, pain that needed to be endured, or as one of several 'building blocks' which helped to create a modern state" (Newby and Krataari 2018, 99). This is reflected in the primarily regionally based and initiated monuments to the Finnish hunger years, which frame the famine in a narrative of endurance and faith in God, rather than as a critique on the domestic government's policies of non-interference. Examples of this are the monument in Rantsila, which depicts a Christian cross and outstretched hands, as well as the large Christian cross in Sotkamo's parish churchyard, which is accompanied by "Verse 49 in the Finnish Lutheran Hymnal" which expresses a steadfast belief in God's goodness (Newby 2017, 205). By contrast, in Ireland, deprived of home rule since 1801, a narrative that frames the Famine as shared victimhood under a foreign colonial oppressor has enabled the widespread emergence of memory templates, which cast the London government's neoliberal politics as wilful neglect. These significant distinctions between the scripts that have informed processes of nationhood formation and struggles for independence on one hand Ireland (1919–1921), and on the other Finland (1917–1919) may also clarify why there is no national famine monument or commemoration in Finland. By contrast, Ireland has had its national famine monument—John Behan's bronze emigrant ship in Murrisk, Co. Mayo—since 1997, and its annual Famine commemoration day since 2008.

3 Famine Memory and Charity

The previously discussed recurrent template which critiques inadequate governmental policies in alleviating famine distress reveals that periods of mass starvation are often remembered through narratives focussing on (lack of) relief. What matters most in the economic framing of legacies of European hunger crises appears to be the issue of accountability in delivering or failing to supply adequate aid. This concept of relief also permeates a second major narrative scheme (Zerubavel 2003, 11) that can be found in Famine remembrance, namely one that foregrounds acts of charity which the afflicted received. This becomes evident when looking at recent legacies of the Finnish hunger years, Ireland's Great Famine, German Post World War II famine (1945–1948) and the Dutch Hunger Winter (1944–45). The famine-stricken Finnish population received aid from the British Society of Friends, who, two decades earlier, had set up soup kitchens and other relief initiatives in Ireland (Newby 2023, 135–36; see also Kinealy 2013). This relief offered by British Quakers to both the Irish and the Finnish suffering population was commemorated in the travelling exhibition "Nälkä!: The Great Finnish Famine" (2019), which was curated by Andrew Newby and which was hosted by, amongst others, National Famine Museum Strokestown Park, the Irish Workhouse Famine in Portumna, the Culture Centre Valve in Oulu, and the University of Tampere. The exhibition showcased a panel entitled "Charity from Home and Abroad" which provides information about the fundraising campaigns and relief operations set up by British Quakers in both Ireland and Finland (see also Newby 2014); in the latter during a period of hunger after the Crimean War (1856), and later during the Great Hunger years themselves (1866–68). In so doing, it broke ground by incorporating comparative, international perspectives and by contributing public knowledge about Finland as a recipient of transnational solidarity.

Irish Great Famine legacies of more recent years have increasingly given attention to the charity received from abroad by the hunger-stricken Irish. During the annual national Famine commemoration ceremony in Dublin, on 17 May 2020, Minister of Culture, Heritage and the Gaeltacht Josepha Madigan paid a tribute to those who donated from across the world, such as Polish Count Strzelecki: "We also remember the contributions received from abroad – from Britain, Turkey and diverse communities in the United States including the Jewish Community in New York and the Committee of Coloured Citizens in Philadelphia" (Great Famine Voices 2020). The earlier analysed painting by Farrell contrasts Britain's unwillingness to offer adequate relief with a reference to the Turkish Sultan Abdülmdjid, who at the time donated an amount equivalent to 1000 pounds to the suffering Irish: in the background, one can perceive a group of Ottomans.

In recent Famine legacies, the donation of $170 by the Choctaw Nation to the Irish, a substantial sum back in 1847, has acquired a significant place. In her speech at the 2020 Famine commemoration, Minister Madigan singled out this international act of generosity. She stated that this gesture of empathy was called "[o]ne of the most enduring memories of the international impact of the Great Famine", coming from deprived people who had just survived displacement from their lands and hunger during the trail of tears, and in return, prompting donations by the Irish to the COVID-19 stricken Navajo and Hopi tribes in March 2020 (Great Famine Voices 2020). This so-called "Choctaw gift" had gained a more prominent place in the collective memories of the Great Famine previously. In 2016, Irish sculptor Kieran Tuohy created "Thank you to the Choctaw", an artwork that depicts a set of fragile hands holding up a group of emaciated people, showing the solidarity and support of one economically vulnerable community to another. Two years later, saw the installation of the monument "Kindred Spirits" (2018), created by Alex Pentek, at Bailivk Park in Midleton, County Cork. Consisting of large, stainless-steel feathers which together form a bowl shape to represent a gift of food, this memorial to a donation "that sparked a bond between the two cultures that continues today" engrains humanitarian aid in Irish Famine legacies (Taggart 2021).

Relief and aid are also central to several monuments related to hunger during and after World War II. The Dutch Hunger Winter, caused by transportation blockades imposed by the German occupier as well as the Allied forces, and intensified by the ongoing railway strike, took place in a very different temporal and geographical context. Nonetheless, we see a similar tendency in collective memory to emphasise charity and relief. In 1947, a monument expressing gratitude to the Frisian people on the part of the population of Amsterdam-Watergraafsmeer, for their aid during the dire months of famine, was revealed in Lollum (see also Jensen and de Zwarte 2024, 101). The images of wheat sheaves and bread epitomise the food aid that was provided to the children, who, through the "Interkerkelijk Overleg", an interconfessional organisation instrumental had been evacuated to areas in the north of the Netherlands not cut off from food distribution (de Zwarte 2020, 231–56). The depicted pelican—a Christian symbol for self-sacrifice—expresses the solidarity of the Frisians in times of general scarcity.

A more recent monument to famine charity, that moreover foregrounds transnational relief, is the Operation Manna monument in Rotterdam, designed by Ruud Reutelingsperger and unveiled on 4 April 2006, to commemorate the food droppings that took place between 29 April and 8 May 1945 on ten locations in the Netherlands. Representing stacked food packages in the steel "belly" of a plane, the memorial eulogises the British and American military forces who operated more than 5300 flights to distribute food (see also Jensen and de Zwarte 2024, 104). The inscription of the column cites one of the bomber pilots, as a way to underscore the significance of Operation Manna in terms of relief: "For five years we spread death and destruction and in the last week we saved thousands from starving". In various respects, Reutelingsperger's monument is not unlike Eduard Ludwig's Luftbrückendenkmal (1951) at the former Tempelhof airport in Berlin, which, also in a rather abstract form, commemorates food aid through air forces. The airlift, organised by America, Britain and France, freed the population of West Berlin from its 332-day isolation and brought supplies of food to West Berlin's citizens (Weinreb 2017, 114, 117). With the two identical memorials that were placed at the Royal Air Force base in Celle (1985) and the Rhein-Main Air base in Frankfurt (1988), the Berlin Luftbrückendenkmal foregrounds a narrative of relief in its remembrance of food shortages, just like many monuments and artworks discussed in this section. It must be remembered, however, as Alice Weinreb has also argued, that this programme of food aid was primarily driven by geopolitical ambitions to curtail the influence of the Soviet Union (Weinreb 2017, 114).

4 Narratives of Agency

Famine legacies—in the form of, for instance, texts, visual representations or monuments—often express narratives of helplessness and victimhood, depicting those vulnerable to starvation through their class, ethnicity, age and gender. For example, in Finland, the Mäntsälä monument to the hunger refugees, designed by sculptor Heikki Varja and unveiled in July 1984 (Newby 2017, 199), shows the lean figures of homeless wanderers, clearly members of the poor, rural classes who have taken to the road in a vain quest for food and work, but who find themselves and their families perish with hunger. Rowan Gillespie's Famine Memorial, commissioned by Norma Smurfit and presented to the City of Dublin in 1997, consists of the sculpture of a famished dog and six bronze-cast figures of haggard persons—four men and two women—who, clutching their few belongings, appear to make their way towards a migrant vessel that is to take them to America (see also Mark-FitzGerald 2013, 221–23). The monument gives shape to phenomena that were common during the Great Famine years: evicted from their homes by their often Anglo-Irish Protestant landlords when, due to the failed potato crops, they could no longer pay the rent, many former Catholic Irish tenants wandered by the roadside, nearly collapsing with hunger (Ó Gráda 1999, 44–45). Often, these famine legacies which convey helplessness centre on maternal figures. An example is Heinrich Zille's "Hunger" (1924), a contribution to a series of lithographs by seven well-known, mostly left-wing artists published in 1924, for the benefit of the "International Workers' Aid", which aimed to collect money for hunger aid when poverty, unemployment and famine prompted commitment. What is striking about Zille's lithograph is the fact that the depicted mother is incapable of providing her underfed children with food, and looks so worn that one wonders whether she will manage to breastfeed her baby sufficiently. This image of a mother failing to keep her newborn alive is also poignantly present in Costas Valsamis's monument to the Greek Famine, "Mother of the Occupation" (Η Μάνα της Κατοχής, 1979), which is located in the "First Cemetery" of Athens. The bronze sculpture, based on a real scene the sculptor witnessed in Piraeus, during the winter of 1941, represents a naked, gaunt and almost lifeless woman, with a child suckling her empty breast (see also Boerman 2025).

The dominant focus on victimhood, even in present-day famine legacies, can be explained through ongoing processes for justice and recognition. Valsamis's monument can be interpreted against the background of ongoing claims for financial reparations for the economic damage caused by Germany during World War II, especially by Tsipras's party between 2015 and 2019. Narratives of victimhood fit in with this political ambition. Similarly, there appears to be a correlation between the long-standing campaigns for recognition of the Ukraine famine as genocide, driven on by Ukraine and its North American diaspora, and the prevalence of narratives of victimhood that mark Holodomor heritage. For example, Nina Marchenko's "The Children of the Holodomor" (2017) includes a painting of starving children and their emaciated mother, whose legs have begun to swell from starvation. As her haggard son, with a distended stomach, holds out an empty bowl to her, she cannot offer any food (HREC Education 2022). Naturally, the narrative of victimhood that has dominated cultural memories of the Holodomor can also be attributed to the fact that the tragedy partially unfolded as a result of the enforced collectivisation of farms—and with this, lack of autonomy amongst Ukraine's peasant class (Graziosi 2008), which may have reinforced this narrative. Nevertheless, Ukraine's effort for international recognition of its 1932–33 famine as genocide should also be seen as impacting this prevalent famine memory template.

In contrast with these representations of emaciated bodies, as symbols of helpless agony calling out for empathy and charity, recent Famine legacies more often present examples of resilience and inventiveness. These alternative memories of European Famine pasts, namely the active ways in which those stricken by hunger sought survival or helped in distributing food, have long remained invisible and inaccessible in the public sphere. As Jefferson Singer and Martin Conway have argued, some pasts are not really forgotten, but less accessible in the public sphere: this happens when certain legacies are "available", but may not be widely "accessible" at any given time, because it remains hidden in archives, or because people have kept back testimonies of such a past for personal or political reasons. This implies, however, that such legacies "can potentially be retrieved and through the retrieval process might enter consciousness and so influence experience and behavior" as well (Singer and Conway 2008, 280).

In Spain, for instance, "[m] emories of hunger were restricted to the individual and family domains" for a very long time (Arco Blanco and Madden 2024, 213). Oral history projects in the post-Franco years, as well as the excavation of hitherto private archives of letters and photographs, have laid bare long-suppressed memoirs of the hunger years, which included the active role played by mothers and housewives in trying to make their families survive. These alternative memories of the Francoist era, and the *años del hambre*, found their way into recent legacies of the Spanish hunger years. Paco Roca's autobiographical graphic novel *Regreso al Edén* (2020), which develops around a family photograph taken at the Nazaret beach in Valencia in 1947, centres on the artist's mother Antonia, who grew up in these famine years, and her working-class family. Antonia's mother is shown to negotiate black market corruption regularly to obtain scraps of food for her husband and children (Roca 2020), thereby presenting an image of steadfast agency.

Similar narratives of women's agency and inventiveness were presented at the recent exhibition "La Hambruna Silenciada" (2022), which was curated by, amongst others, Miguel Ángel del Arco Blanco, Carmina Gústran Locos and Gloria Román Ruiz from the University of Granada. Whilst displaying data about famine mortality, as well as showing explicit pictures of dire poverty and hunger, especially amongst cave dwellers in the neighbourhood of Almeria, this exhibition also accentuates ways in which the Spanish people under Franco's regime attempted to survive the so-called years of hunger. The panels showed recipes invented by housewives to cook meals with very little that was available, such as "arroz de Franco" (Arco Blanco et al. 2022, panel 17). Furthermore, the panels show original photographs of the black markets (*estraperlo*) and food aid centres (Arco Blanco et al. 2022, panel 20–21), and specifically endorse women's agency in acquiring and distributing food, through photographs of an old woman illegally selling potatoes by Alan Lomax (1952) and trying to barter for food on a black market in Malaga (Arco Blanco et al. 2022, panel 21). Analogous narrative templates of (female) agency feature in mementoes to the Dutch Hunger Winter. The recently reorganised displays about the Dutch Hunger Winter at the Amsterdam Resistance Museum (2023) also focus on the actions the hunger-stricken undertook to acquire (access to) food. The material objects on display clearly serve to draw today's audiences into this distant past, for materiality is often a prerequisite for "emotional investment and identification" with the past (2013, 12). These include pots of pickled sugar beets (which was normally food destined for cattle), and tulip bulbs—which were frequently prepared by women and eaten in the absence of any other food. Furthermore, this section of the museum engages with personal testimonies and memories, and the belongings of those who went in search of food. There is, for instance, a letter from December 1944, written by 16-year-old Toby Vos (1918–2019), who walked from Amsterdam to the countryside, to tempt farmers into bartering precious personal belongings for food stuff. These artefacts and the accompanying storyboards generate a sense of the World War II-related famine past that seeks to transcend narratives of passive endurance and defeat.

Most monuments to the Dutch Hunger Winter integrate Christian symbolism, with the exception of Tineke Bot's monument of a young woman on a bicycle (1981), called "De Koerierster" (The Courier) and located at the Noorderplantage in Leeuwarden, Friesland. As Lotte Jensen and Ingrid de Zwarte contend, the monument "allegedly expressed the important role of female couriers in the Dutch resistance" (2024, 96). However, based on the earliest mentions of the monument in the newspaper, the *Leeuwarder Courant*, in May 1981 and 1982, the sculpture "seems to have been intended to symbolise all women who ventured out to search for food during the final year of the war" (Jensen and de Zwarte 2024, 102) and was alternatively called "The Food Bringer". In this light, the monument expresses (women's) agency and resilience during the Dutch famine years, in the acquisition and distribution of food.

5 Conclusion

As has been demonstrated, famine legacies increasingly address the global contexts in which these calamities took place, in terms of analogous or shared pasts, transnational solidarity and charity, as well as constellations of power and money that directed economic policies with regard to food markets, distribution and market regulation. Famine memories often address inequalities between those who have political or economic power on the one hand and those who suffer from want of food on the other; and in what respects this unevenness of power is related to entitlement.

Who are the deserving or undeserving poor in terms of relief measures taken by local, national or imperial governments? These are the bigger issues at stake in the recurring narrative templates that censure nineteenth-century European economic policies in contexts of famines. Whether such templates are omnipresent in famine legacies or not depends to a large extent on the dominant narratives of nationhood that have informed processes towards political independence. Furthermore, whether representations of victimhood—often in the form of emaciated bodies and depictions of suffering—prevail in heritage also appears to be inextricably connected to future political ambitions and agendas on a (trans)national level. The stronger emergence of narratives which remember acts of resilience on the part of the famine-stricken goes hand in hand with the recovery of famine memories which have long been kept out of official histories, or concealed within families. Society's stronger attention for diversity may also have stimulated attention for such additional recollections of active perseverance. At the same time, the template of charity that crops up in many famine memory practices foregrounds the message that donations and solidarity matter and can make a difference in regenerating famine-stricken societies, even if relief is not without its own political and economic motivations. Steven Vertovec's key study imagines the transnational as "sustained, cross-border relationships spanning nation-states" (Vertovec 2009, 5). Famines take place in global contexts, and societies that recollect the catastrophes tap into similar repertoires of remembrance. It is additionally the transnational circulation of aid, money and empathy that alleviate disaster, and may avert future hunger crises.

References

Allison, William P. 1847. *Observations on the famine of 1846–7, in the highlands of Scotland and in Ireland*. Edinburgh and London: William Blackwood & Sons.

Amin, Azril M. 2024. Holodomor of Palestinians calls for urgent global attention. *New Straits Times* (14 March): http://www.nst.com.my/amp/opinion/columnists/2024/03/1025692/holodomor-palestinians-calls-urgent-global-attention.

Anderson, Lara. 2020. *Control and resistance: Food discourse in Franco Spain*. Toronto: University of Toronto Press.

Arco Blanco, Miguel del. 2022. *La Hambruna Silenciada*. Exhibition panels. University of Granada.

Blanco, Arco, Miguel Á. del, and Deborah Madden. 2024. In *Famines and the making of heritage*, ed. Marguérite Corporaal and Ingrid de Zwarte, 204–226. London: Routledge.

Blanco, Arco, Á. del Miguel, et al. 2021. Ícaros de posguerra: Turning to crime to survive famine and malnutrition in early Francoism (1939–1952). In *Franco's famine: Malnutrition, disease and starvation in post-civil war*

Spain, ed. Miguel Á. del Arco Blanco and Peter Anderson, 114–136. London: Bloomsbury.

Boerman, Charley. 2024. Famine landscapes: Finland's 'skeleton track' in memorials and museums. In *Famines and the making of heritage*, ed. Marguérite Corporaal and Ingrid de Zwarte, 183–203. London: Routledge.

Boerman, Charley. 2025. Framing famines: Memory, museums and visual culture. PhD diss., Radboud University.

Boylan, Thomas A., and Timothy P. Foley. 1992. *Political economy and colonial Ireland: The propagation and ideological function of economic discourse in the nineteenth century*. London: Routledge.

Coleman, Jasmine. 2015. Greek debt crisis triggers memories of world war two. *BBC News*, 9 July. http://www.bbc.com/news/blogs-eu-33467931.amp.

Corporaal, Marguérite. 2020. Political economy?: The economics and sociology of famine. In *Irish literature in transition, vol. 3, 1830–1880*, ed. Matthew Campbell, 78–92. Cambridge: Cambridge University Press.

Corporaal, Marguérite, and Ingrid de Zwarte. 2021. Heritages of hunger: European famine legacies in current academic debates. *International Journal of Heritage Studies* 28:30–43.

Cox, Mary. 2019. *Hunger in war and peace: Women and children in Germany, 1914–1924*. Oxford: Oxford University Press.

de, Quincey, Thomas. 1844. *The logic of political economy*. Edinburgh: William Blackwood & Sons.

Devereux, Stephen. 2006. *The new famines: Why famines persist in an era of globalization*. London: Routledge.

de, Waal, Alex. 2018. *Mass starvation: The history and future of famine*. Cambridge: Polity Press.

de, Zwarte, Ingrid. 2020. *The hunger winter: Fighting famine in the occupied Netherlands, 1944–1945*. Cambridge: Cambridge University Press.

Erll, Astrid. 2014. From 'district six' to *district 9* and Back: The Plurimedial production of travelling schemata. In *Transnational memory: Circulation, articulation, scales*, ed. Chiara de Cesari and Ann Rigney, 29–50. Berlin/New York: De Gruyter.

FitzGerald, Emily Mark. 2013. *Commemorating the Irish famine: Memory and the monument*. Liverpool: Liverpool University Press.

Gray, Peter. 1999. *Famine, land, and politics: British government and Irish society, 1843–1850*. Dublin: Irish Academic Press.

Graziosi, Andrea. 2008. Why and in what sense was the Holodomor a genocide? In *Holodomor: Reflections on the great famine of 1932–1933 in soviet Ukraine*, ed. Lubomyr Luciuk and Lisa Grekul, 139–158. Kingston: The Kashtan Press.

Great Famine Voices. 2020. National Famine Commemoration Speech—17/5/2020. http://greatfaminevoices.ie/minister-josepha-madigans-full-address-for-the-national-famine-commemoration-day-ceremony-may-17th-2020/.

Häkkinen, A. K. O. 2018. The great famine of the 1860s in Finland: An important turning point or setback? *Journal of Finnish Studies* 21:158–179.

Häkkinen, A. K. O., and Henrik Forsberg. 2015. Finland's 'famine years' of the 1860s: A nineteenth-century perspective. In *Famines in European economic history*, ed. Declan Curran et al., 99–123. New York: Routledge.

Hionidou, Violetta. 2006. *Famine and death in occupied Greece, 1941–1944*. Cambridge: Cambridge University Press.

HREC. 2022. Commemoration Art. https://education.holodomor.ca/educational-resources-list/photo-gallery/commemoration-art/.

Ingram, John K. 1888. *A history of political economy*. Edinburgh: Adam & Charles Black.

Jensen and de Zwarte. 2024. Relative absence: Dutch memory culture and monuments of the hunger winter of 1944–45. In *Famines and the making of heritage*, ed. Marguérite Corporaal and Ingrid de Zwarte, 95–114. London: Routledge.

Kinealy, Christine. 2013. *Private charity to Ireland during the great hunger: The kindness of strangers*. London: Bloomsbury Press.

Mannion, Teresa. 2024. Gaza famine 'repellent' to Irish psyche. *RTÉ* (19 May): www.rte.ie/news/2024/0519/144997-famine-commemoration-longford/.

McKenna, Marita Conlon. 2020. *The hungry road*. Dublin: Transworld.

Meinander, Henrik. 2011. *A history of Finland*. Oxford: Oxford University Press.

Merry, Andrew [Mildred Darby]. 1910. The Hunge. London: A. Melrose.

Mitchel, John. 1854. *Jail journal; or five years in British prisons*. New York: The Citizen.

Newby, Andrew G. 2014. 'Rather peculiar claims upon our sympathies': Britain and famine in Finland, 1856–68. In *Global legacies of the great Irish famine*, ed. Marguérite Corporaal et al., 61–80. Bern: Peter Lang.

Newby, Andrew G. 2017. Finland's 'great hunger years' memorials: A sesquicentennial report. *COLLeGIUM* 22:173–214.

Newby, Andrew G. 2023. *Finland's great famine, 1856–68*. London: Palgrave.

Newby, Andrew G., and Eliza Krataari. 2018. Memory of the great hunger years revisited: Finland's 1860s famine memorials, mass graves and a commemorative craft initiative. *Thanatos* 7:90–126.

Ó Gráda, Cormac. 1999. *Black '47 and beyond: The great Irish famine in history, economy, and memory*. Princeton: Princeton University Press.

O'Brien, Dillon. 1866. *The Dalys of Dalystown*. St. Paul: Pioneer Printing Company.

Ray, Kalyan. 2014. *No country*. New York: Simon & Schuster.

Reese, Heidi. 2017. Lack of resources, information and will: Political aspects of the Finnish crisis of 1867–68. *COLLeGIUM* 22:83–102.

Reijonen, Juho. 2018a. During the year of hunger (a Karelian tale). *Trans. Andrew Newby. Part* 1: https://katovuodet1860.wordpress.com/2018/12/25/nurmes-juho-reijonen-during-the-year-of-hunger-a-karelian-tale-part-1/.

Reijonen, Juho. 2018b. During the year of hunger (a Karelian tale). *Trans. Andrew Newby. Part* 2: https://katovuodet1860.wordpress.com/2018/12/25/nurmes-juho-reijonen-during-the-year-of-hunger-a-karelian-tale-part-2/.

Rothberg, Michael. 2009. *Multidirectional memory: Remembering the holocaust in the age of decolonization*. Stanford: Stanford University Press.

Rigney, Ann, and Chiara de Cesari. 2014. Introduction. In *Transnational memory: Circulation, articulation, scales*, 1–21. Berlin: De Gruyter.

Roca, Paco. 2020. *Regreso al Edén*. Bilbao: Astiberri Ediciones.

Russell, William Howard. 1869. *The adventures of doctor Brady*. London: Tinsley Brothers.

Singer, Jefferson A. and Martin A. Conway. 2008. Should we forget forgetting. *Memory Studies* 1: 279–285.

Taggart, Emma. 2021. Feather sculpture pays tribute to native American generosity to Irish during the great famine. *My Modern Met*. 1 April. https://mymodernmet.com/kindred-spirits-sculpture/

Tönsmeyer, Tatjana, et al., eds. 2021. *Fighting hunger, dealing with shortage: Everyday life under occupation in world war II Europe: A*. Source ed. Leiden: Brill.

Trevelyan, Charles. 1848. *The Irish crisis*. London: Longman, Brown, Green and Longmans.

Vertovec, Steven. 2009. *Transnationalism*. London: Routledge.

Weinreb, Alice. 2017. *Modern hungers: Food and power in twentieth-century Germany*. Oxford: Oxford University Press.

Wertsch, James. 2002. *Voices of collective remembering*. New York: Cambridge University Press.

Zerubavel, Eviatar. 2003. *Time maps: Collective memory and the social shape of the past*. Chicago, IL: University of Chicago Press.

Structural Change of Industrial Societies

Industrial Heritage as a Consequence of Structural Economic Transformations—Rival Conceptualizations in Comparative Perspective

Stefan Berger

1 Introduction

Ever since Barry Bluestone's and Bennett Harrison's pathbreaking book on *The Deindustrialization of America* (1982), the study of deindustrialization has been developing as a multidisciplinary field of scholarship along the lines of often incredibly insightful local studies, many of which have used oral history approaches to find out about the impact of deindustrialization primarily on working-class communities in the global north (see e.g. High 2018; Strangleman 2019; MacKinnon 2020). Deindustrialization is an economic process, but it is also a politically framed one,

This article was first published in Spanish in Ruben Vega Garcia and Irene Diaz (2022).

S. Berger (✉)
Ruhr University Bochum, Bochum, Germany
e-mail: Stefan.Berger@ruhr-uni-bochum.de

S. Berger and T. Fetzer (eds.), *Collective Memory of Economic Crises and Transformations*, Palgrave Macmillan Memory Studies,
https://doi.org/10.1007/978-3-032-09094-2_4

and it has social and cultural implications which, in turn, impact on political and economic decision-making. It is often managed from above, by economic and political elites, but it is also influenced by social movements and reactions from civil society from below. It is experienced by people and people have to make sense of the changes around them. Their understanding will lead to actions that, in turn, can influence the pathways of deindustrialization. It is important to take into account both perspectives, top-down and bottom-up, if we aim to understand the history of deindustrialization. Although there have been important comparative and transnational studies on the impact of deindustrialization, their proliferation is a relatively recent trend (Mah 2012; Raphael 2019; High et al. 2017; Voigt 2021). The DEPOT project led by Steven High, which started in 2020, is the first major collaborative attempt to study the impact of deindustrialization comparatively, including scholars from Canada, the US, Britain, France, Germany, and Italy (Depot 2021). What remains largely uncharted territory to date is the incorporation of perspectives from the global south into the picture and a move towards truly global comparative perspectives on deindustrialization and the development of industrial heritage (Steiner 2020).

What I want to propose in this article are very preliminary and experimental ideas on how to relate regimes of deindustrialization to regimes of heritagization. I propose four different regimes which should not be seen as internally united and which certainly also have overlaps with each other. In other words, the borders of those regimes are fuzzy, both externally and internally. The first regime can be allocated geographically to the Anglo-world, incorporating places such as the US, Canada, Britain and Australia. The second regime comprises continental Western Europe, i.e. countries such as France, Germany, Italy, Spain, the Scandinavian countries and the Low Countries. The third regime is one associated with the post-communist countries of Eastern Europe and the wider world. It can be subdivided further into those countries in the global north and those in the global south. Furthermore, this third regime is divided between those countries in which we still have the dictatorship of a Communist Party and those in which it has been removed. The fourth and final regime would be the global south insofar as it has been reigned over by capitalist economic processes in the nineteenth and twentieth centuries. I will introduce each of these regimes briefly in what follows and relate processes of deindustrialization to the development of industrial heritage.

Heritage is always about memory. Industrial heritage memorializes an industrial past. It does so through narrativizations, which are invariably supported by visualizations. Memory activists are crucial in developing such narrativizations and visualizations. They can be state representatives, politicians or administrators, or they can be industrialists or trade unionists, or ordinary workers and citizens, or they can be social movements, or artists, intellectuals, university lecturers and writers. We will also comment on what regimes of heritagization produce which memory activists. Given the close proximity of heritage and memory, it makes sense to ask what memory landscapes are present in the heritagization of former industrial regions. Here, I will work with the theory of agonistic memory, as it was introduced by Bull and Hansen (2016), Berger and Kansteiner (2022).

The theory of agonistic memory distinguishes between antagonistic, cosmopolitan and agonistic memory. Antagonistic memory works according to an 'us' vs. 'them' narrative. It knows clear heroes, belonging to the 'us' and clear villains belonging to the 'them'. It is non-dialogic and only oriented towards the 'us'. It works through the passion of belonging. Nationalist memory is one of the most clear-cut forms of antagonistic memory. Cosmopolitan memory also knows an 'us' and a 'them' in the sense that it is based on universal cosmopolitan values, such as human rights, freedom, liberty, the rule of law, social justice and democracy. The exact mix of the universalism in question may change, but the 'us' is the group adhering to the set of universal values and the 'them' are those who (allegedly) object to them. Cosmopolitan memory is dialogic and accepts multiperspectivity. In line with the theory of deliberative democracy (Bächtiger et al. 2018), developed by, among others, Jürgen Habermas, cosmopolitan memory seeks to find, through dialogue, political consensus. Once this consensus has been reached, cosmopolitan memory draws borders towards those outside the consensus, who then become 'the other'. It works through the passion of empathy with the victims of dictatorship, totalitarianism and all enemies of deliberative democracy. Agonistic memory, finally, is skeptical of any binary divides between an 'us' and a 'them'. Instead, it seeks to historicize all groups in society, victims, perpetrators and bystanders, in an attempt to understand how we arrive at the radical multiperspectivity that characterizes each present. That multiperspectivity cannot be harmonized into a consensus to which all adhere. Instead, it is the basis of the political process that necessarily knows adversaries, yet adversaries are not enemies, as they are mutually accepted by one another as adversaries operating within the rules of liberal democracies. Agonistic memory is polyphonic (Vice 1997), and it is open towards different futures. It is politicizing memory, as it accepts different narrativizations of the past as the basis of the contemporary political struggle about the future. It works through the passion of solidarity with the poor and the disadvantaged in society.

I will attempt in this article to relate regimes of heritagization to types of memory, antagonistic, cosmopolitan and agonistic. Which memory actors, I will ask, tell which narratives in order to promote which memory politics? Throughout, I wish to highlight to what extent the making of industrial heritage is related to power imbalances that ultimately are often decisive in determining heritagization regimes (Smith 2006). I will conclude with some reflections on how, in different parts of the world, these memoryscapes construct a 'practical past' (White 2014) through industrial heritage that aims to chart diverse paths into the future.

2 Deindustrialization, Heritagization and Memory in the Anglo-World

In large parts of the capitalist English-speaking world, deindustrialization took place under conditions of market radicalism. The influence of neoliberal economic thought worked towards the assumption that markets should not be influenced by macroeconomic steering by government or other political processes. Self-regulating markets were the ideal. They would be able to overcome economic crises by weeding out those companies that had ceased to be profitable and making room for new companies, replacing older ones and providing new opportunities for the people who were once employed by the old companies. Under the Conservative governments of Margaret Thatcher in Britain after 1979, and under the Republican Presidency of Ronald Reagan in the US after 1980, neoliberalism became politically dominant in two of the Anglo-countries. The Thatcher and Reagan governments provided a political frame for neoliberalism. The state in Britain and the US withdrew from any large-scale interventions in the economic sphere and gave up macroeconomic steering (Prasad 2006; Diamond and Sugrue 2020). Instead, they actively sought to remove all obstacles that stood in the way of market self-regulation. One of the key obstacles, in their logic, was trade unions. While the trade union movement in the US had always been comparatively weak in the face of strong corporate interests that tended to be impeccably hostile to unionization (Zieger and Gall 2002), Britain was quite a different story. British unions were among the biggest and most powerful in the world. In the nineteenth century, they had been the first to organize workers and to conduct successful wage bargaining, becoming largely accepted by employers, whose collective organization was much weaker than in the US. In alliance with the Liberal Party after 1850 and with the Labour Party after 1908, the union movement brought about important social legislation that benefitted its core constituency, working folk (Reid 2004).

The close cooperation of trade unions and the state continued during the first two-thirds of the twentieth century. In the nationalized coal industry after the Second World War, the crisis of that industry was effectively co-managed by the powerful National Union of Mineworkers and the state during the 1950s and 1960s (Supple 1988; Ashworth 1986). However, at the shopfloor level, a new militancy was emerging that resulted in increasingly antagonistic industrial relations. There were those on the left who wanted to change that and who pleaded for a return to a more conciliatory culture of industrial relations. Barbara Castle's white paper *In Place of Strife* from 1969 was the most ambitious attempt to set industrial relations on a new (old) course, but it was not to be (Dorey 2019). The radicalization of the union movement continued into the 1970s. When Arthur Scargill replaced Joe Gormley at the head of the NUM in 1981, he implemented an anti-capitalist strategy that went far beyond traditional concerns of trade unions. The NUM and union militancy more generally is sometimes credited with bringing down the government of Edward Heath in 1974. Although this has to remain highly doubtful, the mythology worked its own way into the Conservative Party. Hence, it was no coincidence that Margaret Thatcher chose the NUM to set an example of her determination to defeat the trade union movement in order to allow for more self-regulation of markets. The confrontation famously culminated in the 1984/5 Miners' Strike, when the miners went on strike for more than a year, which brought the country to the brink of civil war before they had to admit defeat. Thatcher's government used the full force of the state, including police violence and legal action against the NUM, to unleash a class war from above, in which she was victorious. What followed was not only the rapid closure of many mines, but also a whole host of anti-union legislation, which left the unions in Britain a mere shadow of their former selves.

Although arguably developments were not as dramatic in the US, the Reagan administration famously expanded employers' rights and helped defeat the strike of air-traffic controllers in 1981, setting a precedent for the 1980s (Shostak and Skocik 1986). The decline of organized labour in the US during the first half of the 1980s was due to a complex mixture of factors, including the massive decline of employment in the most unionized sectors of the economy, but anti-union politics certainly also played an influential role (Goldfield 1987). Once the most important obstacles to self-regulating markets had been removed, the economic policies of the Reagan and Thatcher governments worked in favour of the big corporations and their desire to deregulate markets and flexibilize employment. The state had abandoned its post-war commitment to be an arbiter of social justice.

Things were certainly less straightforward in other parts of the Anglo-world. Thus, in Canada, opponents of neoliberalism and deregulation harnessed the power of nationalism to mobilize against radical forms of deindustrialization (High 2003). The state could be mobilized in that way to be more proactive and interventionist in its attempts to steer the process of deindustrialization. Nevertheless, in the early 1980s, Canada abandoned a commitment to full employment, and although Keynesian economic policy remained attractive to successive Liberal governments, it was Stephen Harper's election victory in 2006, which marked a sharp turn to neoliberalism also in Canada. His government's monetary policies restricted credit and raised interest rates. As fighting inflation became the No. 1 priority of the government, it deliberately risked mass unemployment. The 1989 free trade deal with the US also worked in the direction of a major downturn of the Canadian industry. It created downward pressure on Canadian wages and standards and meant a complete abandonment of any national development plan for the Canadian economy. In the end, it contributed to a reliance on Canada's extractive industries and natural resources, as most Canadian export industries were nose-diving. Industrial productivity as a whole was rapidly declining. The oil boom benefitted western Canada—at substantial environmental costs—, but most of its petroleum industry was foreign-owned. Government spending declined between 1993 and 2013 by 10 per cent (Evans and Smith 2015).

Australia had been a laboratory for social reform at the beginning of the twentieth century, with a strong labour movement influencing national and federal policies to a considerable extent. It was the first country to adopt the eight-hour day, after strong union campaigns, and it championed a whole host of progressive social legislation throughout the twentieth century (Patmore and Stromquist 2018). Yet, from the 2000s onwards, we also see in Australia typical neoliberal reforms, e.g. of the taxation system that lowered tax rates, and, to give another example, of the welfare state, cutting benefits and allowances for the poor. The employment security of workers diminished through outsourcing and competitive tendering. Hire and fire policies became possible. Wages of less-skilled workers entered a downward spiral to a degree where it was often impossible to feed a family on a single wage. The flexibilization of labour markets led to an increase in long-term unemployment. While it was in Australia, as elsewhere, a policy first designed by conservative politicians, labour can be seen as being complicit in designing or taking over neoliberal policy premises, in the UK and in Australia (Humphreys 2019).

Although there clearly were, within the Anglo-world, important differences in terms of their respective neoliberal pathways, we can observe that the consequences of neoliberalism amounted to a rapid and brutal deindustrialization that, in many industrial areas, did not result in economic rejuvenation but rather in lasting economic and social deprivation and ruination. We see this most clearly in the landscapes of the 'rust belt' of the US and in many of the industrial landscapes of Northern England, Scotland and Wales. Insofar as we can observe any heritagization in those landscapes, the drivers of processes of heritagization are most often social movements from below or political forces associated with those movements. Neoliberal governments and the leaders of industry in neoliberal regimes tended to have little interest in the production of industrial heritage. Rather, they were in the vanguard of erasing the memory of industry and preferred the construction of postindustrial landscapes in which there were few traces of a previous industrial past. Alternatively, they simply left those landscapes to decay and to fend for themselves, watching decline and immiseration from the sidelines.

For reasons of space, I will only give the example of the South Wales valleys, where, following the Miners' Strike of 1984/5, most of the mines were closed in quick succession. Most of the buildings were destroyed, and the valley floors that were dotted by mines became spaces for new housing estates, sports centres, new commercial centres or community halls, where little reminded people of what had been there previously. Obliterating the landscape of the industrial past was, as I have argued elsewhere, an attempt of obliterating the memory of the industrial past (Berger 2008). Opposition to this trend came from below, in the form of some of the labour-run councils in the valleys, supported by left-of-centre academics, intellectuals and artists and also some of the residents, often connected to the closed mines, including many former miners and their families, who wanted to save somewhat of the former mining landscape and therewith the memory of a past that had been their lives. The few places of industrial heritage that exist in the valleys today have their origins in these bottom-up and oppositional movements. Thus, today's UNESCO World Heritage site 'Big Pit' in Blaenavon would not have been saved, had it not been for the Torfaen County Council, which decided to buy the mine from the Coal Board after closure. It was subsequently developed as a memorial site in which former miners were closely involved. Similarly, the Rhondda Heritage Park was an initiative around the preservation of a former mine in the Rhondda valley, in which labour politicians, such as Hywel Francis, and social historians, such as Dai Smith, played a crucial role. Both sites celebrate the culture of mining communities and its values against neoliberal attempts to condemn them to the dustbin of history (James 2018; Dicks 2020).

The Anglo-Saxon pathway of deindustrialization and its accompanying heritage regime favour, I would argue, types of antagonistic memory. The memory landscapes that are produced by industrial heritage tend to be counter-cultural in a Gramscian sense. They seek to break the silence of the dominant neoliberalism on the industrial past and oppose the neoliberal framing of deindustrialization as being without alternatives. They seek to work against the denial of industrial heritage and the eradication of historical memory that is associated with such denial. The memory landscapes that are thus produced work with 'us' vs. 'them' distinctions, and they have formulated a clear idea about who the 'heroes' and who the 'villains' are in the stories of deindustrialization and the industrial past they seek to establish. The respective memory landscapes speak, above all, to the 'we' group of former industrial workers and their interest organizations who are mobilized, above all, through the passions of belonging to an often idealized and heroized working class community that has been wilfully destroyed in the process of deindustrialization.

3 Deindustrialization, Heritagization and Memory in Continental Western Europe

In continental Western Europe, as it was forged on the divided continent during the Cold War in the second half of the twentieth century, we find, in contrast to the Anglo-world, much stronger traditions of corporatism, in which strong employers' federations and strong trade unions are working in a system of industrial relations in which the state is a strong arbiter setting standards in terms of social welfare and macroeconomic policies that are far more interventionist than is the case in the Anglo-world (Berger 2002). Like in the Anglo-world, there is no uniformity. Thus, the dirigisme of the state in France was stronger than in many other West European countries (Hall 1986). At the same time, the formal organizing power of the French unions was weaker, but this said nothing about the ability of the French unions to mobilize workers in the event of conflict. Big employers' and trade union confederations were nowhere as strong as in Sweden (Fulcher 1995). The system of 'Rhenish capitalism' describes a specific relationship between state, employers and trade unions in the Federal Republic of Germany (Hockerts and Schulz 2016; Abelshauser 2011). The authoritarian and illiberal variant of corporatism in Spain has given way to tripartism since the 1970s, but with more significant working-class militancy in deindustrializing areas, such as Asturias, than we find elsewhere in Western Europe (Smith 1995).

The list of specificities could be continued, but within all the differences that mark the systems of corporatism in Western Europe, we can still identify a greater willingness than in the Anglo-world to manage deindustrialization and to intervene in markets in order to facilitate a smoother transition from an industrial past to a postindustrial, or at least less industrial, or differently industrial future. Thus, in Germany, for example, the ongoing belief that industry has a strong place in the future German economy has resulted in a semantic dislike of the term 'deindustrialization'. The German term 'Strukturwandel', literally translated as 'structural change', is used to describe the transition from an industrial past to something else that still includes, among other things, industrial futures. Structural change also includes the notion that economic developments can be moulded and directed, given a structure (Goch 2002). It is not a natural force that has to find its own way, as in the neoliberal Anglo-Saxon countries. Of course, neoliberal elements have not been completely absent from the continental West European countries, but they have arguably been far weaker and less radical than in many of the Anglo-Saxon countries. As governments, often together with employers and unions, sought ways of moving regions of declining industries forward into futures that would not stand for desolation but for reinvention and innovation, there was also a much greater willingness of governments, employers and trade unions to become champions of industrial heritage and foster memorial landscapes in which the industrial past played a major role.

The clearest example of this can be found in the Ruhr region of Germany, the former heartland of the coal and steel industry, which has been able to reinvent itself as a space in which a still considerable industrial sphere of the economy stands next to a thriving service industry. Although it does not belong to Germany's economic boom regions, it is a far cry from the landscapes of economic deprivation that can be found in postindustrial spaces in the US and the UK. And it is no coincidence that it is here that we find the development of an extensive landscape of industrial heritage (Berger et al. 2018). Indeed, the Ruhr has become the leading superpower in all things to do with industrial heritage, with a strong reputation in industrial heritage circles around the globe. It is, interestingly, also a landscape that started to emerge from below, through a variety of citizens' initiatives, urban social movements supported by intellectuals, preservationists, artists and academics, plus local residents and workers (Wicke 2017). The machine hall of Zeche Zollern, a mining site in Dortmund, was the first industrial building in Germany to be put under preservation in 1968. It followed a sustained campaign by art historians, preservationists and intellectuals who managed to build enough political support for the project. In the early 1970s, the working-class housing estate Eisenheim in Oberhausen was 'saved' from destruction by an alliance of local working-class residents and preservationist-academic, Roland Günter. These are typical examples of urban social movements struggling to preserve industrial heritage at a time when few others were thinking about it. However, during the course of the 1970s and 1980s, the idea gained increasing political support from the ruling Social Democratic Party in Düsseldorf, which sought to instrumentalize industrial heritage to create a memory landscape in which its key clientele, ordinary working people, would find themselves represented in a proud story of industrialization and well-managed deindustrialization. Eventually, employers and trade unions also came to support the heritagization of an entire industrial landscape, so that the movements from below and above coincided to a certain extent, to form a remarkably unitary and powerful mindscape (Berger 2019).

The dominant memory regime in that heritage landscape was that of cosmopolitan memory, in which a powerful corporatist 'us' comprised key representatives of the 'old' industrial society and important institutions who were involved in forging the 'new' society in a process of 'structural change'. This 'us' subscribed to a set of values which can be described in terms of solidarity, a strong commitment to a welfare state and social justice—in other words, Social Democratic values that had been universalized. Those universal values work through the passion with the victims of those in the past, who stood for these values in the forging of the industrial society in the nineteenth and twentieth centuries. The 'them' in the cosmopolitan memory are the enemies of liberal corporatism, i.e. neoliberalism on the right and a left-wing perspective denouncing the idea of social partnership that has been at the heart of liberal corporatist ideas.

The cosmopolitan memory of the industrial landscape of the Ruhr is multi-perspectival, as it incorporates different political and social perspectives that negotiate the exact outlook of the universal values that they all subscribe to. But, after reaching consensus, there are those who stand outside of that consensus and form the 'them' of the cosmopolitan memory frame. Market radicals, neoliberals, right-wing populists and also left-wing populists and class warriors are all in the 'them' group.

There are parts of Scandinavia in which we find similarly unified memory landscapes based on industrial heritage. In France, Italy and Spain, by contrast, we certainly find more division. Nevertheless, it is, in my view, justified to incorporate also these countries of Western Europe into a corporatist type of deindustrialization. After all, we do see considerable attempts to construct industrial heritage in all of these countries, and they are often connected to attempts to underpin regional identities by creating memory landscapes of industrial pasts and transitions to something else. In France's Nord-Pas-de-Calais, for example, an entire industrial landscape, comprising 17 pitheads, 21 headgears and 51 slag heaps, as well as dozens of buildings and locations, including schools, places of worship, housing estates and sports facilities, was declared world heritage by UNESCO (Fontaine 2018). Like in the Ruhr, it was meant as a sign of recognition of the importance of the region's industrial, mining past, but also as an important ingredient in a strategy to revive the fortunes of that region after the closure of the coal mines. In the northwestern triangle of Italy, between Genoa, Milan and Turin, efforts to preserve an industrial landscape associated with steel, cars and ports were more localized, but all of the major cities in the region developed ideas around industrial heritage as participating in the urban regeneration of former industrial areas (Berger et al. 2022).

In the former coal-mining region of Asturias in Spain, the preservation of industrial heritage is more localized and it is in constant competition with other forms of heritage, in particular the medieval heritage of Asturias and the natural beauty of the Asturian landscape, but we also find local communities, politicians, usually from the left, industrialists and managers from the state-owned coal company, among those constructing a landscape of industrial heritage. However, we also find a movement from below contesting the narratives that are contained in that heritage and establishing rival narratives about working-class militancy and betrayal by those in power, in the industry, in the unions and in government (Vega Garcia 2018, 2020). Here, we have a cosmopolitan memory landscape that is rivalled by an antagonistic one. Overall then, we find many specificities and differences between the countries of continental Western Europe, but also, to varying degrees, at least the dominance of a cosmopolitan memory landscape associated with diverse forms of industrial heritage within deindustrialization regimes managed by corporatist forms of government.

4 Deindustrialization, Heritagization and Memory in Post-communist Countries

When it comes to regimes of deindustrialization, Europe remains divided between east and west. The rapid demise of Communism in Eastern Europe around 1990 brought back capitalism and a reintegration of the post-communist world into world markets, in which the Communist industries were either not competitive and declined or taken over and destroyed by its capitalist rivals. The transformation process was by no means uniform in the different post-communist countries. Indeed, there were huge differences even within countries. Yet, the policies themselves, leading to transformation, followed a one-size-fits-all logic: privatization of state-owned companies, price liberalization and macroeconomic stabilization formed the triad applied everywhere across the post-Communist bloc. And everywhere, the move to a liberal capitalist economy produced deep scars, not only economic ones, but also social and cultural ones that left a legacy that plays a major role in all of these post-Communist societies today (Gevorkjan 2018).

The transition policies were way too simplistic to deal with the specificities of complex economic processes, and they resulted, among other things, in the rapid deindustrialization that came to industrial regions of Eastern Europe rather suddenly in the 1990s. Many of the governments in post-Communist countries followed the market-radical and neoliberal gospels that were still dominant in the 1990s. A lack of macroeconomic steering and a weak commitment to social justice and welfare produced landscapes of ruination not dissimilar to what happened in the Anglo-countries earlier. The main victims of deindustrialization, the industrial working class, found that it had nowhere to turn for support (Németh 2018; Valuch 2020; Kideckel 2018). Its unions, insofar as they were still the old Communist ones, were discredited by the fall of Communism and, in any case, not used to formulate policies against governments or to organize workers on behalf of their interests. Industrial workers had been the archetypal proletarians—the heroes of the Communist regimes for whom they allegedly existed. Even if these workers had never belonged to the ardent supporters of Communism, they now suffered from the association with the Communist regimes.

Poland was an exception in East Central and Eastern Europe, for here it had been workers who had formed the key opposition to Communism. Forming an independent union in the early 1980s, Solidarnosc, they had been the germ that ultimately was to bring down Communism in Poland and the entire Eastern Bloc. This might explain why Polish governments have been far more sympathetic to the construction of industrial heritage (Tomann 2017). Especially where memorializing workers could be linked to memorializing opposition to Communism, industrial heritage was thriving in Poland. It followed a strongly antagonistic memory regime in which a positive anti-Communist 'us' was juxtaposed with a Communist 'them'. But there was also, intriguingly, a certain nostalgia for the Communist times among Polish workers whose moral economy functioned according to values and norms that had been shaped under Communism and that resisted the impact of market liberal reforms on the organization of their everyday existences (Wawrzyniak 2020).

Yet, this story was not repeated in other parts of East Central and Eastern Europe, where we find relatively few efforts to promote industrial heritage, neither from above nor from below, as there was no strong civil society from where social movements could have organized resistance to deindustrialization and constructed industrial heritage as a memorial landscape that would provide a counter-narrative to the dominant neoliberal narratives in post-Communist societies. Hence, in many regions of the post-Communist world, we truly have silence on the industrial past, with no significant memory regime being implemented in the desolate landscapes that were once industrial.

This looks entirely different if we move from post-Communist Eastern Europe to post-Communist China, where we still have a communist dictatorship presiding over a fast-expanding turbo-capitalist regime. After the economic reforms of the Deng government of the late 1970s and 1980s, we witnessed massive and rapid industrialization, especially in the newly established private sector and in special economic zones created by the Communist state (Garnaut et al. 2018). As a new industrial giant awoke, there were also pockets of deindustrialization, especially in the established state-sector industries. One of the first and foremost regions of heavy industry in China was traditionally the North-East of the country. Here, Japanese imperialism had created the puppet state of Manchukuo in the 1930s and promoted industrialization and modernization. After 1945, the Soviet allies of Communist China continued on that path, and after the break with the Soviet Union, the North East remained heavily industrialized and focussed around steel and coal. Yet, in the new turbo-capitalist China, these state-owned industries increasingly found themselves in crisis. Industries declined and companies closed (Wang et al. 2014). In China's rust belt, we have seen many protests by industrial workers against dismissals, including unofficial strikes, street demonstrations and attempts to use the law to enforce their legal rights. Deemed 'protests of desperation' by Ching Kwan Lee, they are characterized by attempts to defend a perceived 'moral order' associated with the Communist regime before 1978 (Lee 2007).

Seeking to find strategies for reviving the fortunes of the northeast region of China, the Communist Party and government developed a whole arsenal of new ideas, among them the use of industrial heritage for economic regeneration. China began developing its own heritage ideas and lobby. It became internationally active in promoting Chinese heritage at different levels (Zhu and Maags 2020; Yan 2018). Industrial heritage was a latecomer to the Chinese heritage boom and rarely could be found before the 2000s. Thereafter, it developed rapidly, but it always was and remains a top-down affair. There certainly are many innovative and intriguing ideas that, for example, base conceptualizations of industrial heritage on the danwei system of Chinese cities, i.e. a system where workplaces, residency and social facilities are combined in strong neighborhood communities (Bonino and De Pieri 2014). Yet, a lot of the heritage sites in China, not only industrial heritage ones, suffer from Disneyfication and the construction of imagined pasts that indulge in kitsch nostalgia for touristic purposes (Xu and Sofield 2018).

The memory narratives we encounter in industrial history museums and industrial heritage sites are narratives foregrounding both national and Communist achievements. Hence, industrial heritage is closely tied to the promotion of nationalism, regionalism (i.e. regions being particularly important in the nation's history of industrialization and modernization) and Communism (Lam 2020). There are a number of tensions inherent in these narratives. Thus, for example, the strong nationalism silences the foreign, in particular the colonial aspects of the industrial past (Xin and Xiaofan 2020). In the Northeast of China, for example, the industrialization that was carried out under Japanese colonialism is rarely mentioned at all. If it is mentioned, it is in the context of the Japanese aggression against the Chinese nation and the Chinese resistance against Japanese imperialism. The same is true for Russian colonialism in the nineteenth century on the Russian–Chinese border. And the Soviet help for Chinese industrialization after 1945 is also not given prominent attention in industrial heritage initiatives in the Northeast.

There is tension not only between the national narratives and colonialism, but also between the heroization of Communism and the depiction of working-class life. Most industrial heritage sites celebrate the role of Communist officials and the Communist Party leadership in the history of industrialization. Industrial heritage thus becomes part and parcel of 'red tourism' in China that proliferates since the early 2000s. Celebrating the Communist heritage, it aims at a domestic touristic market and combines economic with political goals (Wall and Zhao 2017). There is complete silence about any failure of the Chinese Communist Party in its industrialization attempts. Events such as the 'Great Leap Forward' or the Cultural Revolution are dealt with, if they are dealt with at all, with rose-tinted spectacles, depicting them as stepping stones on the road to economic success or, in the latter case, as a happy meeting point between urban elites and the peasantry, where both mutually learnt from each other. If industrial workers appear in the narratives that we encounter at industrial heritage sites, it is in the propaganda photos of the Communist Party: happy and laughing workers entering or leaving factory gates, workers building a bright future for the country under the direction of the Communist Party and nostalgic views at depoliticized everyday rituals like marriage customs. A critical, multi-perspectival look at the everyday life of workers is mostly absent. The working class remains, at best, present as a propagandistic backdrop to the main theme of the heroic actions of the Communist Party leading the nation to greatness. Quite apart from the rather overt, in-your-face propagandistic qualities of industrial heritagization discourses in China, there also is a marked trend to commodify and commercialize industrial heritage in major theme parks constructed for tourists, where they can consume an entertaining and depoliticized past. As a result, there is a growing presence of industrial heritage in Communist China but is one entirely constructed from above in a highly homogeneous and uncritical fashion (Li 2021).

The dominant memory regime that can be found in post-Communist China's industrial heritage sites is that of antagonistic memory, where it is part and parcel of a clear 'us' versus 'them' narration: the Chinese nation, led by the Communist Party, is pitted against other hostile nations seen as clear enemies. A strong Communist China is depicted as necessary to avoid bringing new dependencies like the ones under which China suffered in the nineteenth and the first half of the twentieth centuries. Industrial heritage thus serves the purpose of underpinning, stabilizing and strengthening Communist Party rule in China, as the country challenges the global dominance of the US as the foremost economic and political nation in the world. This antagonistic memory is highly monologic, as it seems primarily directed at a domestic touristic market, and it frequently combines the aim of economic regeneration with political ideologization. It seeks to stir the passions of belonging, and the highly dramatized and staged depictions at Chinese heritage sites also work in the direction of boosting the 'us' group against its imagined enemies.

5 Deindustrialization, Heritagization and Memory in the Global South

With the exception of China, we have so far been talking about the global north of the twentieth century—Europe, North America and Australia. It is, indeed, here that the history of deindustrialization and the accompanying histories of industrial heritage have found most attention. There is, therefore, an urgent need to bring deindustrialization and heritagization processes in the global south more into conversation with the global north (MacKinnon and High 2020). The fact that deindustrialization in the global north and industrialization in the global south have often been perceived to be mirror processes since the 1970s should not deflect from the fact that we have seen significant pockets of deindustrialization in the global south during the same period. Free trade agreements between near or distant parts of the world have sometimes resulted in job losses, where companies decided to shift production to different countries, which suddenly looked more attractive, i.e. cheaper places to produce (Brady et al. 2011; Cowie 1999). In cities such as Mumbai and Ahmedabad in India, Johannesburg in South Africa, the Zambian Copperbelt or São Paulo in Brazil and Buenos Aires in Argentina, we have witnessed massive deindustrialization of key industries, such as textiles and mining.

In Latin America, a range of largely right-wing military dictatorships led market-radical reforms, e.g. in Chile and Argentina, that produced, in their wake, a trail of destruction through some of these countries' industrial sectors. Latin America was the first playground for the neoliberal ideologues coming from the Chicago School of Milton Friedman and a range of other neoliberal economists (Martins 2020). They abandoned national industrialization strategies and introduced economic liberalization, especially trade liberalization. This was accompanied by the dictatorships' policies of quashing their countries' union movements and either killing their activists or driving them into exile. Manufacturing jobs declined rapidly as a result. Only when the military dictatorships had ended, did resistance to deindustrialization become more widespread, as evidenced in a widespread factory occupation movement in Argentina in the early 2000s (Ranis 2005).

Latin America, in particular, has seen widespread debates surrounding deindustrialization (Cypher 2015), and there have also been attempts to compare paths of deindustrialization between different regions of the global south, i.e. between Latin America and Southeast Asia (Kim and Lee 2014). If we take the example of Brazil, deindustrialization has been brought about through a mixture of factors: exchange rate policies which reduced the international competitiveness of the national economy, the unregulated commercial opening of the country with the lifting of protectionism, high interest rates leading to decreasing investment, foreign direct investment, aggressive trade policies developed both by China and the US as well as the slowdown of the world economy after 2007 (Cano 2012).

During the Cold War, the global south was divided between adherents to the capitalist West and the communist East. In those countries of former world communism, where Communist Parties still cling to power, such as Vietnam or Cuba, industrial heritage, like in China, is largely a top-down affair emphasizing both nationalism and the heroic deeds of the ruling Communist Party. But where Communist Parties have lost power, or in those parts that had always belonged to the capitalist West, attempts to preserve industrial heritage often run into the difficulty of how to justify its preservation. After all, many countries in the global south have other heritage than industrial heritage to preserve. This includes the pre-colonial heritage of empires and kingdoms in Latin America, Africa and Asia, the colonial heritage of the colonizers, the heritage of the anti-colonial resistance movements, the post-colonial national heritage, quite apart from the stunning natural heritage that characterizes many regions of the global south. The stiff competition that industrial heritage often faces makes it difficult for those pleading to preserve industrial heritage.

An added difficulty is that industrial heritage in the global south cannot lay any claim to originality and authenticity. In Britain, the US and Germany, we have observed how industrial heritage plays an important part in laying claim to being the first (in industrialization), the most innovative in producing particular technologies (for industrialization), the biggest in terms of industrial output and other superlatives could be added here. As the global south found itself, also in terms of its industrialization and deindustrialization, in what Dipesh Chakrabarty famously called 'the waiting room of history' (Chakrabarty 2000, 8), its industrial heritage had little that could not already be claimed for the industrial heritage of the global north. In addition, it faced the problem that it was part of a colonial heritage, reminding the people of the global south of its entanglements with the global north that were characterized by power imbalances working in favour of the global north. All of this taken together does not make for convincing justifications for the preservation of industrial heritage.

Hence, although we have many global interchanges among preservationists and others dealing with industrial heritage, in particular through The International Committee for the Conservation of Industrial Heritage (TICCIH) (Douet 2013), industrial heritage remains a (growing) minority concern in the global south. In many places across the global south, there are now initiatives to preserve industrial heritage sites, which often suffer from a lack of investment in industrial heritage. Many examples could be given here. Let me just, again for reasons of space, pick one, namely the intriguing attempts to preserve the heritage of Brazilian railway towns that are often company towns, i.e. towns developed almost entirely through railway companies, such as Paranapiacaba, Mairinque, Caieiras and Três Barras, all established between the 1890s and the 1910s. In many of these company railway towns, the active functioning of the railways has made the preservation of industrial heritage more complex, but not impossible (Romero de Oliveira 2017).

The adaptive reuse of industrial heritage has been thriving in a number of countries from the global south (Louw 2018), including places such as Iran (Samadzadehyazdi et al. 2020), but such searches for preserving, through new uses, industrial heritage were often little related to preserving memories and experiences of workers who used to work in those industries and whose lifeworld circled around them. The growing attempt in places located in the local south, like the diamond-mining areas of Gauteng province in South Africa (Van der Merwe and Rogerson 2018; Xie 2015; Conlin and Jolliffe 2011), to develop local, national and international tourism around industrial heritage primarily aims at economic regeneration and the commodification and commercialization of industrial heritage—aims that are often contrary to concerns about preserving mindscapes of workers previously employed in that industry.

More interesting from the perspective of memory narratives are more immaterial attempts to recover lost worlds of industrial workers. Thus, for example, the meatpacking plants of Berisso in Argentina, fifty miles from the capital Buenos Aires, have all but disappeared and left only empty spaces. Yet, they have found a historian, Daniel James, who, through one subject, Doña Maria Roldán, found ways to recall, through oral history, stories of everyday life of workers and their families, for whom that physical and social space of work and neighbourhood had been a place of suffering and hate, but also of love, joy, friendship and solidarity. Mourning for this place through memory was one way of recovering experiences and bolstering identities that might still be meaningful for contemporary struggles (James 2000, 149).

Yet, the recovery of lost worlds through oral history cannot always be made meaningful in the present. As Joshi Chitra's wonderful history of the 'lost worlds of Indian labour' exemplifies, the lives of workers in the textile mills of Kanpur that emerged as early as the 1860s and dominated the lives of the working poor until deindustrialization hit in the 1990s and caused most mills to close, can be brought back to life through oral history, something her book achieves in an enviable way. In a postscript to the volume, she can even provide a richly textured account of how that mill-centred world collapsed in the 1990s and 2000s. Its disappearance had a disastrous effect on workers' households, changed gender relations profoundly and remade the spatial order of the city. Perhaps, most importantly, it led to changing self-perceptions of the laboring poor who found it increasingly impossible to relate in any meaningful sense to the history of working-class lives under the mill regime. The latter being an increasingly distant memory and seemingly unrelated to the pressing concerns of the present, the memories and experiences of the past are not easily actualized to be meaningful in the present (Chitra 2003).

It is a similar story in Mumbai, a metropolis that thrived on its textile industry before diversifying into engineering, pharmaceuticals and chemicals. Well into the second half of the twentieth century, about two-thirds of its working-class population worked in textile mills. The city was the site of the first Indian cotton mill that started in 1856. Girangaon became the central textile district in the city—a 25 square kilometer area in which a dense working-class infrastructure emerged around shared housing patterns and shared organizations, including trade unions. With deindustrialization, the issue of redevelopment of this district became a pressing one and with rising real estate prices, we see that the original inhabitants were increasingly pushed out of their housing and into more informal housing that accompanied a more precarious work environment. Like in Kanpur, the memory of the lifeworld of the mills was soon a distant and seemingly irrelevant one for the everyday struggles of the laboring poor (Adarkar and Phatak 2005).

Overall, in the global south, industrial heritage is rarely pushed by social movements from below, and, where in existence at all, it is mostly developed by governmental agencies from above. Because of its post-colonial and post-communist overtones, it often tends to work towards antagonistic forms of memory, in which there is a clear 'us' versus 'them' dichotomy. It is sometimes in the form of a post-colonial 'us' against the colonial metropoles of yesterday and today, and it is sometimes a post-communist 'us' against the capitalist West. Like all antagonistic regimes of memory, it works in highly monologic ways, and is directed exclusively at the 'us' group, mobilizing passions of belonging that are above all national(istic) and ideological, producing two-dimensional and highly binary ideas about the past of industrial societies and the pathways of deindustrialization.

6 Conclusion: The Need for Agonism in Global Memory Regimes of Industrial Pasts and Deindustrialization

The approach that this brief article has tried to follow seeks to bring together deindustrialization studies, heritage studies, memory studies and social movement studies. So far, it is a rare combination, as, more often than not, these things are studied by separate scholarly communities. Economists and social scientists examine the history and present of deindustrialization; heritage scholars, mostly from urban planning, geography, and the humanities study the making of heritage, focussing on the hardware; memory studies scholars, coming from a range of different disciplines, look at the narrativizations that we encounter in connection with industrial heritage; and social movement scholars look at urban movements, seeking to influence the pathways of deindustrialization, protecting workers from job losses and the gentrification of neighbourhoods. It seems to me that all these fields would benefit from a conversation that would bring their concerns together: what kinds of deindustrialization produced which types of industrial heritage? What memory narratives were told through these sites of industrial heritage? How contested were they and what role did social movements play in the contestation of dominant memory narratives?

The briefest of analyses that I have given here is necessarily highly schematic and, to a degree, even simplistic. It is painted on a huge canvas with a broad brush. It will certainly have to be modified and the many gaps will have to be filled in—in the hope that the texture will become more dense, the brush strokes finer and the arguments more differentiated. Nevertheless, at this early stage of comparative investigation, I would suggest that it makes sense to differentiate between, on the one hand, market-radical neoliberal pathways of deindustrialization that we can often find in Anglo-countries, but also in parts of post-communist Eastern Europe and parts of the capitalist global south, and, on the other hand, corporatist pathways of deindustrialization that are dominant, above all, in continental Western Europe. In the market-radical and neoliberal regimes, we encounter very few, if any attempts from above to institutionalize forms of industrial heritage. The memory of an industrial past is eradicated as far as possible as it is seen as hindering the evolution of the future post-industrial society. In some cases, we find the emergence of counter-discourses, often carried by social movements from below that seek to preserve a counter-hegemonic discourse to the dominant neoliberal one. These tend to be weaker in post-communist Eastern Europe, as there is less of a developed civil society in former working-class strongholds that have been abandoned by politics after the collapse of communism, not least as these archetypal proletarian places were often (wrongly) associated with the Communist regimes of the past.

Most of the memory regimes that we encounter in Anglo-countries, post-communist countries and the global south are characterized by antagonistic forms of memory, with clear divisions between a positive 'us' and a negative 'them', between 'heroes' and 'villains'. Antagonistic memoryscapes are monologic and directed only at the 'in'-group. There is little multiperspectivity and memory works through a mobilization of belonging. This is also true for post-Communist China, where the Communist Party is clinging to power and overseeing the development of a turbo-capitalism that is challenging the world economic and political dominance of the US. Here, we see a massive deployment of industrial heritage in deindustrializing regions, but it is always functionalized by the Communist Party to underpin its variant of red nationalism and to allow for economic regeneration through touristification and commodification. The only places where we do not find dominant antagonistic memory regimes in association with industrial heritage are in continental Western Europe, where strong corporatist traditions have led to more negotiated pathways of deindustrialization, where markets remained embedded to a greater degree in state action and where stronger trade unions prevented a complete turn to market radicalism. Within such corporatist attempts to direct structural economic and social change, we also witness the emergence of powerful landscapes of industrial heritage, which often underpin claims of a successful transition from an industrial to a postindustrial society, and it is this success story that allows for a positive look back at the industrial past. Here, we encounter rather homogeneous cosmopolitan memory regimes that are more multi-perspectival and dialogic but still differentiate between a corporatist 'us' and a 'market radical' them, claiming moral and economic superiority over market radicalism. Having managed deindustrialization without producing the kind of social immiseration and ruination that is characteristic of market-radical forms of deindustrialization belongs to the proudest claims of the cosmopolitan memory regime of deindustrialization in continental Western Europe. It is passionate for the victims of deindustrialization and claims to take better care of them as its alternatives in the Anglo-world.

Yet, we have seen, over recent decades, in continental Western Europe, just as in the Anglo-world, the emergence of populist right-wing movements that appealed to the losers in deindustrialization processes, among others (Mudde 2019). Trumpism in the US and Brexit in the UK, both thrived on their appeal to white working-class electorates in the deindustrialized rust belt of the US and the many deindustrialized regions of northern England and South Wales that felt betrayed by political elites from the centre-left that had followed the pied piper of neoliberalism in both countries. The Democrats under Bill Clinton and the Labour Party under Tony Blair had been hesitant to roll back the advances made by neoliberalism in both countries. Disillusioned with their former left-of-centre allegiances, they turned to the popular right. Yet, we find similar phenomena in continental Western Europe. The Rassemblement National in France, the Alternative für Deutschland (AfD) in Germany, the Lega Nord in Italy—they all successfully mobilize among White working-class electorates in deindustrialized regions of those countries. They could do so on the same basis as their sister organizations in Anglo-countries mobilized White working-class voters: on a charge of the alleged betrayal of the latter's interests. This is a clear sign that many workers do not buy into the memory narratives of corporatism. They do not share the feeling that the structural transformation that regions of industry have seen in Western Europe has benefitted them. The cosmopolitan memory frame that has been built here does not incorporate them and is therefore useless in trying to integrate those who are feeling dispossessed by the processes of deindustrialization. It is here, I would argue, that agonistic forms of remembrance, that are nowhere dominant and are in fact rarely present at all in the memory landscapes of deindustrialization, need to be brought in. Agonistic memories would allow for the setting up of left-wing counter-hegemonic discourses that would work in favour of the marginalized. It would give voice to those who did not emerge as winners from the structural transformation of industrial society and empower social movements speaking on their behalf. Agonistic memory would also be capable in this way to repoliticize memory discourses by delegitimizing market radicalism and pointing out the deficits in the corporatist crisis management of continental Western Europe that still left many feeling stranded in the transition from an industrial society to something else. Such agonistic memory discourses would make for an industrial heritage that enables agency of ordinary working people through their association in social movements fighting for their interests. It thus also understands industrial heritage as an integral part of an ongoing political struggle. Agonism, I would contend, remains a future challenge for memory landscapes in postindustrial regions, but it is one very necessary if we want to combat right-wing populism in those regions.

References

Abelshauser, Werner. 2011. *Deutsche Wirtschaftsgeschichte von 1945 bis zur Gegenwart*, 2nd ed. Munich: C.H. Beck.

Adarkar, Neera, and Vidyadhar K. Phatak. 2005. Recycling mill land. Tumultuous experience of Mumbai. *Economic and Political Weekly*, December 17, 5365, 5368.

Ashworth, William. 1986. *The History of the British Coal Industry, vol. 5: 1946–1982: The Nationalized Industry*. Oxford: Oxford University Press.

Bächtiger, André, John S. Dryzek, Jane Mansbridge, and Mark E. Warren, eds. 2018. *The Oxford Handbook of Deliberative Democracy*. Oxford: Oxford University Press.

Berger, Stefan. 2002. Social partnership 1880–1989: The deep historical roots of diverse strategies. In *Policy Concertation and Social Partnership in Western Europe: Lessons for the 21st Century*, ed. Stefan Berger and Hugh Compston, 335–352. Oxford: Berghahn Books.

Berger, Stefan. 2008. Von „Landschaften des Geistes“ zu „Geisterlandschaften“: Identitätsbildungen und der Umgang mit dem industriekulturellen Erbe im südwalisischen Kohlervier. *Mitteilungsblatt des Instituts Für Soziale Bewegungen* 39: 49–66.

Berger, Stefan. 2019. Industrial heritage and the ambiguities of nostalgia for an industrial past in the Ruhr Valley, Germany. *Labor: Studies in Working-Class History* 16 (1): 37–64.

Berger, Stefan, ed. 2020. *Constructing Industrial Pasts: Heritage, Historical Culture and Identity in Regions Undergoing Structural Economic Transformation*. Oxford: Berghahn Books.

Berger, Stefan, and David Broughton, eds. 1995. *The Force of Labour. The Western European Labour Movement and the Working Class in the Twentieth Century*. Oxford: Berg.

Berger, Stefan, and Hugh Compston, eds. 2002. *Policy Concertation and Social Partnership in Western Europe: Lessons for the 21st Century*. Oxford: Berghahn Books.

Berger, Stefan, and Wulf Kansteiner, eds. 2022. *Agonistic Memory and Representations of War in Twentieth-Century Europe*. Basingstoke: Palgrave MacMillan.

Berger, Stefan, Jana Golombek, and Christian Wicke. 2018. A post-industrial mindscape? The mainstreaming and touristification of industrial heritage in the Ruhr. In *Industrial Heritage and Regional Identities*, ed. Christian Wicke, Stefan Berger, and Jana Golombek, 74–94. London: Routledge.

Berger, Stefan, Stefano Musso, and Christian Wicke, eds. 2022. *Deindustrialization in Twentieth-Century Europe: The Northwest of Italy and the Ruhr in Germany in Comparison*. Basingstoke: Palgrave MacMillan.

Bluestone, Barry, and Bennett Harrison. 1982. *The Deindustrialization of America. Plant Closings, Community Abandonment, and the Dismantling of Basic Industry*. New York: Basic Books.

Bonino, Michele, and Filippo De Pieri, eds. 2014. *Beijing Danwei. Industrial Heritage in the Contemporary City*. Berlin: Jovis.

Brady, David, Yunus Caja, and Gary Gereffi. 2011. Stagnating industrial employment in Latin America. *Work and Occupations* 38 (2): 179–220.

Bull, Anna Cento, and Hans Lauge Hansen. 2016. On agonistic memory. *Memory Studies* 9 (4): 390–404.

Cano, Wilson. 2012. A desindustrialização no Brasil. *Economia e Sociedade* 21: 831–851.

Chakrabarty, Dipesh. 2000. *Provincializing Europe. Postcolonial Thought and Historical Difference*. Princeton: Princeton University Press.

Chitra, Joshi. 2003. *Lost Worlds: Indian Labour and its Forgotten Histories*. New Delhi: Permanent Black.

Conlin, Michael V., and Lee Jolliffe, eds. 2011. *Mining Heritage and Tourism: A Global Synthesis*. London: Routledge.

Cowie, Jefferson. 1999. *Capital Moves. RCA's Seventy-Year Quest for Cheap Labor*. New York: Cornell University Press.

Cypher, James M. 2015. Emerging contradictions of Brazil's neo-developmentalism: Precarious growth, redistribution, and deindustrialization. *Journal of Economic Issues* 49 (3): 617–648.

Depot. https://deindustrialization.org/. Accessed on 4 May 2021.

Diamond, Andrew J., and Thomas J. Sugrue, eds. 2020. *Neoliberal Cities: The Remaking of Postwar Urban America*. New York: New York University Press.

Dicks, Bella. 2020. Industrial heritage as place making: The case of Wales. In *Constructing Industrial Pasts: Heritage, Historical Culture and Identity in Regions Undergoing Structural Economic Transformation*, ed. Stefan Berger, 68–90. Oxford: Berghahn Books.

Dorey, Peter. 2019. *Comrades in Conflict: Labour, the Trade Unions and 1969's in Place of Strife*. Manchester: Manchester University Press.

Douet, James, ed. 2013. *Industrial Heritage Re-Tooled. The TICCIH Guide to Industrial Heritage Conservation*. Lancaster: Carnegie Publishing.

Evans, Bryan M., and Charles W. Smith, eds. 2015. *Transforming Provincial Politics. The Political Economy of Canada's Provinces and Territories in the Neoliberal Era*. Toronto: University of Toronto Press.

Fontaine, Marion. 2018. Regional identity and industrial heritage in the mining area of Nord-Pas-de-Calais. In *Industrial Heritage and Regional Identities*, ed. Christian Wicke, Stefan Berger, and Jana Golombek, 56–73. London: Routledge.

Fulcher, James. 1995. Sweden. In *The Force of Labour. The Western European Labour Movement and the Working Class in the Twentieth Century*, ed. Stefan Berger and David Broughton, 7–38. Oxford: Berg.

Garcia, Rubén Vega. 2018. Looking back: Representations of the industrial past in Asturias. In *Industrial Heritage and Regional Identities*, ed. Christian Wicke, Stefan Berger, and Jana Golombek, 32–55. London: Routledge.

Garcia, Rubén Vega. 2020. Sounds of decline: Industrial echoes in Asturian music. In *Constructing Industrial Pasts: Heritage, Historical Culture and Identity in Regions Undergoing Structural Economic Transformation*, ed. Stefan Berger, 216–227. Oxford: Berghahn Books.

Garnaut, Ross, Ligang Song, and Cai Fang, eds. 2018. *China's Forty Years of Reform and Development, 1978–2018*. Canberra: ANU Press.

Gechert, Juliane. 2017. *Geschichtskultur im Strukturwandel: Öffentliche Geschichte in Kattowice nach 1989*. Berlin: de Gruyter.

Gevorkjan, Aleksandr V. 2018. *Transition Economies: Transformation, Development, and Society in Eastern Europe and the Former Soviet Union*. London: Routledge.

Goch, Stefan. 2002. *Eine Region im Kampf mit dem Strukturwandel: Bewältigung von Strukturwandel und Strukturpolitik im Ruhrgebiet*. Essen: Klartext.

Goldfield, M. 1987. *The Decline of Organized Labor in the United States*. Chicago: University of Chicago Press.

Hall, Peter A. 1986. *Governing the Economy: The Politics of State Intervention in Britain and France*. Cambridge: Cambridge University Press.

High, Steven. 2003. *Industrial Sunset. The Making of North America's Rustbelt, 1969–1984*. Toronto: Toronto University Press.

High, Steven. 2018. *One-Job Town: Work, Belonging and Betrayal in Northern Ontario*. Toronto: Toronto University Press.

High, Steven, Lachlan MacKinnon, and Steven Perchard, eds. 2017. *The Deindustrialized World: Confronting Ruination in Post-Industrial Places*. Vancouver: UBC Press.

Hockerts, Hans Günter, and Günther Schulz, eds. 2016. *Der „Rheinische Kapitalismus" in der Ära Adenauer*. Paderborn: Schöningh.

Humphreys, Elizabeth. 2019. *How Labour Built Neoliberalism. Australia's Accord, the Labour Movement and the Neoliberal Project*. New York: Haymarket Books.

James, Daniel. 2000. *Dona Maria's Story: Life, History, Memory and Political Identity*. Durham: Duke University Press.

James, Leighton S. 2018. Mining memories: Big Pit and industrial heritage in South Wales. In *Industrial Heritage and Regional Identities*, ed. Christian Wicke, Stefan Berger, and Jana Golombek, 13–31. London: Routledge.

Kideckel, David. 2018. Identity and mining heritage in Romania's Jiu Valley coal region: Commodifications, alienation, renaissance. In *Industrial Heritage and Regional Identities*, ed. Christian Wicke, Stefan Berger, and Jana Golombek, 119–135. London: Routledge.

Kim, Chong-Sup., and Seungho Lee. 2014. Different paths of deindustrialization: Latin American and Southeast Asian countries from a comparative perspective. *Journal of International and Area Studies* 21 (2): 65–81.

Lam, Tong. 2020. Ruins for politics: Selling industrial heritage in postsocialist China's rust belt. In *Constructing Industrial Pasts: Heritage, Historical Culture and Identity in Regions Undergoing Structural Economic Transformation*, ed. Stefan Berger, 251–269. Oxford: Berghahn Books.

Lee, Ching Kwan. 2007. *Against the Law: Labor Protests in China's Rustbelt and Sunbelt*. Berkeley: University of California Press.

Li, Zhengdong. 2021. Constructing Industrial Heritage in China and Germany. Forging Collective Identities Through Industrial Heritage – Tangshan, Shenyang and the Ruhr Region in Comparison. PhD thesis, Ruhr-Universität Bochum.

Louw, Michael, ed. 2018. *Industrial Heritage Protection and Redevelopment*. Mulgrave: Images Publishing.

MacKinnon, Lachlan. 2020. *Closing Sysco: Industrial Decline in Atlantic Canada's Steel City*. Toronto: Toronto University Press.

MacKinnon, Lachlan, and Steven High. 2020. Deindustrialization. In *The Routledge Handbook to the Political Economy and Governance of the Americas*, ed. Olaf Kaltmeier, Anne Tittor, Daniel Hawkins, and Eleonora Rohland, 57–67. London: Routledge.

Mah, Alice. 2012. *Industrial Ruination, Community and Place: Landscapes and Legacies of Urban Decline*. Toronto: Toronto University Press.

Martins, Carlos Edoardo. 2020. *Dependency, Neoliberalism and Globalization in Latin America*. Leiden: Brill.

Mudde, Cas. 2019. *The Far Right Today*. Cambridge: Polity.

Németh, Györgyi. 2018. Contested heritage and regional identity in the Borsod industrial area in Hungary. In *Industrial Heritage and Regional Identities*, ed. Christian Wicke, Stefan Berger, and Jana Golombek, 95–118. London: Routledge.

Patmore, Greg, and Shelton Stromquist. 2018. *Frontiers of Labor: Comparative Histories of the United States and Australia*. Champaign/Illinois: The University of Illinois Press.

Perchard, Steven, Steven High, and Lachlan MacKinnon, eds. 2017. *The Deindustrialized World: Confronting Ruination in Post-Industrial Places*. Vancouver: UBC Press.

Prasad, Monica. 2006. *The Politics of Free Markets. The Rise of Neoliberal Economic Policies in Britain, France, Germany and the United States*. Chicago: University of Chicago Press.

Pohl, Norman, Michael Farrenkopf, and Frederieke Hansell, eds. 2020. *Lebenswerk Welterbe. Aspekte von Industriekultur und Industriearchäologie, von Wissenschafts- und Technikgeschichte*. Berlin: Diepholz.

Ranís, Peter. 2005. Argentina's worker-occupied factories and enterprises. *Socialism and Democracy* 19 (3): 1–23.

Raphael, Lutz. 2019. *Jenseits von Kohle und Stahl: Eine Gesellschaftsgeschichte Westeuropas nach dem Boom*. Munich: C.H. Beck.

Reid, Alastair J. 2004. *United We Stand: A History of Britain's Trade Unions*. London: Allen Lane.

Romero de Oliveira, Eduardo. 2017. A cultura industrial como herança: Questões sobre o reconhecimento do patrimônio da industrialização "tardia" no Brasil. *Oculum Ensaios* 14 (2): 311–330.

Samadzadehyazdi, Sepideh, Mojtaba Ansari, Mohammadjavad Mahdavinejad, and Mohammadreza Bemaninan. 2020. Significance of authenticity: Learning from best practice of adaptive reuse in the industrial heritage of Iran. *International Journal of Architectural Heritage* 14 (3): 329–344.

Shostak, A. B., and D. Skocik. 1986. *The Air Controllers' Controversy: Lessons from the PATCO Strike*. New York: Human Sciences Press.

Smith, Angel. 1995. Spain. In *The Force of Labour. The Western European Labour Movement and the Working Class in the Twentieth Century*, eds. Stefan Berger and David Broughton, 171–210. Oxford: Berg.

Smith, Laurajane. 2006. *Uses of Heritage*. London: Routledge.

Steiner, Marion. 2020. Begegnungen mit Helmut: Raucherpausen, lokale Initiativen und globale Ambitionen zur Industriekultur. In *Lebenswerk Welterbe. Aspekte von Industriekultur und Industriearchäologie, von Wissenschafts- und Technikgeschichte*, eds. Norman Pohl, Michael Farrenkopf and Frederieke Hansell, 55–69. Berlin: Diepholz.

Strangleman, Tim. 2019. *Voices of Guinness: An Oral History of Park Royal Brewery*. Oxford: Oxford University Press.

Supple, Barry. 1988. *The History of the British Coal Industry, vol. 4: 1913–1946: The Political Economy of Decline*. Oxford: Oxford University Press.

Tomann, Juliane. 2017. *Geschichtskultur im Strukturwandel: Öffentliche Geschichte in Kattowice nach 1989*. Berlin: de Gruyter.

Valuch, Tibor. 2020. A special kind of cultural heritage: The remembrance of workers' life in contemporary Hungary – Case study of Ózd. In *Constructing*

Industrial Pasts: Heritage, Historical Culture and Identity in Regions Undergoing Structural Economic Transformation, ed. Stefan Berger, 242–250. Oxford: Berghahn Books.

der Merwe, Van, D. Clinton, and Christian M. Rogerson. 2018. The local development challenges of industrial heritage in the developing world: Evidence from Cullinan, South Africa. *GeoJournal of Tourism and Geosites* 21 (1): 186–199.

Vice, Sue. 1997. Polyphony: Voices with equal rights. In *Introducing Bakhtin*, 112–148. Manchester: Manchester University Press.

Voigt, Sebastian, ed. 2021. *Since the Boom. Continuity and Change in the Western Industrialized World after 1970*. Toronto: Toronto University Press.

Wall, Geoffrey, and Ning Ryan Zhao. 2017. China's red tourism: Communist heritage, politics and identity in a party-state. *International Tourism Studies* 3 (3): 305–320.

Wang, Mark, Zhiming Chen, Pinju Zhang, Lianjun Tong, and Yanji Ma. 2014. *Old Industrial Cities Seeking New Road of Industrialization: Models of Revitalizing Northeast China*. Singapore: World Scientific Publishing.

Wawrzyniak, Joanna. 2020. Transforming industry: On the corporate origins of post-socialist nostalgia in Poland. In *From Revolution to Uncertainty: The Year 1990 in Central and Eastern Europe*, ed. Joachim von Puttkammer, Włodzimierz Borodziej and Stanislav Holubec, chap. 10. London: Routledge.

White, Hayden. 2014. *The Practical Past*. Evanston/Illinois: Northwestern University Press.

Wicke, Christian. 2017. Urban movements à la Ruhr? The initiatives for the preservation of workers' settlements in the 1970s. In *Cities Contested: Urban Politics, Heritage and Social Movements in Italy and West Germany in the 1970s*, ed. M. Baumeister, B. Bonomo and D. Schott, 347–371. Frankfurt/Main: Campus.

Xie, Philipp Feifan. 2015. *Industrial Heritage Tourism*. Bristol: Channel View Publications.

Xu, Honggang, and Trevor H. B. Sofield, eds. 2018. *Heritage Tourism and Cities in China*. London: Routledge.

Yan, Haiming. 2018. *World Heritage Craze in China: Universal Discourse, National Culture, and Local Memory*. Oxford: Berghahn Books.

Zhao, Xin, and Qu Xiaofan. 2020. The heritage of the Chinese Eastern Railway: Symbol of colonization and international cooperation. In *Constructing Industrial Pasts: Heritage, Historical Culture and Identity in Regions Undergoing Structural Economic Transformation*, ed. Stefan Berger, 270–287. Oxford: Berghahn Books.

Zieger, Robert H., and Gilbert J. Gall. 2002. *American Workers, American Unions: The Twentieth Century*, 3rd ed. Baltimore: The Johns Hopkins University Press.

Zhu, Yujie, and Christina Maags. 2020. *Heritage Politics in China: The Power of the Past*. New York: Routledge.

Industrial Mnemoscapes of Post-socialism: Heritage Legacies and Diverging Economic Memories

Joanna Wawrzyniak, Linara Dovydaitytė, and Ruzanna Tsaturyan

1 Introduction

In recent decades, the study of post-socialist industrial heritage has attracted growing interest (Guerin and Szcześniak 2024; Kochetkova and Petrova 2022; Kisiel 2021; Sklokina and Kulikov 2021; Wager 2000). However, much of the ongoing research either remains confined to single-country cases or extrapolates national experiences across the broader post-Soviet and post-socialist region. Moreover, it is often asserted that the collapse of socialist economies resulted in widespread deindustrialization, leaving behind a void filled with ruins and nostalgia (Grgić 2024; Petrović 2017; Pusca 2010; Wawrzyniak 2021). While this

J. Wawrzyniak (✉)
University of Warsaw, Warsaw, Poland
e-mail: wawrzyniakj@is.uw.edu.pl

L. Dovydaitytė
Vytautas Magnus University, Kaunas, Lithuania

R. Tsaturyan
Yerevan State University, Yerevan, Armenia

S. Berger and T. Fetzer (eds.), *Collective Memory of Economic Crises and Transformations*, Palgrave Macmillan Memory Studies,
https://doi.org/10.1007/978-3-032-09094-2_5

claim holds some truth, a more precise characterization would acknowledge that the collapse of socialist economies triggered profound transformations in industrial landscapes, reshaping collective memory and cultural heritage in complex and varied ways (Tomann 2025). As time has passed since the threshold years of 1989–1991, these divergent trajectories have become increasingly apparent. Across the former Eastern Bloc, industrial sites were rapidly closed, abandoned, or adapted for new functions, forcing communities to redefine their relationship with the industrial past. Some former industrial centers have repurposed their heritage as assets for tourism, cultural revitalization, and economic development, while others, either due to limited resources, lack of recognition, or a perception of these sites as unwanted relics of a difficult past, have allowed them to fall into decay.

While the experience of socialist rule and subsequent economic transition suggests commonalities, this chapter argues that the ways in which industrial heritage is remembered, silenced, or forgotten vary significantly across different national and local contexts. It focuses on Poland, Lithuania, and Armenia as case studies of post-socialism due to their distinct positionalities within the Soviet and post-Soviet transformation processes. Poland's relative economic autonomy under state socialism, Lithuania's direct integration into the Soviet centrally planned economy, and Armenia's specialized industrial base of "planned cities" shaped distinct experiences of socialism. Moreover, Poland underwent neoliberal reforms and EU integration, Lithuania's industrial decline was tied to post-Soviet collapse, neoliberal reforms, and Europeanization, whereas Armenia faced economic contraction due to war, sanctions, and political instability.

Central to this chapter is the concept of economic memory—the ways in which past modes of production and labor are interpreted and repurposed in the present (Hilmar 2023; Pehe and Wawrzyniak 2023). In (post)industrial contexts, economic memory encompasses how technological transformations are narrated, how former workers' experiences are commemorated (or marginalized), and how industrial sites are framed within contemporary political and cultural discourses. This process occurs within broader mnemoscapes, or landscapes of memory, where the industrial past is selectively preserved, reimagined, or erased depending on contemporary economic and political constraints. Through a comparative literature review and our own research expertise in Poland, Lithuania, and Armenia, the chapter explores four interrelated questions to analyze the trajectories of economic memory in these three countries: (i) How has industry been—or not been—transformed into heritage? (ii) Which periods of industrialization are most frequently commemorated, and which are overlooked? (iii) What historical and political factors have shaped the remembrance, silencing, or erasure of industrial sites? (iv) How have top-down and bottom-up initiatives influenced post-socialist processes of industrial heritagization?

Juxtaposing these three cases makes it apparent that, while the level of resources is a crucial factor in shaping how economic memory functions in relation to industrial heritage within post-socialist mnemoscapes, historical legacies, political frameworks, and cultural narratives also play significant roles in defining how industrial pasts are remembered, reinterpreted, or marginalized. The interaction between these elements creates distinct trajectories of industrial heritage preservation and erasure in former socialist countries.

2 Eclectic Economic Memory: Solidarity and the Shifting Narratives of Industrial Legacies in Poland

Today, the industrial heritage landscape of Poland, as showcased in major cities, suggests a long-standing tradition of industrial prowess. The recent proliferation of heritage sites in smaller towns, celebrating glass factories, textile mills, or coal mines, further reinforces this impression. Yet, this carefully curated image stands in contrast to a long history in which Poland remained predominantly rural, with industrialization arriving late and often as a byproduct of foreign rule (Koryś 2018). Much of this industrial heritage originated in territories that historically belonged to different states due to shifting borders, and many of these sites were developed under foreign rule rather than by Polish initiatives. The nineteenth-century industrial expansion was often driven by the partitioning empires—Prussia, Austria, and Russia—whose economic strategies influenced the nature and scope of industrial development. In some cases, this led to the cohabitation and struggle of local elites with imperial authorities, as seen in the textile industry of Łódź, which thrived under Russian rule (Zysiak et al. 2019), or the mining boom in Silesia under Prussian administration (Schoffer 2023).

The interwar period (1918–1939) saw limited industrial progress due to economic instability and political fragmentation, though state-led initiatives, such as the construction of the Central Industrial Region (Centralny Okręg Przemysłowy, COP), aimed to modernize key sectors. During World War II, industrial infrastructure was repurposed for the war economy under Nazi occupation, with many factories, mines, and transportation networks integrated into the German war effort. While this led to forced labor and inhuman working conditions for workers, some sites were also expanded or modernized to meet wartime demands. However, as the war progressed, many of these industrial sites faced widespread destruction due to the strategic moves of German or Soviet forces.

Under socialism, industrialization became a cornerstone of national economic policy. The communist government embarked on ambitious projects, expanding heavy industry, while urbanization accelerated as millions of people migrated from rural areas to work in state-run enterprises. This transformation created a strong working-class identity and reshaped Poland's economic landscape. However, inefficiencies, environmental degradation, and labor unrest—culminating in the Solidarity movement (1980–81)—highlighted the contradictions of state-controlled industry (Staniszkis 1984; Ost 1991).

The post-1989 transition to a market economy brought widespread privatization and structural shifts. During the 1990s, little was done in terms of industrial heritage preservation, as economic restructuring took priority over cultural and historical concerns (Sadowy and Lisiecki 2019). This period reflected a broader shift in official economic memory, where the focus was on pointing out the inefficiencies of the socialist command economy and the positive outcomes of market liberalization and privatization. Many former workers' experiences were marginalized in public discourse, and industrial sites were often abandoned, repurposed without heritage considerations, or demolished outright, symbolizing a selective erasure of the socialist economic past.

However, following Poland's accession to the European Union in 2004, a growing number of initiatives emerged to protect and reinterpret industrial heritage (Konior and Pokojska 2020; Koj 2024; Jabłoński et al. 2024). Access to EU structural funds and knowledge exchange led to a significant expansion of heritage projects across the country. Cities such as Łódź, Gdańsk, Katowice, Kraków, Warszawa, and Wrocław have actively repurposed industrial sites into cultural hubs, museums, and business districts. Grassroots initiatives have further enriched Poland's industrial heritage landscape. Activist groups, historians, and local communities have engaged in documenting, preserving, and advocating for industrial sites that might otherwise have been neglected.

This shift illustrates a transformation in economic memory marked by two key processes. First, the legacy of the Solidarity movement has played a crucial role, albeit not always an explicit role, in shaping industrial memory. The labor activism of the 1980s not only challenged the socialist regime but also cemented the cultural and historical significance of industrial sites, particularly in Gdańsk, where the Gdańsk Shipyard has been preserved as a site of both labor and democratic struggle (discussed below). This intertwining of industrial heritage with Poland's broader national narrative has made industrial sites key arenas for public memory and institutional commemoration, since the mid-2000s often becoming points of contention between the country's two major political parties (Civic Platform, PO and Law and Justice, PiS), each seeking to shape the legacy of labor activism of Solidarity and its role in Poland's post-socialist identity.

Second, the integration of these sites into broader mnemoscapes allowed for a reimagining of Poland's industrial past as part of a European narrative of modernization and labor history, where industrial sites began to be framed within regional and branch discourses rather than a solely post-socialist phenomenon. The Silesian region has become a focal point for industrial heritage projects, including the transformation of former coal mines into museums and cultural centers (Dzięgiel 2021), such as the Guido Mine in Zabrze[1] (Koman 2020; Coal Mining Museum 2025) or the Silesian Museum in Katowice (Tomann 2017; Silesian Museum 2025). UNESCO has recognized lead, silver, and zinc ore mines in Tarnowskie Góry (also in Silesia) (Silver Mine and Black Trout Adit 2025) for its historical significance, further embedding Poland's industrial past within global heritage frameworks. European Route of Industrial Heritage (ERIH) has worked to integrate Polish industrial sites into heritage tourism and foster cross-border collaboration (Szromek et al. 2021). Their project on the Industrial Monuments Route in Silesia promoted one of the most comprehensive regional heritage networks by systematically mapping key cultural landmarks in Silesia (Staszewska

[1] The mine is part of the larger heritage complex of the Coal Mining Museum [Muzeum Górnictwa Węglowego] in Zabrze.

and Żemła 2013). This was accompanied by the efforts of the Industrial Heritage Foundation in Silesia, which has facilitated collaboration between local cultural professionals, historians, and policymakers in the region (Foundation for the Preservation of Industrial Heritage 2025). Also, the Polish chapter of the International Committee for the Conservation of the Industrial Heritage (TICCIH) (Polish Committee for Industrial Heritage 2025), founded in 1999, has played a role in shaping expertise discourse on industrial heritage conservation in Poland. The rise of industrial tourism has helped bring greater attention to the significance of industrial heritage, but these initiatives also reflect a broader societal interest in reclaiming and reinterpreting industrial memory as a crucial component of remaking regional identity.

And yet, while major cities have successfully integrated industrial heritage into their cultural and economic strategies, smaller towns and rural areas struggle with underfunded and neglected sites (Barski and Zathery 2018). Moreover, while aspects of Poland's industrial past—particularly those associated with labor activism of Solidarity—are actively commemorated, other elements, such as the austerity measures and hardships of industrial labor under post-1989 transformation, are often overshadowed by triumphalist narratives of democratic transition.

The European Solidarity Centre (ECS) (European Solidarity Center 2025), established in 2014, represents a paradigmatic example of industrial heritage that transcends economic history to become a central site of political memory (Szcześniak 2024). Located in the aforementioned former Gdańsk Shipyard—widely recognized as the birthplace of the Solidarity movement—the ECS embodies the entanglement of labor history with Poland's transition from socialism to democracy. The shipyard, once a major industrial hub employing thousands of workers, became the focal point of resistance against the communist regime in the 1980s. The site's repurposing as a museum, educational center, and civic space is often mobilized in the service of national narratives of political struggle and democratization. However, the ECS has also been a site of political contention, criticized by conservative factions for what they perceive as an overly liberal or Eurocentric framing of Solidarity's legacy. Some argue that the museum downplays the movement's Catholic and nationalist dimensions, while others point to the exclusion or marginalization of shipyard workers' voices in favor of elite political actors. Additionally, debates persist over the site's transformation from a center of labor activism into a tourism destination, with critics questioning the absence of the economic struggles and job losses experienced by former shipyard workers after 1989 (Peters 2015) (Fig. 1).

In central Poland, Łódź, known as the "Manchester of Poland," was once the epicenter of the country's textile industry. Its collapse in the 1990s left the city with massive unemployment and an array of abandoned factories. Unlike the Gdańsk Shipyard, where industrial heritage is framed through the lens of political democratic activism, Łódź's approach has been predominantly one of urban regeneration, in which industrial spaces are repurposed for commercial and cultural use. The scale of this process makes Łódź a leading center of post-socialist industrial revitalization (Walczak and Kępczyńska-Walczak 2024). The city's post-industrial transformation has been shaped by a mix of municipal authorities, private investors, and cultural institutions, often leading to tensions between heritage preservation and economic revitalization (Fig. 2).

For example, the Manufaktura complex (Manufaktura 2025)—one of the most emblematic cases of industrial repurposing—has turned a nineteenth-century textile factory into a vast commercial and entertainment center (Cudny 2016). While celebrated as a model of adaptive reuse, Manufaktura has also sparked debates over the extent to which gentrification erases the memory of working-class life. Parallel to these commercial projects, efforts have been made to institutionalize memory at sites such as the Central Museum of Textiles (Central Museum of Textiles 2025), which highlights the history of industrial labor in the city, and the revitalized Księży Młyn district, where former factory housing has been converted into lofts and cultural venues (Hanzl 2015). The Museum of the City of Łódź, housed in the former Poznański Palace, also engages with the city's industrial past, foregrounding factory owners, while workers also appear but less visibly (Rek-Woźniak and Woźniak 2020).

Amid these dominant narratives of revitalization and entrepreneurship, alternative memory projects—such as those initiated by the *Topografie* group—have sought to reclaim the voices and experiences of workers. Active since the early 2000s, *Topografie* is an independent collective that has documented the everyday life of Łódź's industrial past through oral history projects, exhibitions, and urban interventions (Topography Association 2025). By gathering testimonies and photos from former textile workers and mapping sites of vanished labor culture, they challenge the selective memory of deindustrialization that often privileges the history of entrepreneurship and architectural aesthetics

Fig. 1 European Solidarity Centre, Gdańsk, Poland. © Joanna Wawrzyniak (2024)

Fig. 2 Manufaktura complex in Łódź, Poland. © Joanna Wawrzyniak (2023)

over social histories. Their initiatives, including guided memory walks and city games, have drawn attention to the erasure of socialist-era labor history in favor of a sanitized post-industrial cityscape. While they push for a stronger emphasis on labor narratives and the social consequences of deindustrialization, the dominant commemorative discourse tends to celebrate entrepreneurship and the city's nineteenth-century boom rather than its twentieth-century socialist past.

Overall, Poland's current approach to economic memory is multifaceted, intertwining narratives of nineteenth-century entrepreneurship, Solidarity's labor activism, regional histories, and European modernization. This can be described as an "eclectic economic memory"—a framework in which the Solidarity movement and labor activism serve as central reference points, while other aspects of the industrial past are selectively remembered. Sites linked to workers' resistance and democratic struggle receive prominent commemoration, yet the hardships of economic restructuring after 1989 garner far less attention.

3 Disavowed Economic Memory? Industrial Heritage and the Politics of Soviet Legacy in Lithuania

While Poland's industrial heritage has been shaped to an extent by narratives of national labor activism, post-1990 Lithuania's engagement with its industrial past has initially followed a different trajectory—one in which industry is often framed as a Soviet imposition rather than an integral part of national identity. Historically, Poland and Lithuania, once united under the Polish-Lithuanian Commonwealth, shared a predominantly agrarian economy, with industrialization arriving relatively late in both regions. In Lithuania, the absence of significant raw material deposits and the delayed emergence of industrial enterprises meant that large-scale industrialization only began in the mid-twentieth century. The period of the First Republic (1918–1940) saw some growth in manufacturing, but these efforts were disrupted by World War II and subsequent occupations, leaving the most significant phase of industrial expansion to occur under Soviet rule.

The rapid industrial development of Lithuania was the result of the country's integration into the centrally governed economic system of the Soviet empire. The Soviet economic reform of 1959–1965, known as Sovnarkoz, marked a change in local industry, with the introduction of chemical, electronics, and other new industries, and the production of metals and machinery becoming Lithuania's main industry (Drėmaitė 2012). Over a relatively short period of twenty years, employment in industry and construction peaked at around 40% of the total population. (Meškauskas 1994). Similarly, to Poland, industrialization fueled urban expansion and reshaped the social structure, transforming a predominantly agrarian society into one where city life and industrial labor became defining features within a few decades.

In the 1980s, however, the enthusiasm for modernization was replaced by "a rustic turn," which saw the country's industrialization and urbanization as a result of forced post-war collectivization and deportations, while at the same time, shaping and affirming a national identity as a rural rather than an industrial (Davoliūtė 2013). This attitude was further reinforced by the environmental protests, which gradually evolved into a national, anti-Soviet movement in Lithuania. Mass public actions, such as the "The Ring of Life" rally around the Ignalina nuclear power plant in 1988, which attracted tens of thousands of participants, shaped what political scientist Jane I. Dawson has called eco-nationalism, turning large industrial projects into a symbol of colonial oppression, through which social dissatisfaction and questioning the Soviet rule are expressed (Dawson 1996).

Lithuania's transition from a state-planned economy to a free market after regaining independence in 1990 led to significant economic changes, which resulted in factory closures and job losses. In the period of neoliberal reforms and deindustrialization, the emphasis on economic survival rather than memory work did not lead to a broader industrial heritage movement (Dovydaitytė 2021). Furthermore, public interest in industrial heritage remained weak, as much of the industrial legacy associated with the Soviet era was viewed negatively, as "alien," associated mostly with land pollution, a Russian immigrant workforce, and poor-quality products. The emphasis on national identity has allowed only a small part of the heritage to be considered "Lithuanian," e.g., industrial objects of the First Republic of Lithuania. The listing of industrial heritage, which started in 1995, was limited to vernacular objects such as watermills and historic bridges, or has been selective, e.g., recognizing the nineteenth-century "brick-style" facades of a former factory but excluding its Soviet-era extensions. The 2000s saw a few former industrial sites converted by business companies into mainly commercial premises such as shopping centers, preserving only selected pre-Soviet architectural elements (Drėmaitė 2002, 2012).

The Energy and Technology Museum (Energy and Technology Museum 2025), which opened in 2003 in the capital Vilnius, represents how industrial heritage has come to be associated not only with national but also with professional identities (Fig. 3). It is also an early example of the international knowledge exchange networks on the cultural uses of the industrial past. The energy sector activists, nurturing the ideas of "technical heritage" for two decades and encouraged by international industrial heritage specialists in mid-1990s, got the capital's first public power plant listed as a heritage site in 1997, where a new museum was inaugurated a few years later (Burokas and Urnieže

Fig. 3 The Energy and Technology Museum, Vilnius, Lithuania © Joanna Wawrzyniak (2023)

2023). Co-owned by the municipality and several energy companies, the museum began with a small exhibition in the authentic Turbine Hall and operated for some time as a small, semi-closed memory institution for the energy community.[2] It was also one of the first museums in Lithuania to benefit from EU financial support, which allowed for the adaptation of the remaining premises of the power plant for exhibitions and, since 2008, has transformed into a central institution promoting industrial heritage. In terms of museum type, the Energy and Technology Museum combines features of a historical industry museum with the ones of a science center. At the beginning, the focus was on the authentic environment and equipment of the old power plant through the pre-Soviet and Soviet periods—gas boilers, turbines, generators, and control panel. More recently, the museum has increasingly focused on edutainment. Students are the target audience to visit The Transformation Hall, which is the latest 1000 sq. m. space designed as an interactive exhibition about the human relationship with energy, where visitors collect points through live testing of hands-on devices and overcoming challenges. Technology education is a key concern of the museum, a result of its founding history (the energy community) and its shareholders (energy companies). From 2024, it will be rivalled by the Science Island, a new science center built in Kaunas, Lithuania's second-largest city, with EU support, dedicated exclusively to interactive learning about science and technology (see Science Island 2025).

The perception of industrial heritage has been changing over the last decade. Pre-Soviet heritage is still emphasized at national level (for example, there are only few industrial objects from the second part of twentieth century listed), more visible at international level (for example, old industrial sites and objects dominate the European Route of Industrial Heritage portal (see European Route of Industrial Heritage 2025)), but a growing number of memory initiatives focus on (post-)Soviet heritage. Moreover, engaging with the economic memory of the Soviet period encompasses a broad and diverse spectrum, including not only material and technological aspects, but also social dimensions, working-class testimonies, labor history, and the contested, dissonant aspects of that past. The emergence of these initiatives is partly conditioned by the diversification of the museum sector[3] and the corporate interest of the surviving

[2] Linara Dovydaitytė's interview with a collection keeper at the Energy and Technology Museum, Vilnius, March 8, 2022.

[3] Mention can be made of some regional museums, such as the Alytus Museum of Ethnography and Tauragė Regional Museum, which have recently included the history of local industry, including the Soviet period, in their new exhibitions.

industrial enterprises to start preserving organizational memory.[4] Private companies have started to use industrial heritage stories to promote the conversion of abandoned Soviet era industrial sites into commercial and residential premises (Tranavičiūtė 2023). The contested industrial past has begun to be reconsidered as a valuable resource for local identity maintenance and economic revitalization at the municipal level. The following two cases will show that new actors, such as artists and cultural practitioners, as well as transnational networks and global processes, have also contributed to the new understanding of industrial heritage.

Community platform Backup Stories (*Mažosios istorijos*), founded in 2017 by artist and activist Auksė Petrulienė, is the most prominent (and still rare) attempt to commemorate the experiences of former workers in the Soviet-era factories as well as to engage with difficult stories of deindustrialization (Fig. 4). This is a long-term curatorial project at the National M. K. Čiurlionis Museum of Art, which includes temporary exhibitions about the past of the industrial city of Kaunas. Backup Stories exhibition series is co-created with former factory employees and is based on their biographical testimonies, which are displayed as short stories alongside personal belongings: photographs, production samples, memorabilia, and related artifacts found in museum collections. The storylines of the exhibitions present everyday life and working-class experiences, ranging from working conditions and gender issues in the Soviet industrial environment to workers' strikes during the neoliberal reforms. Backup Stories, which presents itself as "a megaphone for the voices of the communities, amplifying them and helping them to be heard," uses working-class memories to create powerful, affective stories about the vanished industrial way of life with its positive and negative aspects. Thanks to this project, certain artifacts—such as a sample of an artificial aorta invented in a textile factory in the 1960s and preserved by its designer, or the company's annals rescued from the archives of a closed enterprise—entered the museum collection (Dovydaitytė 2023).

An artistic rather than academic approach has recently been used in other museum-type projects on (post)Soviet industry, such as the collection and exhibition of the history of the local cotton mill at the Alytus Museum of Ethnography (2022), or creative documentation of the first

[4] Over the past decade, the successors of large industrial companies have published their own history books, such as Jonas Vaičys (2016) on the TV factory in Šiauliai, or Aldona Jankauskienė (2019) on a machine factory in Alytus.

Fig. 4 Arturas Bumšteinas, Sound installation *Clay Throats* at the exhibition *The Great Industry*, Community platform Backup Stories, M. K. Čiurlionis National Museum of Art, Kaunas, Lithuania. © Darius Petrulis (2017)

residential building in atomic town by the public company Urban Stories (2024) (see Urban Stories 2025). However, these grassroot initiatives, though often realized in the museums, are mainly dependent on project-based funding, including international funds, which does not ensure continuity or the systematic collection and preservation of industrial tangible and intangible heritage. They might be treated as emerging industrial memory activism, stemming not from the former industry workers but from the creative sector, which results in both making sense of working-class experiences and pointing to the complexity and ambiguity of the industrial past (Dovydaitytė 2023; compare with Berger 2023).

Another case, showing the growing interest in Soviet-era industrial legacy as a resource of economic revitalization, is the Visaginas City Museum, opened in 2024 and dedicated to the history of the satellite settlement built for the employees of the Ignalina Nuclear Power Plant in the 1970–1980s (see Visaginas City Museum 2025). After the nuclear power plant shutdown in 2009, the mono-industrial town experienced social and economic decline, recording the highest emigration and unemployment rates in Lithuania. Nuclear heritage was not recognized as a valuable resource for urban regeneration at the municipal level until the global success of the HBO TV series "Chernobyl" (2019), which was filmed at the Ignalina Nuclear Power Plant and stimulated international tourism afterwards (Dovydaitytė and Denisenko 2025). After a decades-long process of developing and negotiation, Visaginas now hosts a local museum owned by the municipality, which collects and exhibits the social history of the nuclear industry and its decommissioning. In addition to everyday life and nuclear labor, the inaugural exhibition also includes the difficult legacy of the industrial past, presented through the personal testimonies of the local "Chernobyl Liquidators" association, whose members were once involved in the cleanup of the nuclear disaster. The museum is a low-budget institution with only a few staff and operates in temporary premises in the gymnasium building. However, Visaginas Municipality, which in recent years has been involved in a few international research networks, has included nuclear cultural heritage in its strategic priorities since 2020 and is planning larger heritage projects, such as repurposing the simulator of the nuclear power plant for cultural needs and integration of nuclear-themed objects in public spaces to attract tourists. Despite the increasing recognition of industrial heritage at the municipal level, wider national and industry involvement is still limited (Rindzevičiūtė et al. 2024).

Overall, in the last decade, new projects started to reconsider the role of industrial heritage in Lithuania. While the rejection of Soviet industrialization remains a dominant framework, the increasing inclusion of diverse agents—ranging from artistic interventions to corporate-sponsored memory work to municipal policy—suggests a gradual shift in how Lithuanians engage with their industrial heritage. This evolving approach signals that economic memory in Lithuania, once predominantly shaped by the disavowal of industry, is gradually becoming more pluralistic.

4 Islands of Economic Memory: Industrial Heritage and Cultural Engagement in Armenia

Armenia's shift toward socialism began shortly after World War I—roughly three decades earlier than in East-Central Europe. Before that, during the Russian imperial period, Armenian industry was largely limited to copper mining and alcohol production. Consequently, Armenia has little cultural memory of pre-Soviet industrialization. The establishment of Soviet rule between 1920 and 1922 ushered in a period of rapid industrial expansion. This process accelerated particularly following the economic reforms of 1959–1965, transforming Armenia within a few decades into a key industrial hub of the Soviet system. Industrialization drove rapid urbanization and the development of "planned cities" including Vanadzor (then Kirovakan), Charentsavan (initially, Lusavan), and others. Heavy industry—metallurgy, precision instrument manufacturing, and chemical production—remained under direct control from Moscow, while light industries such as textiles and food processing were managed by the Armenian SSR. Armenia's integration into the broader Soviet economic network ensured employment stability and facilitated urban expansion, yet it also relegated the republic to a peripheral role as a site for extractive and environmentally hazardous industries. This transformation profoundly reshaped Armenian society, fostering an industrial workforce with relatively high levels of education.

Armenia's industrial sector began to decline even before the dissolution of the Soviet Union. The 1988 earthquake, one of the most devastating seismic events in the modern history of the Caucasus, destroyed major industrial cities, Spitak, Gyumri (then Leninakan), and Vanadzor, crippling production and infrastructure (Campbell 1991/1995; Verluise 1995). The earthquake also contributed to the partial closure of Armenia's nuclear power plant in Metsamor and the ensuing energy and economic crisis. The collapse of Soviet economic structures was accompanied by the activation of the Artsakh movement, the first war in Nagorno-Karabakh (1988–1994), and the blockade imposed by Turkey and Azerbaijan, which further exacerbated the economic crisis (Iskandaryan et al. 2016; Zürcher 2007). By the mid-1990s, Armenia's industrial economy had largely collapsed, with privatization efforts often resulting in the transfer of state enterprises into private hands without strategies for sustainability or possibilities of reintegration into new markets (Melkumyan 2018; Azizbekyan 2004). Until the mid-2020s, many industrial sites remained functionally obsolete, with privatized factories either abandoned, repurposed without heritage considerations, or used for small-scale production. The privatization has further complicated processes of preservation as private ownership restricts access to the abandoned sites (Khatchadurian 2022). Consequently, industrial heritage has not been widely recognized as a cultural asset. Former industrial sites have been typically perceived either as "economic zones" designated for redevelopment or as mere "ruins"—troubling vestiges of the decline of once-thriving Soviet-era spaces evoking both nostalgia and broader anxieties surrounding unjust patterns of property accumulation and growing social polarization (Khatchadurian 2022) (Fig. 5).

The few maintained industrial heritage sites exist as isolated enclaves amidst a broader landscape of decay. Among the notable exceptions is the sustained Russian influence over the railway system, which also serves a heritage purpose. This is exemplified by the dedicated railway museum at the Yerevan central station (Armenian Railway Museum 2025), where aspects of this industrial legacy are displayed. Beyond its function as a historical site, the railway museum symbolizes Armenia's enduring infrastructural and economic ties to Russia, reflecting both the legacy of the

Fig. 5 Abandoned industrial premises in Vanadzor, Armenia. © Joanna Wawrzyniak (2022)

Russian empire and Soviet-era connectivity and the continued geopolitical and economic dependencies that shape post-Soviet Armenia.

Another noteworthy exception is the commercial valorization of the food industry. Grand Tobacco, Grand Candy, and the Ararat brandy factory refer to the local traditions. Especially, the Museum of Ararat (Ararat Museum 2025), operated by the Yerevan Brandy Company, a subsidiary of the French beverage conglomerate Pernod Ricard since 1999, illustrates how industrial heritage can be strategically repurposed as both a cultural and economic asset. By tracing the historical evolution of Armenian brandy-making, including its expansion during the Soviet period and subsequent global recognition, the museum highlights the intersection of industrial production, heritage preservation, and national identity. However, as a corporate initiative, the site primarily serves commercial interests, shaping historical narratives to align with brand identity rather than fostering critical engagement with the broader socioeconomic transformations that have defined Armenia's industrial past. While the museum ensures the material preservation of certain aspects of industrial heritage, it does so in a highly curated manner, privileging marketable histories over more complex or contentious ones. This raises broader questions about the extent to which commercial enterprises can serve as stewards of industrial heritage and whether alternative models of preservation might allow for a more nuanced and inclusive representation of Armenia's industrial legacy (Fig. 6).

Armenian public museums showcase a rich array of heritage, including ancient artifacts, medieval manuscripts, religious relics, folk art, but only occasionally incorporate industrial topics, in temporary exhibitions such as "The 'Porcelaine' History of Soviet Yerevan" (2024) and "Women and the Economy of Soviet Yerevan" (2021), occasionally exhibited at the Yerevan History Museum (Yerevan History Museum 2025). While business, state, and institutional recognition of industrial heritage remains limited in Armenia, grassroots activists and artists have played some role in reshaping perceptions of abandoned industrial sites. These efforts, though represent a critical counterbalance to state neglect and the commercial privatization of industrial spaces, are often fragmented and facing financial and legal constraints. In places like Alaverdi, where the legacy of Soviet-era mining and metallurgy continues to impact local communities, grassroots organizations have campaigned for environmental justice and the responsible management of industrial ruins, without much success. In Vanadzor, a former chemical industry hub, and

Fig. 6 Ararat museum, Yerevan, Armenia. © Joanna Wawrzyniak (2022)

in Metsamor, initiatives aimed at reinterpreting industrial heritage have struggled to advance. The challenges are attributed to a misalignment between the projects' objectives and the local communities' needs and perceptions. In Vanadzor, the absence of a platform of communication on industrial heritage between the local authorities, NGOs, and academic circles has hindered progress. In Metsamor, efforts to repurpose industrial sites have faced difficulties due to a lack of community engagement (Melkumyan 2018; Manukyan 2021).

Charentsavan is another case at hand of the opportunities and challenges of preserving Soviet industrial heritage in Armenia's planned industrial cities. They were studied in-depth by Ruzanna Tsaturyan, a contributing author of this chapter, in multilevel discussions with stakeholders, during her work within a project for cultural development strategy design of Charenstavan in (2021–2022). Founded in 1948 as Lusavan and later renamed in honor of the poet Yeghishe Charents, Charentsavan was established as a center for metallurgy, machinery, and tool manufacturing. The city exemplifies the functionalist principles of mid-twentieth-century Soviet urban planning, integrating industrial facilities with cultural institutions and residential zones. Notable architectural landmarks include the city hall, railway station, music school, city park, Charents' memorial hall, and socialist-era monuments and statues, as well as elements of industrial design, such as the mosaics of the former Centrolit factory (Tsaturyan 2023).

Charentsavan's economy collapsed in the 1990s, leaving many of its factories abandoned or operating at reduced capacity. Although the city's industrial spaces still exist physically, they have faded from its present-day narrative. And yet, the material remnants of Charentsavan's industrial past—factories, workers' housing, and public spaces once central to industrial life—offer significant opportunities for heritage-making and historical reinterpretation (Fig. 7).

However, gaining broader recognition of industrial heritage among stakeholders remains a significant challenge. City authorities are reluctant to acknowledge Soviet-era architecture as part of the local cultural

Fig. 7 Centrolit factory gate, Charentsavan, Armenia. © Ruzanna Tsaturyan (2022)

landscape because they are used that in Armenia cultural heritage is rather associated with ancient history, religion, folk art, and culinary traditions. The city's identity, as represented in official city narratives and tourism materials, is either vaguely defined or entirely absent. Charentsavan's cultural and toponymic landscape does not fully capture its industrial foundations, as envisioned by its architect, Tiran Marutyan, in the late 1940s and 1950s. Older generations often associate socialist factories with the economic security of a bygone era but struggle to perceive them as cultural heritage, while younger residents frequently regard them as meaningless ruins. Factory owners—many of whom acquired these properties during the privatization process—remain largely indifferent to their historical or cultural significance, prioritizing commercial viability over heritage preservation. Activists' efforts to engage with industrial history—such as proposals to document and archive Charentsavan's Soviet-era urban development—face substantial obstacles due to a lack of institutional support (Tsaturyan 2023).

Ultimately, Armenia's industrial past exists in a state of partial remembrance, shaped by material neglect and present-day economic pragmatism. While it is not entirely dismissed, industrial heritage remains marginal, lacking strong institutional support or broader societal recognition. The factory ruins scattered across the country, neither preserved nor erased, serve as stark reminders of the broader challenge of incorporating Armenia's Soviet-era industrial legacy into its contemporary cultural memory.

5 Conclusion

A recurring theme in memory studies is that memory is more about the future than the past. This is particularly evident in how societies engage with their industrial heritage, shaping narratives of economic transformation and positioning themselves within imagined futures. In Poland and Lithuania, industrial heritage practices have, to some extent, been shaped by patterns established in Western European countries. While German (corporatist) and British (neoliberal) approaches to cultural heritage redevelopment differ significantly (Berger, this volume), both have provided accessible frameworks for representing industrialization and industrial decay. Moreover, EU heritage policies encourage postindustrial regions to repurpose their industrial past. In both countries, integrating industrial memory into heritage economies strengthens a broader European narrative of modernization, technological advancement, and social progress, framing the industrial past as merely a phase in a larger trajectory toward innovation, cultural renewal, or ecological restoration. At the same time, certain cultural meanings attached to industrial memory remain distinct. In Poland, the legacy of the Solidarity movement shapes interpretations of the socialist industrial past, while in Lithuania, the negative perspective on Soviet history, introduces layers of ambiguity to industrial heritage. In contrast, Armenian industrial memory has not yet developed a structured or "usable past." This is partly due to the nature of its post-Soviet transition. Unlike EU member states, Armenia does not have access to heritage funding or institutional frameworks that promote industrial heritage as an economic or cultural asset. As a result, the memory of industry in Armenia is associated with loss rather than renewal, and it remains largely unclaimed within national or regional narratives.

The contrast between Poland, Lithuania, and Armenia highlights the broader question of how memory practices mediate access to imagined futures. In Poland and Lithuania, industrial heritage is leveraged as part of a Europeanization process, integrating local narratives into transnational frameworks of economic and cultural development. In Armenia, however, the absence of a structured industrial memory practice reflects broader geopolitical uncertainties. Without a clear trajectory toward the future, industrial heritage remains in limbo, neither fully remembered nor actively repurposed. This raises further questions about what happens when a past is not "usable"—whether nostalgia takes over, ruins become sites of alternative memory, or forgetting itself becomes a strategy.

Acknowledgements The authors' collaboration was made possible through *COST Action "Slow Memory: Transformative Practices for Times of Uneven and Accelerating Change"* (CA20105). Linara Dovydaitytė's research was funded by the Estonian Research Council under the grant "*Practices and Challenges of Mnemonic Pluralism in Baltic History Museums*" (PRG1097). Joanna Wawrzyniak's research is part of the project *MEPOST: Remembering (De)industrialisation: Moral Emotions in the Memory of Post-Socialist Transformation in Lithuania and Poland*, National Science Center (NCN) in Poland (2024/52/L/HS2/00283). Ruzanna Tsaturyan's research was supported by the European Union within the framework of the EU4Culture project, which supports non-capital cities in the Eastern Partnership (EaP) region in developing and implementing cultural strategies. The content on Charentsavan is the sole responsibility of the Culture for Sustainable Development–Armenia Organization and the author, Ruzanna Tsaturyan, and does not necessarily reflect the views of the European Union.

References

Ararat Museum in Yerevan (Ararat). https://en.araratbrandy.com/museum/. Accessed on 13 March 2025.

Armenian Railway Museum. https://www.railway.am/arm/musey. Accessed on 13 March 2025.

Azizbekyan, R. 2004. Manifestations of the reconstruction policy in Armenia 1985–1990. *Banber YSU* 3 (114): 144–152.

Barski, J., and M. Zathey. 2018. Industrial heritage and post-industrial situation in the post-transformation era in Lower Silesia (Poland). *GeoScape* 12(1) (June).

Berger, S. 2023. Deindustrialized spaces. In *The Routledge handbook of memory activism*, ed. Y. Gutman and J. Wustenberg, 253–258. London and New York: Routledge.

Burokas, V., and G. Urniežė, eds. 2023. *Elektra. Kaip nušvito Vilnius?* Vilnius: VšĮ Lietuvos energetikos muziejus.

Campbell, R. 1991/1995. The December 7, 1988 Armenia earthquake: Effects on selected power, industrial, and commercial facilities. https://inis.iaea.org/collection/NCLCollectionStore/_Public/30/052/30052386.pdf. Accessed on 29 September 2019.

Central Museum of Textiles [Centralne Muzeum Włókiennictwa w Łodzi]. Website. https://cmwl.pl/public/. Accessed on 13 March 2025.

Coal Mining Museum [Muzeum Górnictwa Węglowego]. Guido Mine [Kopalnia Guido] website. https://kopalniaguido.pl. Accessed on 13 March 2025.

Coal Mining Museum [Muzeum Górnictwa Węglowego]. Institutional website. https://www.muzeumgornictwa.pl. Accessed on 13 March 2025.

Cudny, W. 2016. Manufaktura in Łódź, Poland: An example of a festival marketplace. *Norsk Geografisk Tidsskrift – Norwegian Journal of Geography* 70(5): 276–291.

Davoliūtė, V. 2013. *The Making and Breaking of Soviet Lithuania: Memory and Modernity on the Wake of War*. London and New York: Routledge.

Dawson, J. I. 1996. *Eco-nationalism: Anti-nuclear Activism and National Identity in Russia, Lithuania, and Ukraine*. Durham and London: Duke University Press.

Dovydaitytė, L. 2021. The pedagogy of dissonant heritage: Soviet industry in museums and textbooks. In *Learning the Nuclear: Educational Tourism in (post)industrial Sites*, ed. N. Mažeikienė, 65–110. Berlin: Peter Lang.

Dovydaitytė, L. and O. Denisenko. 2025. Nuclear urbanity as heritage. *Urban History*: 1–17. https://doi.org/10.1017/S0963926825100382.

Dovydaitytė, L. 2023. Curating industrial memories in a museum: An artistic approach. *Kunstiteaduslikke Uurimusi / Studies on Art and Architecture / Studien Für Kunstwissenschaft* 32 (3–4): 193–224.

Drėmaitė, M. 2002. *Pramonė kaip paveldo objektas. Kultūros paminklai* 9: 110–118.

Drėmaitė, M. 2012. Industrial heritage in a rural country: Interpreting the industrial past in Lithuania. In *Industrial Heritage Around the Baltic Sea*, ed. M. Nisser, M. Isacson, A. Lundgren, and A. Cinis, 65–78. Uppsala: Uppsala Universitet.

Dzięgiel, M. 2021. The geotouristic attractiveness of the underground trails in Zabrze, Dąbrowa Górnicza, and Tarnowskie Góry towns (Silesian Upland). *Geotourism/geoturystyka* 17 (1–2): 23–38.

Energy and Technology Museum [Energetikos ir technikos muziejus]. Website. https://etm.lt. Accessed on 13 March 2025.

European Route of Industrial Heritage (ERIH). Website. https://www.erih.net/. Accessed 13 Feb 2025.

European Solidarity Center [Europejskie Centrum Solidarności]. Website. https://ecs.gda.pl/. Accessed on 13 March 2025.

Grgić, A. 2024. Industrial ruins, malaise, and ambivalent nostalgia: Reflections on the post-socialist condition in contemporary Balkan cinemas. In *Visual Culture of Post-industrial Europe*, ed. F. Guerin and M. Szczesniak, 171–194. Amsterdam: Amsterdam University Press.

Guerin, F., and M. Szczesniak, eds. 2024. *Visual Culture of Post-industrial Europe: Cities and Cultures*. Amsterdam: Amsterdam University Press.

Hanzl, M. 2015. Księży Młyn in Łódź, Poland – An example of a successful rehabilitation thanks to social engagement. In *Cities Save the World. Let's Reinvent Planning*, Proceedings ISOCARP 2015. Amsterdam–Rotterdam.

Hilmar, T. 2023. *Deserved: Economic Memories After the Fall of the Iron Curtain*. New York: Columbia University Press.

Iskandaryan, A., A.H. Mikaelian, and S. Minasyan. 2016. *War, Business and Politics: Informal Networks and Formal Institutions in Armenia*. Yerevan: Caucasus Institute.

Jabłoński, W., A. Podstawka, M. Przednowek, D. Sęk, W. Smagieł, and J. Sroczyńska. 2024. The image of transformations of industrial facilities in Poland – A case study of the Żnin Sugar Factory industrial complex. *Architecture, Urban Planning, Interior Design* 19.

Jankauskienė, A. ed. 2019. *Astra. Keturios kartos*. Alytus: [Machine Factory Publication].

Khatchadourian, L. 2022. Life extempore: Trials of ruination in the twilight zone of Soviet industry. *Cultural Anthropology* 37 (2): 317–348.

Kisiel, P. 2021. When we say post-industrial – we mean ruins. *Heritage & Society* 14 (1): 20–45. https://doi.org/10.1080/2159032X.2021.2022070.

Kochetkova, E., and A. Petrova. 2022. Abandoned, but not forgotten heritage: Former industrial enterprises in cultural and urban Russian landscapes. *Heritage & Society* 15 (3): 277–298.

Koj, J. 2024. Adaptive reuse of industrial heritage in a polycentric metropolitan area: The case of GZM (Silesian Province, Poland). *Bulletin of Geography. Socio-Economic Series* 65: 141–153. https://doi.org/10.12775/bgss-2024-0029.

Koman, W. 2020. Podziemna przestrzeń kulturalna Zabrza w Kopalni 'Guido'. *Konwersatorium Wiedzy o Mieście* 33(5): 141–151. https://doi.org/10.18778/2543-9421.05.11.

Konior, A., and W. Pokojska. 2020. Management of postindustrial heritage in urban revitalization processes. *Sustainability* 12: 5034. https://doi.org/10.3390/su12125034.

Koryś, P. 2018. *Poland from Partitions to EU Accession: A Modern Economic History, 1772–2004*. London: Palgrave Macmillan.

Manufaktura. Website. https://www.manufaktura.com/. Accessed on 13 March 2025.

Manukyan, L. 2021. Interpretation and utilization of industrial heritage values: Vanadzor City, Armenia. Vienna: CEU. [unpublished MA thesis].

Melkumyan, H. 2018. Soviet ideology, utopian futures & daily transformations of urban space in Metsamor. In *Utopia and Collapse: Rethinking Metsamor – The Armenian Atomic City*, ed. A. Franke, S. Kichatov, and K. Šira, 212–216. Zurich: Park Books.

Meškauskas, K. 1994. *Lietuvos ūkis 1940–1990*. Vilnius: Lietuvos istorijos institutas.

Ost, D. 1991. *Solidarity and the Politics of Anti-politics: Opposition and Reform in Poland Since 1968*. Philadelphia: Temple University Press.

Pehe, V., and J. Wawrzyniak, eds. 2023. *Remembering the Neoliberal Turn: Economic Change and Collective Memory in Eastern Europe After 1989*. London and New York: Routledge.

Peters, F. 2015. Solidarność yesterday – Solidarity today? The European Solidarity Center in Gdańsk endeavors to combine the past with the present. *Cultures of History Forum*, 12 May. https://doi.org/10.25626/0041.

Petrović, T. 2017. Nostalgia for industrial labor in Socialist Yugoslavia or why the post-socialist affect matters. In *Nostalgia on the Move*, ed. M. Velikonja, 14–29. Belgrade: The Museum of Yugoslavia.

Polish Committee of the International Committee for the Conservation of the Industrial Heritage [Polski Komitet Ochrony Dziedzictwa Przemysłowego]. Website. https://ticcih.pl/. Accessed on 13 March 2025.

Pusca, A. 2010. Industrial and human ruins of postcommunist Europe. *Space and Culture* 13 (3): 239–255.

Rek-Woźniak, M., and W. Woźniak. 2020. Working-class and memory policy in post-industrial cities: Łódź, Poland, and Tampere, Finland, compared. *International Labor and Working-Class History* 98: 5–21.

Rindzevičiūtė, E., A. Storm, and L. Dovydaitytė. 2024. *Nuclear Spaces: Communities, Materialities, Locations of Nuclear Cultural Heritage. Concluding Report*. Kingston upon Thames: Kingston University London. https://nusspaces.eu/concluding-report/.

Sadowy, K., and A. Lisiecki. 2019. Post-industrial, post-socialist or new productive city? Case study of the spatial and functional change of the chosen Warsaw industrial sites after 1989. *City, Territory and Architecture* 6(4).

Schofer, L. 2023. *The Formation of a Modern Labor Force: Upper Silesia, 1865–1914*. Berkeley: University of California Press.

Science Island [Mokslo sala]. Website. https://mokslosala.lt/. Accessed on 10 March 2025.

Silesian Museum [Muzeum Śląskie]. Website. https://muzeumslaskie.pl. Accessed on 13 March 2025.

Silver Mine and Black Trout Adit [Kopalnia Srebra i Sztolnia Czarnego Pstrąga]. Website. https://kopalniasrebra.pl/zabytkowa-kopalnia-srebra/. Accessed on 13 March 2025.

Sklokina, I., and V. Kulikov. 2021. Industrial heritage and its multiple uses in Donbas, Ukraine. *Region* 10 (1): 33–60.

Staniszkis, J. 1984. *Poland's Self-limiting Revolution*. Princeton: Princeton University Press.

Staszewska, A., and M. Żemła. 2013. The industrial monuments route of the Silesian Voivodeship as an example of the regional tourism product enhancing tourism competitiveness of the region. *Czech Journal of Tourism* 2 (1): 37–53.

Szcześniak, M. 2024. Erasure and recovery: Representing labour in the deindustrializing space of the Gdańsk shipyard. In *Visual Culture of Post-industrial Europe*, ed. F. Guerin and M. Szczesniak, 43–66. Amsterdam: Amsterdam University Press.

Szromek A, K. Herman, and M. Naramski. 2021. Sustainable development of industrial heritage tourism—A case study of the Industrial Monuments Route in Poland, *Tourism Management*, vol. 83 https://doi.org/10.1016/j.tourman.2020.104252.

The Foundation for the Preservation of the Industrial Heritage of Silesia [Fundacja Ochrony Dziedzictwa Przemysłowego Śląska]. Website. https://www.muzeatechniki.pl/. Accessed on 13 March 2025.

Tomann, J. 2017. *Geschichtskultur im Strukturwandel: Öffentliche Geschichte in Katowice nach 1989*. Berlin: Oldenbourg De Gruyter.

Tomann, J. 2025. Memorialization of industrial pasts in post-socialist countries. In *The Routledge International Handbook of Deindustrialization Studies*, eds. T. Strangleman, S.L. Linkon, S. High, J. Clarke and S. Berger. 388–418. London and New York: Routledge.

Topography Association [Stowarzyszenie Topografie]. Website. http://topografie.pl. Accessed on 13 March 2025.

Tranavičiūtė, B. 2023. Modernist heritage versus contested legacy: The case of 'Radio City.' *Buildings* 13 (246): 1–22.
Tsaturyan, R. 2023. *Charentsavan: Soviet and Post-Soviet Memory Spaces: Photo Album.* Culture for Sustainable Development. Yerevan. [in Armenian].
Urban Stories. Project website. https://www.facebook.com/urbanstoriesvsg/. Accessed on 10 February 2025.
Vaičys, J. 2016. *Mūsų istorija.* Šiauliai: [TV Factory Publication].
Verluise, P. 1995. *Armenia in Crisis: The 1988 Earthquake.* Detroit: Wayne State University Press.
Visaginas City Museum [Visagino miesto muziejus]. Website. https://www.visaginomuziejus.lt/. Accessed on 12 February 2025.
Wager, H., ed. 2000. *Industrial Heritage in the Nordic and Baltic Countries: Seminar on Cooperation Strategies, Research and Training, 1–3 October 1999.* Copenhagen.
Walczak, B.M., and A. Kepczyńska-Walczak. 2024. Adaptive re-use of industrial heritage in Łódź, Poland. *International Journal of Conservation Science* 15(2).
Wawrzyniak, J. 2021. 'Hard times but our own': Post-socialist nostalgia and the transformation of industrial life in Poland. *Zeithistorische Forschungen / Studies in Contemporary History* 18(1). [Online edition].
Yerevan History Museum. https://yhm.am. Accessed on 13 March 2025.
Zürcher, C. 2007. *The Post-Soviet Wars: Rebellion, Ethnic Conflict, and Nationhood in the Caucasus.* New York and London: New York University Press.
Zysiak, A., K. Śmiechowski, K. Piskała, W. Marzec, K. Kaźmierska, and J. Burski. 2019. *From Cotton and Smoke: Łódź—Industrial City and Discourses of Asynchronous Modernity, 1897–1994.* Łódź: University of Łódź Press.

Systemic Political Transformations

To Remember Impossible to Forget: The Memory of Entrepreneurship in the Late Nineteenth–Early Twenty-First Century in Ukraine

Tetiana Vodotyka

1 Introduction

Memory studies in Ukraine and about Ukraine have a long history but are generally focused on a set of specific issues. These include, for example, analysing ways of remembering nationalist organisations, recognising their role in nation and state building, and, more broadly—dealing with difficult pasts (Yurchuk 2017; Wylegała 2017). Scholars also examine contemporary politics of memory in Ukraine (Kasianov 2022a, 1295–98; Koposov 2017; Stryjek and Konieczna-Sałamatin 2021), such as the processes of decommunisation, intensified by the Revolution of Dignity and Russian invasion (Marples 2018; Plokhii 2017), and how the history, memory and memory wars became casus belli for Vladimir Putin (Mahda and Vodotyka 2021; McGlynn 2022; Nikitin 2022). Finally,

T. Vodotyka (✉)
Kyiv School of Economics, Kyiv, Ukraine
e-mail: tvodotyka@kse.org.ua; tetiana.vodotyka@durham.ac.uk

Institute of Advanced Study, Durham University, Durham, UK

S. Berger and T. Fetzer (eds.), *Collective Memory of Economic Crises and Transformations*, Palgrave Macmillan Memory Studies,
https://doi.org/10.1007/978-3-032-09094-2_6

the memory of several genocides on Ukrainian territory—Holodomor 1932–1933 (Riabchuk 2008; Amiot 2024) and Holocaust 1941–1943—is also addressed (Portnov 2017; Chebotarova 2020; Kotljarchuk 2022). Scholars from the field of memory studies have never drawn their attention to the entrepreneurs as actors in present memory politics or commemorated figures. However, businesses in Ukraine actively shaped and established mnemonical practices in the late ninteenth and early twentieth century, and they also shape them today. At the turn of the twentieth century, the means to this end were the erection of monuments, the naming of streets and settlements, and the patronage and funding of significant social projects, such as schools or hospitals. These initiatives took place primarily in cities but may have been more visible in big ones due to the scope of the funded projects. For example, it is impossible to avoid Kyiv with its' numerous schools, hospitals, and cultural institutions funded and supported by Tereschenko, Brodskyi, Khanenko, and other merchant families. Odesa was famous for its merchant Greek and Jewish dynasties, which sponsored synagogues, church buildings, clinics, and educational and cultural institutions. Oleksiy Alchevskyi in Kharkiv became visible due to the massive support of Ukrainian initiatives, mostly educational ones. The scope of initiatives in smaller cities was accordingly smaller but not less visible or important. On the contrary, financing school buildings in provincial towns such as Hlukhiv (the hometown of the Tereschenko family) was even more influential.

The presence of entrepreneurs in public spaces and the memorial culture they fostered aimed to point out the subjectivity of companies and their visibility in the public realm and the recognition of the importance of these new elites' representatives in the rapidly transforming society. Entrepreneurs were also members of local councils, mayors, and generous donors. As they gained prominence in these structures, they increasingly sought to mark their presence on Ukraine's streets and squares.

After the October Revolution of 1917, the situation changed completely. Most entrepreneurs lost their property and social influence, and many of them lost their lives. As the Bolsheviks tried to ruin the capitalist system, they were highly motivated to destroy any remaining fillip to the memory of their "class enemies". The Bolsheviks renamed the streets and settlements established to honour local entrepreneurs' legacy, destroyed their monuments, and ruined everything that reminded them of the former owners and their contribution to the economic growth of Ukraine. The first years of Soviet rule on the territory of Ukraine were marked by what the Bolsheviks called the "Civil War", but in fact, was a war between the Bolsheviks and Ukraine, actually the Ukrainian War of Independence, and it was fought predominantly on the territory of Ukraine (Руккас et al. 2016; Верстюк 2022; Верстюк 2017) all the significant toponyms marking entrepreneurial presence and legacy were removed, and all the monuments were destroyed.

During the 1930s, under Joseph Stalin's rule, the Communist Party and the Soviet authorities launched a process of writing/creating a new "suitable" version of history. This process included, among other things, political repressions against the researchers whose position was uncomfortable or who tried to oppose the dominant party line; the initiation of a bottom-up movement of collecting data and writing the histories of plants and factories under the leadership of renowned Russian writer Maksim Gorkiy; and the creation of the holistic historical narrative, which emphasised the dominant historical role of the working class and denigrated entrepreneurship as a symbol of the imperial regime of the Romanovs (Юркова 2012a; Юркова 2012b). The Bolshevik state used all possible means of influence—political, ideological, organisational, financial, and punitive. Everything was subordinated to gain control of science in accordance with the doctrinal provision on the possibility of effective use of scientific achievements in socialist transformations. Scholars and historians, in particular, were perceived mainly as enemies*Istoriya vsesoyuznoy kommunisticheskoy partii (bol'shevykov). Kratkiy kurs* (translated into English under the title *History of the All-Union Communist Party [Bolsheviks]: Short Course*), first published in 1938 and edited by Joseph Stalin, became the apotheosis and quintessence of this ideologeme (Stalin 1939).

The decline of the USSR led to tectonic changes in geopolitics and memory regimes across Central and East Europe, including Ukraine. The memory of the entrepreneurial past of some settlements, which were founded by businessmen (and some businesswomen) in the nineteenth century, rapidly returned. New monuments were erected during the last decade of the twentieth and the first decade of the twenty-first century, and quite a few names were brought back from oblivion. This also reflected a massive postsocialist transformation on all possible levels, from the economic to cultural and social ones. In this chapter, I rely on the scholarship in memory studies to explain memory shifts in Ukraine after 1917 and 1991 and to analyse businessmen (and one businesswoman) as commemorated figures. I analyse the changes that the memory of entrepreneurs and entrepreneurship faced during the late nineteenth and the early twenty-first century and how this part of memory culture reflected (and continues to reflect) the social and political reality of the present and the changes and challenges that the Ukrainian society has been through.

Jan and Aleida Assman's concepts of cultural and collective memory are crucial to understanding the changes in memory culture and how the figures of entrepreneurs were introduced into the memorial canon, then moved to the "archive" in an attempt to be erased, and then made their way back (Assmann 2010). The concept of communicative memory helps to understand how the memory of businesspeople survived through the years of denigration and forgetting via informal/vernacular remembering, personal experiences, and emotions. As termed by Jan Assmann, communicative memory is an informal and implicit form of memory lacking a defined structure, a shared experience conveyed within a social group defined by common memories of personal interactions, primarily through verbal communication, spanning a time frame of approximately 80 to 100 years (Assmann 2008). Even though recent publications question the strict distinction between cultural and communicative memory, preferring to talk about two different registers for evoking the past—one regarding the distant and the other regarding the recent past, we would argue that for the purposes of our analysis, such clear distinction is still relevant, as referring more to official vs private/unofficial/vernacular memory (Bodnar 1992).

Eric Hobsbawm's conceptualisation of the invention of tradition in the late nineteenth–early twentieth century will help to place the emergence of entrepreneurial commemoration practices into the broader context. Hobsbawm explains the mechanism of inventing mediums (traditions) for group identification—nation and also class (i.e., sports and schooling as an element of such social self-segregation) (Hobsbawm 2012).The initiation of certain commemorative practices both in the late imperial times and in the early years of Ukrainian independence could be seen as manifestations of this mechanism.

The typology of memory regimes, developed by the research team under the supervision of Jan Kubik, brings us closer to the understanding of changes and perspectives of memory regimes in Ukraine after 1991. Kubik and others argued in their edited volume *Twenty Years After Communism* that different combinations of mnemonic actors in different contexts lead to three types of memory regimes: fractured, pillarised, and unified (Bernhard and Kubik 2014). In 2014, the crucial year marked by the annexation of Crimea and the outbreak of the Russo-Ukrainian war and the year when the book was published, they defined the memory regime in Ukraine as fractured with "the possibility for mnemonic pluralism" (Shevel 2014). However, such approaches require revision in light of the recent events that took place in Ukraine, particularly with respect to the memory of Ukrainian entrepreneurship. While in 2014 and even in 2020, memory wars were still on the table, with the potential to divide Ukrainian society, the potential for this division decreased from year to year. While the histories of entrepreneurs were controversial, it turned out that their memory was one of the least contested ones. It must be admitted that the memory of entrepreneurs was the safe road to take in this respect, as hardly any figure of a businessman from the past caused any discussion or outright rejection. This was a "safe option" to choose from and might become a good ground for a unified memory regime in the future.

The full-scale Russian invasion led to tectonic changes in many ways, including history writing. The invasion has catalysed significant shifts in the optics and methodological approaches within academic and cultural spheres. History and memory have been spotlighted as contentious battlegrounds, as Russia's goal is clearly to question the legitimacy of the Ukrainian state (Mahda and Vodotyka 2021). Consequently, the landscape of knowledge production is transforming, particularly regarding access to archives and the nature of methodological discussions. In this ongoing struggle, the more active decolonisation efforts become, the better chances Ukraine has at reclaiming and asserting its subjectivity.

At the same time, I am conscious that engaging with the postcolonial theory in the case of Ukraine is not easy or unproblematic. As early as 2019, for example, Barbara Törnquist-Plewa and Yuliya Yurchuk used the case of the memory culture about World War II and the Ukrainian Insurgent Army to show that the postcolonial stage is entangled with the anticolonial stage in Ukrainian contexts of remembrance (Törnquist-Plewa and Yurchuk 2019). Madina Tlostanova (2019) highlighted the complexity of the post-Soviet postcoloniality, which "certainly falls out of the postcolonial dichotomous division into the colonisers and the colonised". For her, postcoloniality was a condition, and decoloniality was an option and "an entry point into the agency"; her advice was to use decolonial concepts on a general level of analysis while reserving postcolonial tools for the level of description, in particular, that of various actors and historical figures (Tlostanova 2019, 172).

This approach is appropriate for our case of Ukrainian businesses and their mnemonical practices, particularly if combined with the concept of hybridity. As popularised by postcolonial critics, the concept of cultural hybridity refers to a culture and new transcultural forms within the contact zone produced by colonisation. Hybridisation manifests in various forms, including cultural, political, and linguistic. According to Homi Bhabha (1994), hybridity and "linguistic multivocality" can potentially intervene and dislocate the process of colonisation through the reinterpretation of political discourse. As we will see, the concept of hybridity will help us understand and deconstruct newly emerged memory practices around the figures of entrepreneurs of the nineteenth century.

In the following, I trace the development of predominantly local, though not apolitical, memory until 1917 into politicised and centralised practices during the Soviet era and then back to local agendas after 1991, though economic actors and Ukrainian nation-building also drive the ones. These changes in memory production are analysed in four dimensions/spheres. First, I examine the changes in *knowledge production* and how historical research and the methods of "making history" transformed during the Soviet era and then again after 1991. The second dimension is *the role of mnemonic actors*. Indeed, the initiative for memorialisation moved from the local elites and entrepreneurs themselves in late imperial times to the state and the simulacrums of the civil society institutions in the Soviet era and to the different constellations of the state and local elites after 1991. The third sphere of analysis is *urban toponymy and memorialising projects*, which was easy to change as it required minimal investment but promised a good outcome. The erection of monuments was more costly but also more spectacular and effective. Both toponymic changes and the erection of monuments are the consequences of the changes in knowledge production and the set of actors. Local elites tried to use entrepreneurs of the past to justify their own influence and power.

I will use discourse analysis methodology to navigate these dimensions and explain all the changes that happened over a hundred years. I am assessing how the discourse influenced the language used (written, spoken, and visual) and knowledge production (Smiraglia 2015; Tannen et al. 2015).

2 To Remember: Late Nineteenth Century to 1914

In terms of memory studies, the late nineteenth century was the time of two parallel processes: the formation of the public image of entrepreneurship and the formation of the memory of it. By the end of the century, the first-generation family business owners in Ukraine had already passed away. But their gravitas, social influence, contribution to social and cultural development, and the amount of money spent on charity demanded recognition.

The significant role of the local elites should be pointed out. It was up to the city councils to vote on the changing of streets' names, on the approval of the construction of monuments, or on awarding honorary citizenship to prominent entrepreneurs of the past. Of course, the local communities picked up the "heroes" for such commemoration. What did the community leaders see as significant in fulfilling this role? First was the amount spent by an entrepreneur on charity and important social projects (such as the patronage of schools, hospitals, and donations to building churches). It must be acknowledged that this factor was the primary one in their decisions. The second factor was the position of an entrepreneur in the communities, which was often determined by ethnicity. For example, Jewish entrepreneurs often donated as generously as Russian or Ukrainian ones but were never awarded honorary citizenship (Vodotyka and Vodotyka 2019). The local elites, then, led the process of knowledge production about the role of the businesses in the development of their localities and Ukraine more broadly. While this memory might often appear non-political and linked to local interests and groups, in fact, the story is more complex in that it not only includes some prominent businessmen (and even fewer businesswomen) while excluding others but also those very interests often intertwined with broader imperial programmes. Put simply, local actors were more likely to be recognised and commemorated when the imperial metropolis recognised them, as well.

It is worth examining the cases of some of the significant entrepreneurial figures of the late nineteenth and early twentieth century to explore these aspects in detail. For example, Oleksandr Pol (1832–1890) was a prominent entrepreneur, researcher, collector, public figure, and outstanding organiser. Pol personified a success story not so much for himself but for the whole region of East-Central Ukraine and its two largest cities, Kryvyi Rih and Katerynoslav (now Dnipro). Pol did not contribute to the support of schools, hospitals, or any cultural initiatives. He was a famous collector of antiquities, and this collection, after his death, became the ground for the collection of the Dnipro Local Lore Museum. His memory was predominantly local and limited to this region: his name is primarily associated with the transformation of the Katerynoslav region into the centre of the mining and metallurgical industry of the Russian Empire, which retains this function in present-day Ukraine.[1] In May 1887, at the celebration of the 100th anniversary of Dnipro (then Yekaterinoslav or Katerynoslav in Ukrainian version), the Mayor paid tribute to the role of Oleksandr Pol: "We owe to his remarkable energy, tireless activity and enormous expenditures that our iron ore wealth became famous not only in our country but throughout Europe and that attracted domestic and foreign entrepreneurs with their solid capital" (Кочергін 2018, 78–90).

Pol was awarded the title of an honorary citizen of Katerynoslav in November 1887 for a highly significant contribution to the development of the city and the province (Donik n. d.). At the same time, Pol became the first person to receive this title. In 1889, during his lifetime, the city council discussed the issue of erecting a monument to Alexander Pol. It was also decided that he should place his portrait in the noble assembly hall and establish scholarships in his name at the Mining School of St. Petersburg and the Katerynoslav Secondary School. Also, during his lifetime, in 1890, his bronze bust with the inscription "To the little Russian [i.e., Ukrainian][2] Columbus" was installed in what was then the village of Dubova Balka, owned and researched by Pol, and where later the first iron ore mine started working (now part of modern Kryvyi Rih). Unfortunately, it was stretched to scrap metal in a few years and never restored.

On July 17, 1891, a year after Pol's death, a bronze bust was erected in his honour near the Iron Foundry in Kryvyi Rih suburb, which worked with the ore from the Pol's mines. It was commissioned by the Kryvyi Rih Iron Ore Joint Stock Company, which was extremely successful and profitable at that time. The inscription on the pedestal reads as follows:

[1] See Кочергін 2018 for further reading about O.Pol.

[2] Little Russian (Maloros) is a term used to describe Ukrainians in the times of the Russian Empire (officially) and during Soviet rule (disparagingly). The idea behind the term is to underline the secondary, non-sovereign, subordinate, dependent, and even colonial position of Ukrainians and Ukraine compared to Russians and Russia (Ясь n.d.).

"To honour the useful activity of O[leksandr] Pol in Kryvyi Rih in 1870–1890, from the Kryvyi Rih Iron Ore Joint Stock Company. In 1915, Katerynoslav city council also named one of the streets in honour of Oleksandr Pol".

Similarly, Oleksiy Alchevskyi (1835–1901) was one of the founders and managers of several banks and enterprises in Ukraine and the creator of perhaps the first financial and industrial group in the Russian Empire in the modern sense of the word, which included banks, mines, metallurgical plants, iron ore mines, as well as transport companies.

Alchevskyi financed the maintenance and erection of a building for a Sunday school in Kharkiv, which was established by his wife, Khrystyna. Alchevskyi's donations helped to establish a commercial school and an agricultural institute in Kharkiv. He was also among the most generous donors of the Higher School of Mining in Katerynoslav in 1899. He built schools in villages and a public library in his native Sumy, employed the Ukrainian intellectual elite's representatives, and financed public education initiatives. He was a notable figure in the Ukrainian national movement, worked in an unofficial organisation called *Hromada*, and even had a bust of Ukrainian national poet Taras Shevchenko in the garden of his Kharkiv estate (Семенюк n.d.). Alchevskyi was the head of the Kharkiv Stock Exchange Committee and had unquestionable authority among the Ukrainian entrepreneurs. However, the case of Alchevskyi also demonstrates the level of hybridity that is not untypical for the milieu of Ukrainian businessmen in the late Russian Empire: while supporting the Ukrainian national project, he was also a loyal imperial subject whose contribution was recognised by the state level by granting the Order of St. Stanislaus (and the greeting letter from the Russian imperial Minister of Finances Sergei Vitte) and the title of Commerce Advisor in 1894 (Нестерчук n.d.).

The overproduction crisis of 1899–1902[3] was fatal for the entrepreneur: the manufactured products were increasingly difficult to sell, the number of bankruptcies increased, and the largest factories closed. Alchevskyi asked the government and personally Minister Vitte for help placing state orders for rails at his new plant. This could have saved the business, but the request was refused. On May 7, 1901, seeing

[3] A decrease in the influx of foreign capital into government bonds and industrial enterprise securities instigated this crisis, which led to an abrupt halting of the growth industrialisation of the 1890s. See more, i.e., Lychakov 2021.

no good prospects out of the critical situation, Alchevskyi threw himself under the train at the Tsarsko-Selsky railway station in St. Petersburg. His death had a domino effect and triggered the Kharkiv Crash—the peak of the economic crisis in the early 1900s in the Russian Empire that started from the bankruptcy of the banks located in Kharkiv and affiliated with Alchevskyi (Мошенський 2015).

While Alchevskyi's authority in the business community remained unquestionable even after his death, the way his legacy was commemorated reflected the complexity of his biography. In 1903, at the request of several Russian and Ukrainian industrialists, the railway station Yurivka was renamed Alchevsk. Next to the station grew a village, which gradually became a town where the metallurgical plant owned by Alchevskyi was located. The same year, 1903, one of the first biographies of the entrepreneur was published (Белов 1903).

It is impossible to avoid the Tereshchenko family in discussing Ukrainian imperial entrepreneurship. The Tereshchenkos, who made their fortune in the grain trade and sugar industry, were exemplary entrepreneurs, bankers, philanthropists, and arts patrons. Having earned profits on the intermediary trade in grain, salt, and timber and from lucrative government contracts during the 1840s and 1850s, they went on to rent, buy, and re-organise sugar factories and establish new ones.

Nikola Tereshchenko (1819–1903), a representative of the second generation of the family who would become the face of the family business for several decades, began public and political activities in his native Hlukhiv. In 1851–1860, Tereshchenko was the senior burgomaster; in 1860–1874, he served as the mayor of Hlukhiv. In this capacity, he did everything in his power for the development of the city. In the 1870s, under his leadership and supported by his financial contribution, the programme for the city's improvement and the paving of the central streets began. In 1895, with his financial support, a railway was built that linked Hlukhiv with Kyiv. In the early twentieth century, Hlukhiv was revived as the region's educational and cultural centre (Донік 2008, 131).

In the late 1870s, the Tereshchenkos moved to Kyiv and continued their way to the respected tops of the society while remaining a visible figure in charity projects. Public and political activity was the best way to ensure this path. According to rough estimates, Tereshchenko donated five million rubles to various charitable projects during his life. The list of philanthropic projects included medical and educational institutions, shelters for children and adults, various public institutions, Orthodox churches, and scholarships for students from several educational institutions.

On October 14, 1899, Nikola Tereshchenko celebrated his 80th anniversary and 50 years of public service. In honour of the jubilee, by the decision of the city authorities, Oleksiyivska Street in Kyiv was renamed to Tereshchenko Street (Tereshchenkivska): "Wishing forever to immortalise your unforgettable name among the people of Kyiv, the city administration assigns the nameTereshchenkivska Street to one of the central streets adjacent to your estate" (Донік 2004, 135–137). Ten years later, in 1909, a monument to Tereshchenko was mounted in Hlukhiv. Hundreds of citizens attended the monument's opening, and a delegation from Kyiv was also present. The monument was a cubic pedestal in a chair with a high back, sitting in bronze. Mykola Tereshchenko was in the pose of a calm, wise man, thereby signifying a memory that transcended specific localities but remained within the confines of an officially sanctioned image of a charitable, seemingly non-political businessman, imperial privy councillor, and Kyiv's honorary citizen (Донік 2004, 135–137).

Finally, the memory of businesses in Ukraine during the period of late Russian Empire would be incomplete without a mention of western businesses and what we might call agents of other empires. For example, John James Hughes (1814–1889), an engineer from Wales, was a prominent figure and significant actor in the history of entrepreneurship in the Donbas region. His role in the economic development and the establishment of heavy industry in the Donbas would be difficult to overestimate. Furthermore, the new urban settlement of Yuzivka (now Donetsk), founded in the late 1860s as a factory colony, also carried his name.[4] Hughes was almost impossible to forget: throughout the late nineteenth and the early twentieth century, most of the whole town's inhabitants and nearby villages had a job at the plant and remembered Hughes personally (he died in 1889). Moreover, the salaries at the Donbas plants, including the one belonging to Hughes, were among the highest in the Russian Empire's industry, thereby making Hughes well-known far beyond the area. His plant was marked as the foundational cornerstone of the whole future of Donetsk city, the first chapter in the

[4] In line with Soviet memorial practices, Yuzivka's name was changed in 1924 to Stalino. The city remained under this name until 1961, after which it is known as Donetsk, the main city of the Donbas region.

new industrial region myth, the working class's future stronghold, and the declared ground of Soviet power. Even to the Bolsheviks who aimed to destroy all evidence of memory of the "enemy class" and were particularly keen to present foreigners like Hughes as "economic exploiters", it was clear that they could not simply erase such a figure from the historical narrative. It is interesting to note that, despite his contribution to the development of Ukrainian industries, Hughes received little other memorialisation on the imperial level, or even locally in Yuzivka: no monument or street was carrying his name, and a comprehenvise commemoration programme started only in the Ukrainian independence era. Further research would be needed to establish whether this was because he was perceived as too foreign and lacking the local social base that ensured commemoration during one's lifetime, somewhat foreshadowing Bolshevik practices of the twentieth century.

In Hobsbawmian terms, then, the commemorative practices that the local entrepreneurs forged in Ukraine were in manty ways an "invented tradition", yet an exclusionary one at that: such practices were aimed at separating themselves and celebrating the most distinguished representatives of their social group or class, rather than at the dissemination of a broader popular memory. Honorary citizenship (Pol', Tereshchenko) was granted by city councils, which were elected by a minority of the citizens due to the property qualification, so no wonder many of the city council members were actually entrepreneurs. The town of Alchevske was named after the entrepreneurs' initiative to pay homage to their leader, Olexiy Alchevskiy. The creation of local official commemorative practices did not lead to establishing fully accepted traditions, but was also not yet opposed to vernacular memory. This was, in many ways, a grassroots tradition often linked to a particular locality. Like the Tereshchenko family, Oleksandr Pol and Oleksiy Alchevsky, John James Huges founded and developed enterprises that became critical for the economic development of the newly established Ukrainian Soviet Socialist Republic and the USSR in general. Employees of these enterprises obviously remembered the original owners and were able to compare the working conditions and social benefits during the imperial and soviet eras. This comparison was not always complimentary to the new regime. How should the new rulers resolve the uncomfortable presence of Hughes' legacy? If they could not make people forget someone and ruin the memory via ruining the monuments, they resorted to replacing the good (or neutral) memoirs with the less favourable ones. The most effective way to do so was via publications and renaming, which brings me to the next period in the memory history of entrepreneurs in Ukraine in 1920–1991. But before moving to this period, I would like to point out the almost total absence of women in these stories and narratives. In the context of the late nineteenth-century Russian Empire, it was almost impossible for women to start, run, and maintain successful businesses if their husbands were alive and well. Even the role of the most visible female entrepreneurs has not been recognised yet. The situation will change with time, but not drastically.

3 To Forget: 1920s to 1991

Ruining monuments. Re-erecting new ones. Renaming streets. Tailoring stories. That was how, step by step, the negative image of entrepreneurs of the not-so-distant past was constructed. The whole mindset was transformed to set the general unshakable ideological framework with the set ahead roles, directions, and characteristics. With rare but notable exceptions, entrepreneurs were almost always assessed as villains and oppressors. After seizing power, the Bolsheviks asserted their right to design the urban landscape in the style of the new Soviet symbols. The first step to mark the space and establish the new narrative was *dismantling the monuments*. Most of them, which were erected in the late nineteenth century to mark the contribution of individual entrepreneurs to the economic, social, and cultural development of a particular region or city, were destroyed. Some of them were destroyed demonstratively. For example, this happened to the memorial plaque to the honorary citizens of Katerynoslav (Dnipro) in the city council building, which also listed Oleksandr Pol', and to Tereshchenko's monument in Hlukhiv (Hardly any records remained on the destruction of the monuments. Most sources provide vague mentions of either "vandals" or "Bolsheviks") (Донік n.d.).

As it happened, the destruction was not simply the result of the revolutionaries' fury. It was justified by law. On 12 April 1918, The Council of People's Commissars in Moscow adopted the Decree on Monuments, which stated that monuments erected in honour of tsars and their servants that had neither artistic nor historical value were to be removed from streets and squares and moved to warehouses or used for utilitaractical purposes (Декрет Совнаркома 1918). The Chairman of the Council of People's Commissars of the Ukrainian Soviet Socialist Republic, Khrystian Rakovskyi, signed a decree of the same name on 7 May 1919. To fulfil this legal requirement, dozens of monuments were removed, broken down, or melted to produce new sculptures. For example, in 1919, a bronze statue of Ukrainian businessman and philanthropist Oleksii Bobrynskyi was removed from one of the central alleys of Kyiv. While the monument to Tsar Alexander II disappeared from the former Tsarist Square, and the monument to Tsar Nicholas I was also dismantled on the Nicholas Square (Mykolaivskyi), now renamed Red Park, monuments to entrepreneurs suffered a similar fate (Купченко and Волкотруб 2003, 194–198).

The next step was erecting new monuments in the same places, often using the same pedestals. In 1918, monuments to Lenin and Trotsky had already been placed in St Sophia Square in Kyiv. Dozens of no-name "monuments" to tanks, guns, and trams, literally displaying machinery on pedestals, were erected to show the new power, the new authorities, and the new rules. Cheap and made fast of plaster and concrete, they often quickly deteriorated. However, the idea was not to build something durable or artistically valuable but to mark the urban space and signify the presence of power (Гайдай 2019, 45). Anatoly Lunacharsky, the first Bolshevik Soviet People's Commissar responsible for the Ministry of Education, recounted in his memoirs his conversation with Lenin about monumental propaganda, in which the latter said the following regarding the construction of monuments:

> Do not think that I am imagining marble, granite and golden letters. For now, we should do everything modestly. Let it be some white slabs with inscriptions as clear as possible on them. I'm not thinking about eternity or even duration. Let it all be temporary... It is important that they be accessible to the masses that they catch the eye... (Луначарський 1933)

To rename the streets and settlements was even cheaper and more easily managed. Some were renamed shortly after the Soviet power was established and became powerful enough to mark the new symbolic space of Soviet cities. Tereshchenkivska Street in Kyiv was first re-named Herzen Street in February 1919 in honour of Alexander Herzen (1812–1870)—a Russian writer and thinker, the precursor of Russian socialism and one of the main precursors of agrarian populism. Then, the street was renamed again after Grygoriy Chudnovsky, a Russian Bolshevik revolutionary. From 1955 to 1992, the street was named after the Ukrainian-born Russian painter Ilya Repin (Терещенківська вулиця n.d.).

In other cases, the process started in the 1920s, with some names remaining the same for decades. There could be several reasons why some namings remained untouched for such a long time: first, there was a shortage of time and resources to rename every street and settlement in the country. Secondly, the newly emerged regime did not have enough "heroes" to create a single pantheon. Indirectly, this argument is supported by the range of new names and monuments: a lot of them were not people but things—such as the aforementioned trams, trains, and guns on pedestals—and the new names were often pretty generic, such as the Red Square, the Soviet Street, or the Miners Street (Кузіна 2018).

Furthermore, it would be wrong to underestimate the sentiments that at least some of the Soviet leaders had towards places such as Yuzivka, Kamianske, or Alchevske, which were their homes and places where they were born or spent their youth. They might have wanted to keep the old names as part of their identity. For instance, Leonid Brezhnev, the General Secretary of the Communist Party of the USSR who was one of the top party leaders stemming from Ukraine, consistently referred in his memoirs *Zhizn' po zavodskomu gudku (Life by the Factory Horn)* to his native town as Kamianske,[5] and not Dneprodzerzhynsk (after the head of Soviet secret police Felix Dzerzhinsky), as the Soviets renamed it in 1936 (Брежнев 1981).

Hence, Alchevske kept the name of the wealthiest Ukrainian of the nineteenth century until 1931. The name was changed to Voroshylovske—after the Soviet military officer Klyment Voroshylov, who worked at the metallurgical plant in 1896–1903 (Соколенко et al. n.d.). But in 1959, the city was again re-named Alchevsk; on December 30, 1961, it received a new name, Kommunarsk. The reason for the survival and even return of the original name was that Oleksiy Alchevskyi was the safe choice for the Bolsheviks: not only had he already been dead for quite a long time, and his contribution to the region's economic development was prominent, but also his plant employed at least one prominent future Bolshevik leader and he generally had a good reputation among Bolsheviks. For example, Voroshylov described him respectfully in his memoirs, paying homage to his progressive views, talented family, and the welcoming atmosphere in Alchevskyi's estate. The old Bolshevik

[5] Kamianske was founded by Cossacks in the mid-eighteenth century and kept the name till 1936, when it was renamed into Dniprodzerzhynsk, to commemorate the 10th anniversary of Felix Dzerzhynskiy (one of the Bolshevik leaders and founder of the Soviet political police and secret service) death.

even admitted Alchevskyi's caring attitude to his employees in the time of economic crisis of 1900–1903: "It should be said that at that time the DUMO[6] plant was like an island in the raging ocean of economic crisis—it continued to smelt pig iron and steel and to produce a variety of rolled products, although everywhere else production was being curtailed. However, unlike in previous years, the products were not sold. But the workers were not laid off. And that is why the calamities already sweeping across Russia were not fully felt here" (Ворошилов 1968, 99).

Oleksandr Pol was also seen as a distant and safe enough figure for the Bolsheviks to recognise his large-scale contribution to the economic development of southeastern Ukraine, perhaps partly because of his entrepreneurial failure, although he had a more prominent and visible success as a collector. Soviet historian Pavlo Matviyevsky mentioned Pol'in 1929 and noted his role in the development of the region:

> The ideologue of industrial capitalism ... in southern Ukraine was a local landowner and public figure, O[leksandr] M[ykolayovych] Pol, with whom the history of the manufacturing and mining industries of the south, as well as the beginnings of cultural labour, are associated. (Голуб n.d.)

While Alchevsky and Pol were relatively safe choices for communist commemoration, others, such as Hughes, were equally notable and impossible to overlook, but they were less safe. True to rather xenophobic attitudes many Bolsheviks held against foreigners, good memoirs of Hughes and other "foreign exploiters" needed to be replaced with less favourable ones for these entrepreneurs. It was to this purpose that *Istoriya fabrik i zavodov (The History of Factories and Plants)*, a colossal publishing project (1931–1938) led and promoted by Bolshevik writer Maxim Gorky, was dedicated. It was through such publications that memory became politicised and centralised during the Soviet era. Though not, strictly speaking, started by Gorky, it was driven by his energy and authority. The writer called for the organisation of a mass movement to write the history of large industrial enterprises. The decree of the Central Committee of the Communist Party authorised the initiative on October 10, 1931. This project was critical in establishing a "correct" version of history. The campaign involved Soviet party leaders, writers, historians,

[6] Donetsko-Yurievskoe Metallugricheskoe Obshestvo—Donetsk-Yurievsk Metallurgical Company.

and public figures. The quality of individual entries in *The History of Factories and Plants* was uneven. While some texts were grounded on primary sources, others were more than tailored stories for Bolshevik justification.

On October 10 1931, a resolution of the Central Committee of the All-Union Communist Party was issued, which established the Editorial board of the new series and, at the same time, framed the new historical narrative. "These collections, the Resolution noted, 'should provide a picture of the development of the old factories and the emergence of new ones, their role in the economy of the country, the situation of the workers before the revolution, the forms and methods of exploitation in the old factories, the struggle of the workers with the entrepreneurs, the everyday conditions, the emergence of revolutionary organisations and the role of each factory in the revolutionary movement, the role of the factory and the change of relations in the factory after the revolution, the change in the type of worker, udarnichestvo, socialist competition and the rise of production in recent years (Смирнова 2016)'".

The first books were published in the early 1930s. This is how Hughes was described in one of them:

> Hughes was about 55 years old when he arrived at the Donetsk Basin. Sturdy, with a round face overgrown with a short beard, Hughes pressed heavily on his legs, which had been concave inwards like the legs of a bulldog. With a prayer book, psalter and books of the Old and New Testament in his suitcase, like an English missionary, Hughes landed at Taganrog port. A Montecristo in a cloth case and a revolver slightly interrupted the integrity of the impression. (Гонимов 1934, 65, transl. Vodotyka)

The author of this passage aimed to create a stereotyped image of a British greedy, trickier hogger who used religion as a shield for his businesses and could not have had any of the talents commonly attributed to him. At great length, though without any references, the author of the entry describes Hughes' way to success through corruption, deception, the exploitation of local resources and the receipt of ordinary local peasants.

To achieve their aim of fabricating a less favourable memory of Ukrainian entrepreneurship, the Soviets also changed the entire knowledge production system. This included the establishment of new institutional centres, such as the Institute of History of Ukraine (est.1936), the repressions against the intellectual elite (Юркова 2012b), and the launching of enormous new research and publications projects. *The History of Factories and Plants* was a part of this larger system, which aimed at producing the narrative that emphasised the proletariat's role in history. The narrative, replicated in every text related to the economic and social history of the late imperial times, described entrepreneurship as a predation.

The idea of a foreign entrepreneur as an exploiter became so encompassing and omnipresent that it even migrated to literary fiction. For example, Sophia Faltz-Fein (1839–1919)a famous representative of the Faltz-Fein family, landowners of German origin, prominent businesswoman of the late ninteenth and early twentieth centuries, and founder of the port of Khorly—was killed by Bolsheviks.

Faltz-Fein became the heroine of the novel *Tavriya* by celebrated Ukrainian Soviet author Oles' Honchar, published in 1952. She was described as an ageing, promiscuous, cruel, despotic, and overbearing German landowner who was entirely focused on pursuing commemoration and eternal youth. Honchar acknowledges the talents of Faltz-Feins' family members, their work and the commitment that led this particular part of the Ukrainian steppe to prosperity, but he completely overlooks Sophia's role in this:

> However, despite the various troubles that Sophia sometimes experienced with her steppe empire, she would not have agreed to exchange her possessions for any other. The protection of the Almighty himself must have guarded this land. Nowhere else in the world was it possible to get rich as quickly and easily as here. What was the American Klondike compared to her Ukrainian prairies? Everything literally falls into your lap here. Your wealth grows, and it seems that you don't even have to do anything to make it without any effort on your part.
> Of course, all this resulted from the energy, ingenuity, culture, and, of course... the happiness of three generations of Faltz-Feins. Yes, happiness, of course. The first Fatlz and Fein arrived here, in Transnistria, as scraggly colonists without noble coats of arms. Having intermarried, they became the "Faltz-Feins", and having bred clouds of sheep, they became noble, and having become even more prosperous, they became powerful steppe kreses, before whom even governors now reserve their favours. Fortune! Brilliant fortune plus economic acumen, fertile land, incomparable pastures, and purebred sheep combined to bring the Faltzfeins their millions. (Гончар 2003, transl. Vodotyka)

As demonstrated by this passage, the big names in Soviet Ukrainian literature also followed the rules set by the official memory policy with respect to what to write about the entrepreneurial figures of the past. The mentioning of Klondike and the phrase "everything literally falls into your lap here" diminishes the talents of the people who work on this lend, pushing us to the thought that much less effort was needed to succeed here. The next sentence recognises the energy, ingenuity, and culture of the Faltz-Feins, but there is happiness, meaning luck, at the end of the list. Honchar points to the reader that Faltz-Feins were foreigners and benefited from the marriage within their community. Honchar suggests reading between the lines and assuming that the only goal of the "new-comers" to this blessed land ("protected by the Almighty himself") was to make a profit and build an empire. If we read through the 1950s lenses, we would get this kind of message:

> God protected only rich and noble people. That is why we in our Soviet state deny God, ruin churches and celebrate atheism. Foreigners could come to our homes to suppress, exploit and gain profit from our hard-working people. That is why we have the Iron Curtain – for protection from dishonourable, sneaky, mean foreigners. Of course, they may have some talents, but with our rich resources, they could not have made it.

Even in the last years of Stalin's rule, when *Tavriya* was published, the writer could hardly allow himself any freedom in narration. Ironically, in their narrative of late nineteenth-century entrepreneurship, some of the less diligent entries in *The History of Factories and Plants* resembled more the passages from fiction, such as Honchar's novel quoted above, than scholarly academic articles. In fact, very little has changed in the narrative despite the various changing regimes in Moscow, from the Thaw to Stagnation and perestroika and the fate of Honchar himself, who was persecuted for his attempt to write more freely in the 1960s (Агєєва 2018). As a consequence of this unwavering policy, the memory and legacy of the many British, German, and French investors and entrepreneurs whose role was crucial in the development of Ukraine's industries were hidden and erased with a range of methods up to physical violence and deportations, such as that of the entire German community from Donbas after Second World War. And yet patterns of vernacular memory survived, grounded on the architectural presence of the industrial heritage, the silent occurrence of the graveyards, family oral histories passed through generations, rooted in knowledge of the local activists, rare findings of the archivists and workers folklore (EuroDonbas 2024).

4 To Remember Again

After Ukraine gained independence in 1991, the memory landscape started changing again. The grassroots tradition of late nineteenth–and early twentieth-century commemorations witnessed its continuation—or revival—after 1991 with the newly erected monuments and renamings; however, this time, the renaming was approved by democratically elected councils. The first wave of renaming happened simultaneously. The speed and quality of this process, intensified by the Revolution of Dignity, were not equally effective in different parts of Ukraine (Plokhii 2017). This unevenness, multiplied by difficulties in formulating the state memory policy and shaping national memory traditions, created the image of "divided memory equals divided Ukraine" (Osipian and Osipian 2012; Shevel 2011; Zhurzhenko 2014). Many of those divisions have become obsolete since the beginning of the Russo-Ukrainian war in 2014; however, the extent to which the division line in the memory culture is still present in Ukraine will only be possible to establish by the first independent sociological surveys in the liberated Crimea and Donbas after the end of the war.

Gradual changes took place in knowledge production, ideas, intentions, and values behind creating the narrative about historical businesses in Ukraine. As Ukrainian scholars started carefully examining previously forbidden pages of the past, economic and business history was not always in focus, and in many ways, the critical approach to the results, issues, and consequences of economic growth of the late Imperial times is yet to be done. Still, businesspeople were at least not just the exploiters anymore. Localism of memory was often rearticulated, but it was also more embedded into the processes of nation-building and decolonisation. While knowledge production did not change overnight, it changed significantly. The pendulum of history writing swung to the opposite end to the heroisation of entrepreneurs and the emphasis on their charitable initiatives rather than on their core activities that built the basis of that charity. Hence, it is no wonder that entrepreneurs appeared in the studies mainly related to culture, social initiatives, and the Ukrainian national project. As a result, most of the research devoted to nineteenth—and early twentieth-century entrepreneurs focuses on their charity activities, public life, and contribution to the local communities' development in the social and cultural spheres (Ніколаєва 2005; Нарадько 2000).

The post-1991 memory narrative has thus also been selective, but differently so from its Soviet predecessor. The best example in this regard is the image of the Tereshchenko family. In 1992, the Kyiv City Council brought back the historical name of one of the streets in the city centre, Tereshchenko Street (Tereshchenkivska), thereby laying the path for the family to the modern Ukrainian mnemonical canon. One of the first books on the family, by Vitalii Kovalinskiy, was written in Russian through the Russian imperial lens, even though it was published in Kyiv in 2003. Kovalinskiy focused on the Tereshchenkos' contribution to rising culture and education in late imperial Russia and downplayed/remained silent about their role in developing Ukrainian industry (Ковалинський 2003). At the same time, one of the most prominent books on the history of this entrepreneurial dynasty to date, Oleksandr Donik's *Tereshchenko Family in the History of Charity*, is written through a lens of Ukrainian national history but nevertheless highlights only its' contribution to charity projects in the nineteenth and early twentieth century. Such facts as sympathy for the Russian nationalist and even chauvinist projects of some of the family members are not mentioned at all (Донік 2004). Equally, the documentary series *Tereshchenkos' Legacy*, directed by Natalia and Viacheslav Ponomariv, filmed in 2021 and released in 2022, aimed to show every possible side of the rich and colourful life of the famous family, including aircraft production, charity and museum projects, and political influence, but it is notable that even this 8-series documentary paid hardly any attention to the business itself which, in fact, constituted the financial backbone of every charitable project and donation (Tereshchenko Legacy 2024).

The way the story of the Tereshchenko family has been told so far—and it has been done so epically, highlighting only positive sides, such as philanthropy or aircraft building and avoiding the simple fact that such a level of success and influence in the Russian Empire must have been the result of the imperial approval—could serve as a case of post-colonial hybridity that is not fully recognised in scholarship today. The renaming of the street in Kyiv shows the pendulum's movement: what was denigrated would now be celebrated, and what was forgotten would be remembered. However, the lens of decolonial critique is lacking; a sense of adoration of the family's richness, glam, and imperial glory still permeates contemporary biographies of the Tereshchenkos.

Perhaps the most significant change in the construction of the new memory narrative about Ukrainian entrepreneurs was due to the appearance of the new actors: local communities and local business elites who have willingly restored the practices of commemorating entrepreneurs. Ironically, most of them did so while they could not care less about memory culture and the restoration of forgotten names in the name of historical justice. However, what they cared about was setting the historical stage for the justification of their influence and power. To this end, they ensured that the monuments and memorial tablets were reinstalled, the human remnants of prominent entrepreneurs of the past were reburied with appropriate fanfare, the local councils voted in favour of the re-naming of streets and squares to honour their legacy, and the names of former owners were incorporated into the new business brands. It was thus through the interests, views, and preferences of the contemporary business elite that the memory of historical businesses reacquired its local dimension and meaning.

The case of Robert and Thomas Elworthy is a good illustration of these processes. Brothers Elworthy established the plant for agricultural machinery in 1874 in what Yelysavetgrad was then. It became pivotal for the city economy and the whole agricultural industry of the southern regions of Ukraine (Bosyi 2012, 11–12). In April 1919 (according to other sources in 1920), the Bolsheviks nationalised the plant, and in 1922, they renamed it "The Red Star Plant". The city also changed its name to Kirovograd. After Ukraine gained independence, the situation changed again. The former family house of the Elworthys was turned into a museum in 1994, and in October 1998, the Red Star Plant Museum officially opened. Now, it is the Elworthy Museum, with a memorial plaque to the legacy of the Elworthy brothers on its facade. In 2004, the monument to the Elworthys was installed on the territory of the still functioning plant, its unveiling timed to coincide with the 130th anniversary of the plant opening. The honorary right to cut the ribbon at the monument's inauguration was given to the eldest grandson of the Elworthy family, Michael Clarkson Webb (Музей Ельворті n.d.). The heritors of the original owners remain present in the city's public life, in a way appearing to revive the pre-revolutionary tradition of entrepreneurial charity. Since 2007, they have supported the family museum and a scholarship for a one-year free study in the UK for the most gifted school pupils in the city (Школярі Кіровоградщини 2017; Конкурс Ельворті-HMC). This was part of the larger process of the formation of the new memory regime, under which, in 2016, the city also changed its name from Kirovohrad to Kropyvnytskyi), and the plant did the same under the influence of 2015 decommunisation laws. On April 22, 2016, the Private Joint Stock Company "Red Star" (Chervona Zirka) also changed its name: the company's shareholders unanimously supported the new name of the plant. Although in the processes of translation from Latin to Cyrillic letters and back, the original name was now misspelt as "Elvorti", it nevertheless honoured the original founders of the vast plant, which is still efficient today and provides thousands of people in the city with their jobs.

The images of other entrepreneurs underwent similar transformations. Sophia Faltz-Fein is now seen not as a cruel landlady, dreaming as she was in Honchar's novel of sanity and debauchery at the same time, but a respectful businesswoman who thought strategically and to due to whose energy and ingenuity the whole city Khorly owes its existence. The leading actor in this case was the descendant of the Faltz-Fein dynasty, Baron Eduard von Faltz-Fein, but it would not have been possible without the support of the local elites. On May 28 1993, at the expense of Baron Eduard, a monument and a memorial plaque were erected on Sofia's grave in Khorly (Павленко 2013, 48–61).

Contemporary practices of recognising Oleksiy Alchevskyi as Alchevsk's "founding father" are rooted in the early 1990s. After Ukraine declared independence, at the city referendum held on December 1, 1991, the residents voted to return the city's original name. The early date illustrates how little the seemingly long decades of Soviet memory policy could sometimes mean in some local contexts. In 1996, when Alchevsk celebrated its 100th anniversary, the City Council's decision unveiled a monument on the city's central square. The inscription on the cast-iron ribbon at the memorial's base reads as follows: "To Oleksiy Kyrylovych Alchevskyi, the founder of the city, from [*its*] grateful descendants" (Ямковой 2001, 25–30). In 2004, on the 350th anniversary of Kharkiv, the municipality of Alchevsk presented the monument of Oleksiy Alchevskyi to the city.

Surprisingly, the establishment of the new canon can be traced back even to the production of the commemorative coins by the National Bank of Ukraine. According to historian Georgiy Kasianov, this institution has perhaps the most direct technical connection to the representation of memorable events, historical dates, and historical figures (Kasianov

2022b, 112). As it turned out, some of the entrepreneurs of the nineteenth century were also eligible for the commemoration in coins. For example, on 26 December 2005, the National Bank of Ukraine, continuing the series "Outstanding Personalities of Ukraine", put into circulation a 2-hryvnia commemorative coin dedicated to the 170th anniversary of the birth of Oleksiy Alchevskyi (НБУ 2006, 43).

Kubik et al. demonstrated that the growing role of local communities and their elites was crucial for the establishment of the pluralistic model of historical memory on the regional level (Kubik and Bernhard 2014). However, a closer look at the commemorative practices around the memory of entrepreneurs of the Ukrainian past reveals that the motivation of these new actors was mercenary rather than altruistic: as noted above, the main goal of bringing up this memory was to legitimise their own freshly earned wealth and to increase their political and social influence. To this end, they initiated new memory practices and constructed a new memory culture to distance themselves from the Soviet past and to highlight the "bright side" of capitalism's history. This could sometimes lead to comical situations caused by oxymoron mnemonical layering.

The best example of such layering is the situation with the memory of Oleksandr Pol' in Kryvyi Rih. The late 1990s and the early 2000s brought along a new, positive version of the entrepreneur's memory. On December 19, 1996, a bust to Pol was unveiled in the old part of Kryvyi Rih. The monument was cast in the foundry of the metallurgical plant Krivorizhstal, one of the most important plants in the Ukrainian metallurgical industry. The opening ceremony was chaired by Mayor Yuriy Lyubonenko and included speeches by the direct commissioners of the construction, the directors of important local businesses at the time Mykola Panchishnyi and Mykola Zemlianyi. The choice of speakers and the location bring us back to Hobsbawm's "invention of tradition" as well as remind us of the prevailance of postcolonial hybridity in commemorative practices. By inventing new commemorative practices, the late twentieth-century business elite of independent Ukraine built imaginary bridges between itself and the entrepreneurs of the past by creating a narrative of economic prosperity in its core and its embodiment in the figure to the local hero entrepreneur.

The monument to Pol was installed in the historical part of the city, at the intersection of what was then Karl Marx Avenue (now Postal Avenue) and October Street (Zhovtneva, now Oleksandr Pol' Street). Nobody seemed to care about the conflicting messages generated by the names of the streets and the monuments—in the hybrid postcolonial landscape of that part of Ukraine in the mid-1990s, it was still a part of the norm to have toponyms named after Karl Marx, Lenin, and other idols of the Soviet era alongside new commemorative practices celebrating former "ideological enemies" of the Soviet system. Such layers of clashing meanings hardly bothered anybody until the streets were eventually renamed in 2016 to comply with the decommunisation laws. Eventually, however, the monument became part of the local mnemonical canon. Pol' is now frequently called the Steppe Columbus, and on September 1, the local elites commemorate his date of birth (Кривий Ріг 2024).

Furthermore, local activists and politicians increasingly refer to Pol after the full-scale Russian invasion of 2022 as a means to strengthen local identity and the sense of belonging to Ukraine. For example, the Mayor of Kryvyi Rih, Yuriy Vilkul, said the following on September 1, 2022: "Oleksandr Pol laid the foundation for the establishment and development of industrial Kryvyi Rih region (Kryvbas). Now our city-fortress is battling and working in the most difficult conditions, but the ore mined by our miners will be needed to restore and develop our Ukraine" (Вілкул 2022). Just as in the case of the Tereshenkos, the new memory of Pol seems to exclude uncomfortable and problematic sides of his complex legacy: despite his interest in local history and archaeology, his passion for collecting historic artefacts, and his mixed German-Ukrainian roots, Pol was the subject of the Russian Empire, the Romanovs subject who never saw himself as part of Ukrainian national activities. He never questioned his status of a Russian nobleman whose work was dedicated to the glory of the empire.

A sculpture of Oleksandr Pol has also adorned the central avenue of the city of Dnipro (formerly Dnipropetrovsk) since September 16, 2002. The sculptor visualised the figure of Pol contemplating near a decorative hill symbolising mineral deposits. At the foot of the monument is a stylised mound and blocks of iron ore, and Pol himself is holding a pickaxe. The epitaph on the monument explains: "To the honorary citizen of Dnipro, from grateful citizens". The site was carefully picked to avoid the kind of clash of messages as was the case in Kryvyi Rih. On the contrary, the next changes on the site empower and support the initial idea. For example, onNovember 27, 2020, next to the monument, a glass cube with the fragment of a cross from the grave of Oleksandr Pol (which was ruined after 1917) was placed. That fragment was discovered during archaeological excavations (Пам'ятник О. Полю n. d.). The whole complex now tells that the citizens do remember Oleksandr Pol as someone whose energy and talents brought prosperity to the city—yet again, simplifies his legacy.

John James Hughes was destined to back a local narrative about industrial Donbas, which would not have been possible without him. Commissioned by the municipal government, the monument to Hughes was unveiled in Donetsk in 2001, in the vicinity of one of the academic buildings of Donetsk National Technical University. Hughes's figure stands at human height on a low pedestal that, according to the sculptor, symbolises the human scale of this figure, showing that he saw himself as one "with the people". This indicates the profession of John Hughes, an engineer, and underlines knowledge as a vital part of entrepreneurship in general and in developing Donbas and Donetsk in particular. In the summer of 2014, the same year as for Oleksiy Alchevskyi, a commemorative coin for Hughes was also minted. 2014 became remembered as the year of the Revolution of Dignity, followed by the Russian invasion and occupation of Crimea and part of the Donbas region. All these events set the stage for establishing new commemorative practices in general and for entrepreneurs in particular. The new wave of decommunisation and derussification started, and public attention was drawn to Donbas and its people—and such figures as Alchevskyi and Hughes appeared to be among them (НБУ 2014, 44).

Ukrainian artist Roman Minin, who stems from the Donetsk region, said the following in his interview for Oleksandr Mykhed's book *Я змішаю твою кров з вугіллям* (I will mix your blood with coal) about his encounter with the memory of Hughes:

> I found out about Hughes when I was older. And no one [*at the time*] really focused on this person at all. There was just some person called Hughes. It was only in Belgium, in the Charleroi Museum, that I found out that there were a lot of Belgians here [*in the Donbas*], too. And they brought their technology here. And how many Englishmen came with Hughes? How many of them died here in the Donetsk region? They just stayed there in the ground. The capitalists who worked there [*and*] did so much. Then the guys in the Budyonovkas [*i.e., Red Army soldiers*] came, waved their sabres, and said they were all so good, [*that*] they built everything themselves. And that was it. It was barbaric [*how businessmen such as Hughes and their contribution were forgotten*]. (Михед 2020, 124–125, transl.Vodotyka)

This quote shows an uncritical dichotomy between the capitalists of the past, who were presented as creators, and the Bolsheviks, who were presented as barbarians who appropriated the results of entrepreneurs' efforts. We see the pendulum go to the other extreme point—the unconditional glorification of the entrepreneurs of the past, fueled by the will to separate the history of Ukraine from the history of Russia and the Soviet Union, underlines and stresses the historical connections with European countries, in this case through the connection between the businesses.

5 Conclusions

In Mykhed's book, famous contemporary Ukrainian poet Sergiy Zhadan continues Hughes's theme. He says that the whole point with Hughes, "the Belgians" as he terms them, is that their legacy was very well absorbed locally (Михед 2020, 159). This suggests that the memory of entrepreneurs of the past remained somewhere on the margins of the texts, images, and memory practices despite the attempts of Soviet propagandists to denigrate it into the image of exploiters and oppressors. The memory of Pol, Alchevskyi, Tereschenko, Hughes, and Elworthy was absorbed, as Zhadan says, and eventually formed the layer of identity and culture that made Donbas a unique part of Ukraine.

Looking back at the transformations of memory of the entrepreneurs in Ukraine, figures such as Pol and the Tereschenkos, it becomes evident that their origins lie in the late nineteenth century, sometimes during their lifetime. The first toponym namings, the first monuments and plaques and the localised commemorative practices that surrounded them are the product of the 1890s and very much embedded in the workings of the empire. The revolutionary years of 1917–1921 led to tectonic changes in the political, cultural, and intellectual landscape. It is no surprise that memory practices and, in the end, the memory canon changed so dramatically. However politicised and centralised the production of memory might have been, the memory of entrepreneurs did not go to the archive completely; instead, it was pushed to the margins. The Soviet memory policies aimed to build a secured mnemonical regime via dismantling the monuments, changing the knowledge production system, toponyms, and series of publications such as the *History of Factories and Plants*, where businesses were denigrated. However, the success of this project was short-lived: the memory of the businessmen who established key enterprises in Ukraine was always there but remained silent and unofficial. It survived despite the seventy or so years of conscious ruining precisely because it was so well domesticated/appropriated on the local level.

1991 marked the reemergence of this memory in the public sphere, though skewed towards the entrepreneurs' charitable, cultural projects and nation-building projects. In contrast, their economic success and innovations were very often overlooked and understudied. In this respect, the emergence of the new memory actors, especially local business elites, was pivotal: if not in terms of knowledge production, their role was essential for the changes in memory culture and commemorative practices. Their presence and their interests became game-changing. The transformations of memory they initiated could be truly far-reaching. Potentially, they could signify the Ukrainians' readiness to become a more inclusive political nation, which would have figures in its memory canon that could unite local communities and local elites. This might be especially relevant in war-torn regions such as Donbas. If Hughes, Alchevsky or Pol' were eligible for national commemorative coin minting and for building monuments in their cities of Donetsk or Kryvyi Rih, this could become the point of no return in the sense of leaving behind the "fractured" and "hybrid" memory regime of the 1990s for good and move towards a truly pluralistic and inclusive one. A society that can, in Zhadan's words, absorb business figures of the past and appropriate them could be on its way to Mälksoo'sagonistic mnemonic pluralism, informed by critical historical research (Mälksoo 2015), and move towards a productive discussion on the challenging issues of the past in future.

The full-scale invasion of 2022 had deep and comprehensive consequences, including the ones in memory culture. On March 21, 2023, the Ukrainian Parliament adopted the Law On Condemnation and Prohibition of the Propaganda of Russian Imperial Policy in Ukraine and the Decolonisation of Toponymy. The law provided a legal framework for the decolonisation process, which, ironically, was only launched on a national scale and gained momentum after the Russian invasion of 2022. We might be living through the times when Ukraine is going through one of the final stages of the symbolic appropriation of its public spaces by its citizens. In many cases, when the renaming was on the agenda, there were meaningful discussions as to who and why should be commemorated instead. However, how entrepreneurs such as Tereschenko and Pol are remembered reveals elements of postcolonial hybridity still present in Ukrainian mnemonic practices. While no longer set in sites of clashing meanings and messages, these figures are often celebrated as businessmen, donors, and contributors to the Ukrainian national project, even though they hardly perceived themselves that way.

There is no better example of how the memory of entrepreneurs is newly localised while also remaining deeply entrenched in nation-building and decolonisation processes than a discussion that occurred in the spring of 2022 when the Kyiv City Council was about to vote for the new name for the former Pushkin Street (Pushkinska) in the city centre. Prior to and during the voting, several historians started a campaign explaining that Kyiv needed a street named after Yevhen Chykalenko, a Ukrainian entrepreneur and benefactor and the manager of many Ukrainian projects in the late nineteenth– and early twentieth century, who also helped to shape the idea of the Ukrainian state and Ukrainians as a political nation (Площу Льва Толстого 2022). It is not a coincidence that, for the first time, not only was an entrepreneur chosen as the best candidate for the street's new name but also that, finally, his business credentials were recognised as key for his financial and organisational contribution to the Ukrainian nation-building. By voting for Chykalenko Street in Kyiv on 27 October 2022 (Замість Пушкінської—Чикаленка 2022), the City Council might have started a new tradition, which can only happen in the situation of true mnemonic pluralism backed by a decolonial approach.

Acknowledgements The paper was written in 2022-2023 during guest research fellowship, in Georg-August-University of Göttingen within the program "Flexibel und Dynamisch—Innovative Maßnahmen für niedersächsische Hochschulen und Forschungseinrichtungen" financed by the Niedersächsisches Vorab (a joint venture by Volkswagen Stiftung and MWK. I am deeply thankful to Dr. Markian Prokopovych for his thoughtful mentorship, insightful comments and suggestions, and kind support.

References

Amiot, H. 2024. Framing the Present Through the Past: Ukrainian Diaspora in France, Holodomor Memory and the 2014 Critical Juncture. *Ethnic and Racial Studies* 47 (2): 367–390.

Assmann, A. 2010. Canon and Archive. In *Cultural Memory Studies: An International and Interdisciplinary Handbook*, eds. A. Erll and A. Nünning, 97–108. Berlin/New York: De Gruyter. https://doi.org/10.1515/9783110207262.2.97.

Assmann, J. 2008. Communicative and Cultural Memory. In *Cultural Memory Studies: An International and Interdisciplinary Handbook*, ed. A. Erll and A. Nünning, 109–118. Berlin/New York: De Gruyter.

Агєєва, В. 2018. Націоналізм чи Папа Римський? Чому забороняли «Собор» Олеся Гончара? https://www.bbc.com/ukrainian/blogs-43554895. Accessed on 12 January 2024.

Bhabha, H. K. 1994. *The Location of Culture*. London: Routledge.

Bernhard, M., and J. Kubik, eds. 2014. *Twenty Years After Communism*. New York: Oxford University Press. https://doi.org/10.1093/acprof:oso/9780199375134.001.0001.

Белов, В. Д. 1903. *А. К. Алчевский (1835–1901)*. Москва.

Брежнев, Л. 1981. *Воспоминания: Жизнь по заводскому гудку. Чувство родины*. Москва: Политиздат.

Bodnar, J. 1992. *Remaking America: Public Memory, Commemoration, and Patriotism in the Twentieth Century*. Princeton: Princeton University Press. https://doi.org/10.2307/j.ctv131bw3q.

Ворошилов, К. 1968. Рассказы о жизни. Воспоминания. Кн. 1: О жизни и о себе.

Bosyi, P. 2012. Robert Pearce Elworthy, 11–12.

Chebotarova, A. 2020. Collective Memory of the Holocaust in Post-Soviet Ukraine. In *The Burden of the Past: History, Memory, and Identity in Contemporary Ukraine*, 183–205.

Декрет Совнаркому. 1918. Про пам'ятники Республіки. http://ru.wikisource.org/wiki/Декрет_СНК_РСФСР_от_12.04.1918_О_памятниках_Республики. Accessed on 12 January 2024.

Донік, О. 2008. *Купецтво України в імперському просторі*. Київ.

Донік, О.М. 2004. *Родина Терещенків в історії доброчинності*. Київ.

Donik, O. M. *Pol' Oleksandr Mykolayovych*. http://www.history.org.ua/?termin=Pol_O. Accessed on 12 January 2024.

EuroDonbas – Trailer. https://www.youtube.com/watch?v=4hNfkG4pbTc. Accessed on 9 August 2024.

Hobsbawm, E. 2012. Mass-Producing Traditions: Europe, 1870–1914. In *The Invention of Tradition*, eds. E. Hobsbawm and T. Ranger, 263–308.

Гайдай, О. 2019. *Кам'яний гість. Ленін у Центральній Україні*.

Голуб, І. Поль Олександр Миколайович. https://www.dnipro.libr.dp.ua/index.php?route=information/project&prj_id=108. Accessed on 12 January 2024.

Гончар, О. 2003. *Таврія*. Київ. https://www.ukrlib.com.ua/books/printit.php?tid=3131. Accessed on 12 January 2024.

Гонимов, И. 1934. *Джон Джеймс Юз*. Харьков: Всеукраинская редакция истории фабрик и заводов.

History Of The Communist Party Of The Soviet Union (Bolsheviks). Short Course. 1998. http://www.marx2mao.com/Other/HCPSU39NB.html. Accessed on 12 January 2024.

Замість Пушкінської – Чикаленка. 2022. У Києві перейменували понад 40 вулиць. https://texty.org.ua/fragments/108098/zamist-pushkinskoyi-chykalenka-u-kyyevi-perejmenuvala-ponad-40-vulyc/. Accessed on 12 January 2024.

Kasianov, G. 2022a. Challenges of Antagonistic Memory: Scholars versus Politics and War. *Memory Studies* 15 (6): 1295–1298. https://doi.org/10.1177/17506980221133517.

Kasianov, G. 2022b. *Memory Crash: Politics of History in and around Ukraine, 1980s–2010s*. Budapest: Central European University Press. https://doi.org/10.1515/9789633863817.

Ковалинский, В.В. 2003. *Семья Терещенко*. Київ.

Кочергін, І. 2018. *Олександр Поль. Геній міста на Дніпрі*. Харків.

Кривий Ріг відзначив річницю від дня народження видатного дослідника-археолога, краєзнавця, першовідкривача залізних руд Олександра Поля. https://one.kr.ua/news/36739. Accessed on 12 January 2024.

Koposov, N. 2017. Memory Laws in Ukraine. In *Memory Laws, Memory Wars: The Politics of the Past in Europe and Russia*, 1st ed., 177–206. Cambridge: Cambridge University Press. https://doi.org/10.1017/9781108304047.

Kotljarchuk, A. 2022. Babi Yar and the Nazi Genocide of Roma: Memory Narratives and Memory Practices in Ukraine. *Nationalities Papers* 50 (3): 450–470.

Кузіна, К. 2018. Пам'ятники як місця пам'яті у символічному просторі міст радянської України (1920–1930-ті pp.). *Нові сторінки історії Донбасу* 27. http://nbuv.gov.ua/UJRN/Nsid_2018_27_12. Accessed on 12 January 2024.

Купченко, В., and Г. Волкотруб. 2003. Міське планування в Києві у 1920–1930-х роках. *Студії з архівної справи та документознавства* 10: 194–198.

Kubik, J., and M. Bernhard. 2014. A Theory of the Politics of Memory. In *Twenty Years After Communism*, eds. M. Bernhard and J. Kubik. https://doi.org/10.1093/acprof:oso/9780199375134.003.0002.

Луначарський, А. 1933. *Ленин о монументальной пропаганде*. http://lunacharsky.newgod.su/lib/vospominaniya-i-vpechatleniya/lenin-o-monumentalnoj-propagande/. Accessed on 12 January 2024.

Mahda, Y., and T. Vodotyka. 2021. Battles for History. 'Combats Pour l'histoire' as the Elements of Russian Information Warfare. Ukrainian Case. In *The Russian Federation in Global Knowledge Warfare*, eds. H. Mölder, V. Sazonov, A. Chochia, and T. Kerikmäe, 243–260. Cham: Springer. https://doi.org/10.1007/978-3-030-73955-3_18.

Marples, D. R. 2018. Decommunization, Memory Laws, and "Builders of Ukraine in the 20th Century." *Acta Slavica Iaponica* 39: 1–22.

Mälksoo, M. 2015. 'Memory Must Be Defended': Beyond the Politics of Mnemonical Security. *Security Dialogue* 46 (3): 221–237. https://www.jstor.org/stable/26292349.

McGlynn, J. 2022. Imposing the Past: Putin's War for History. *War on the Rocks*, March 15. https://warontherocks.com/2023/03/imposing-the-past-putins-war-for-history/.

Михед, О. 2020. *Я змішаю твою кров з вугіллям*. Київ.

Музей Ельворті – часточка XIX століття в Кіровограді. https://gre4ka.info/kultura/280-37muzei-elvorti-chastochka-khikh-stolittia-v-kirovohradi. Accessed on 12 January 2024.

Мошенський, С.З. 2015. Фінансові кризи початку XX століття в Україні. *Проблеми теорії та методології бухгалтерського обліку, контролю і аналізу* 1 (31): 281–300. https://doi.org/10.26642/pbo-2015-1(31)-281-300.

Нарадько, А.В. 2000. *Благодійність у розвитку освіти в Україні (др. пол. XIX – поч. XX ст.)*. Запоріжжя.

Нестерчук, Д. В. Лист міністра фінансів С. Ю. Вітте до О. К. Алчевського з приводу надання йому звання комерції-радника. http://dspace.nbuv.gov.ua/bitstream/handle/123456789/121999/10-Nesterchuk.pdf. Accessed on 12 January 2024.

НБУ. 2014. Банкноти і монети України). Випуск 18. https://shron1.chtyvo.org.ua/Banknoty_i_monety_Ukrainy/Vypusk_18.pdf

Ніколаєва, Т.М. 2005. *Внесок підприємців в освітньо-культурний розвиток України (остання третина XIX – початок XX ст.)*. Київ.

Nikitin, V. 2022. Memory Wars in Russia and Ukraine. *The Nation*, March 1. https://www.thenation.com/article/world/ukraine-russia-putin-historical-memory/.

Osipian, A. L., and A. L. Osipian. 2012. Regional Diversity and Divided Memories in Ukraine: Contested Past as Electoral Resource, 2004–2010. *East European Politics and Societies* 26 (3): 616–642. https://doi.org/10.1177/0888325412447642.

Павленко, В. 2013. Родина Фальц-Фейнів: сторінки історії. *Вісник Таврійської Фундації* 9: 48–61.

Пам'ятник О. Полю. https://heritage.dniprorada.gov.ua/culture/pamyatnyk-o-m-polyu/. Accessed on 12 January 2024.

Площу Льва Толстого у Києві слід перейменувати на честь Євгена Чикаленка. 2022. https://tyzhden.ua/ploshchu-lva-tolstoho-u-kyievi-slid-perejmenuvaty-na-chest-ievhena-chykalenka-istoryky/. Accessed on 12 January 2024.

Про введення в обіг ювілейної монети «Олексій Алчевський». *Вісник НБУ*, Лютий 2006: 43. https://journal.bank.gov.ua/archive/2006/2.pdf

Про введення в обіг пам'ятної монети "Джон Джеймс Юз". *Вісник Національного банку України* 9 (2014): 44. http://nbuv.gov.ua/UJRN/Vnbu_2014_9_14. Accessed on 12 January 2024.

Plokhii, S. 2017. *Goodbye Lenin: A Memory Shift in Revolutionary Ukraine*. https://www.harvard.edu/leninfallpaper.pdf. Accessed on 12 January 2024.

Portnov, A. 2017. The Holocaust in the Public Discourse of Post-Soviet Ukraine. In *War and Memory in Russia, Ukraine and Belarus*, 347–370.

Riabchuk, M. 2008. Holodomor: The Politics of Memory and Political Infighting in Contemporary Ukraine. *Harriman Review* 16 (2): 3–9.

Руккас, А., М. Ковальчук, А. Папакін, and В. Лободаєв. 2016. *На бій за волю. Перемога через поразки. Україна у війнах і революціях 1914–1921.* Харків.

Shevel, O. 2011. The Politics of Memory in a Divided Society: A Comparison of Post-Franco Spain and Post-Soviet Ukraine. *Slavic Review* 70 (1): 137–164.

Shevel, O. 2014. Memories of the Past and Visions of the Future: Remembering the Soviet Era and its End in Ukraine. In *Twenty Years After Communism*, eds. M. Bernhard and J. Kubik. https://doi.org/10.1093/acprof:oso/9780199375134.003.0008.

Smiraglia, R. P. 2015. Discourse Domains and Their Role in Knowledge Production Dissemination and Organization. In *Domain Analysis for Knowledge Organization*, 1–18. Chandos Publishing. https://doi.org/10.1016/B978-0-08-100150-9.00001-8.

Семенюк, М. Найперший пам'ятник Тарасу Шевченку в Україні. http://dspace.nbuv.gov.ua/bitstream/handle/123456789/16724/07-Semenyuk.pdf. Accessed on 12 January 2024.

Смирнова, А. 2016. Архивная история «Истории фабрик и заводов». In *Человек труда в истории: актуальные вопросы історичної науки, архівознавства і документознавства*, 338–348.

Соколенко, В., С. Короткова, und А. Жураківський. Проблеми та перспективи розвитку міста Алчевська. https://nvd.luguniv.edu.ua/archiv/NN4/07svmrma.pdf. Accessed on 12 January 2024.

Stalin, J. 1939. History of the Communist Party of the Soviet Union (Bolsheviks): Short course. Moscow: Foreign Languages Publishing House.

Stryjek, T., and J. Konieczna-Sałamatin, eds. 2021. *The Politics of Memory in Poland and Ukraine: From Reconciliation to De-Conciliation*. London/New York: Routledge.

Tannen, D., et al. 2015. *The Handbook of Discourse Analysis*. John Wiley & Sons. https://ebookcentral.proquest.com/lib/durham/detail.action?docID=1895501.

Tlostanova, M. 2019. The Postcolonial Condition, the Decolonial Option and the Post-Socialist Intervention. In *Postcolonialism Cross-Examined*, ed. M. Albrecht, 165–178. London: Routledge.

Törnquist-Plewa, B., and Y. Yurchuk. 2019. Memory Politics in Contemporary Ukraine: Reflections from the Postcolonial Perspective. *Memory Studies* 12 (6): 699–720.

Терещенківська вулиця. https://kyiv-heritage-guide.com/page/tereschenkivska-vulicya. Accessed on 12 January 2024.

Tereshchenkos' Legacy. https://www.youtube.com/watch?v=2Dd_XYHMslc. Accessed on 12 January 2024.

Верстюк, В. 2017. Від "Великой Октябрьской социалистической революції і громадянської війни на Україні (1917–1920)" до "Нарисів історії Української революції": трансформації дослідницької парадигми. *Український історичний журнал* 3. http://resource.history.org.ua/publ/UIJ_2017_3_4. Accessed on 12 January 2024.

Верстюк, В. 2022. Російсько-українські війни 1917–1921 років: теперішнє в минулому. *Проблеми вивчення історії Української революції 1917–1921*, 17. http://resource.history.org.ua/publ/Pviu_2022_17_3. Accessed on 12 January 2024.

Вілкул, Ю. 2022. Олександр Поль поклав початок становленню та розвитку промислового Кривбасу. https://spilkuisia.kr.gov.ua/yu-vilkul-oleksandr-pol-poklav-pochatok-stanovlennyu-ta-rozvytku-promyslovogo-kryvbasu-zaraz-nashe-misto-forteczya-boretsya-i-praczyuye-v-najskladnishyh-umovah-ale-zdobuta-nashymy-shahta/. Accessed on 12 January 2024.

Vodotyka, T., and S. Vodotyka. 2019. Honorary Citizenship of the Cities of Ukraine under Russian Rule in the Second Half of the Nineteenth Century: the Strategies of Gratefulness and Loyalty. *Ukrainian Historical Journal* 6: 58–68. https://doi.org/10.15407/uhj2019.06.058.

Wylegała, A. 2017. Managing the Difficult Past: Ukrainian Collective Memory and Public Debates on History. *Nationalities Papers* 45 (5): 780–797. https://doi.org/10.1080/00905992.2016.1273338.

Yurchuk, Y. 2017. Reclaiming the Past, Confronting the Past: OUN–UPA Memory Politics and Nation Building in Ukraine (1991–2016). In *War and Memory in Russia, Ukraine and Belarus*, 107–137.

Ямковой, А.А. 2001. *Семья Алчевских*. Алчевск.

Ясь, О.В. Мала Русь. http://www.history.org.ua/?termin=Mala_Rus. Accessed on 12 January 2024.

Школярі Кіровоградщини мають шанс безкоштовно повчитися у Великобританії. 2017. http://uc.kr.ua/2017/11/24/shkolyari-kirovogradshhyny-mayut-shans-bezkoshtovno-povchytysya-u-velykobrytaniyi/. Accessed on 12 January 2024.

Юркова, О. 2012a. На українському «історичному фронті» 1934 року: журнал «Історик-більшовик». *Проблеми історії України: факти, судження, пошуки* 21: 195–211.

Юркова, О. 2012b. Наука під більшовиками: рух по синусоїді. In: *Україна радянська. Ілюзії та катастрофи "комуністичного раю"*, ed. Н. Єфіменко, 295–316. Харків.

Zhurzhenko, T. 2014. A Divided Nation? Reconsidering the Role of Identity Politics in the Ukraine Crisis. *Die Friedens-Warte* 89(1/2): 249–267. http://www.jstor.org/stable/24868495.

Memories of Empire and Embedded Banking—Austrian Bankers Investing in Central Eastern Europe in the 1990s

Oliver Kühschelm

1 Introduction

In September 1993, the management of the Waldviertler Sparkasse had every reason to celebrate. Their institute had been awarded a banking license in the Czech Republic. It was the first foreign bank to receive such a license, which allowed it to build a network of branches in southern Bohemia. Director Werner Pohnitzer had pulled off an exceptional feat, one of which he remains proud to this day.

Admittedly, for the Czech banking system a later Austrian investment was of far more consequence: In 2000, the Erste Bank of Vienna—originally also a local savings bank—began its takeover of Česká spořitelna, the largest bank of the Czech Republic. Česká spořitelna had been founded in 1823, following the model set by the Erste Bank. Eventually, the Erste Bank also integrated the Waldviertler Sparkasse into is realm—much to the dismay of Pohnitzer, who saw his life's work destroyed.

O. Kühschelm (✉)
Institute of Rural History, St. Pölten, Austria
e-mail: oliver.kuehschelm@ruralhistory.at

University of Vienna, Vienna, Austria

S. Berger and T. Fetzer (eds.), *Collective Memory of Economic Crises and Transformations*, Palgrave Macmillan Memory Studies,
https://doi.org/10.1007/978-3-032-09094-2_7

The foreign investments of the Waldviertler Sparkasse and of the Erste Bank are episodes of what, from an Austrian vantage point, was called the opening-up of the East ("Ostöffnung"). This chapter sets itself a double task: it will discuss the role cultural memory played in this process and it will do this by taking a microhistorical approach. It will look at two different ways of how entrepreneurial actors—and media interacting with their stories—brought memories of the past into play. We can call it the big bank- and the small bank-version of opening up the East. The prototype of the former was provided by the Creditanstalt-Bankverein. The chapter will contrast this with the small bank-perspective represented by the Waldviertler Sparkasse. The bank and its actors fashioned themselves in opposition to their rivals from Vienna. Among them was the Erste Bank, which in the 1990s transformed into a major bank more in line with the tradition of Viennese universal banks than with that of regional savings banks. The Erste and its chairman Andreas Treichl became the nemesis of the Waldviertler Sparkasse and its director Werner Pohnitzer.

The chapter concerns itself with Austrian elites and their self-fashioning in view of the chances that they wanted to capitalize on by expanding into the former socialist countries. It does not dwell on the perspective of political and managerial elites in Central Eastern Europe who accepted their purchase and cooperation offers. However, in the case of the Waldviertler Sparkasse it can be shown that the story Austrian bankers crafted contained elements that Czech officials could find attractive.

2 Approach and Scope of the Study

The breakdown of the communist regimes in 1989 signified new investment opportunities for Western business. The transition economies were painted as a new frontier. From the perspective of the recipient countries, the surge in foreign direct investment formed a conspicuous part of their transition from socialism to market economies (Bandelj 2008; Marinova and Marinov 2003). In this process Austrian foreign direct investments were of great significance—for the region that received them and for Austria itself. In Austria, the inflow of direct investments had always been much larger than the outflow. In 1989, for the first time, this relation turned on its head. In 1990, outward investments exceeded inward investments by a factor of 2.6; in 1991, by a factor of 3.6.[1] In 1989 former socialist countries that had been successor states of the Habsburg Monarchy represented four percent of the national portfolio of foreign direct investments; at its peak in 2007 the region's share of the portfolio had grown to 36%.[2] Austrian companies often acted as first movers and in most of Eastern and South Eastern Europe they came to own large portions of the capital stock held by foreign investors. In many countries Austria was even the top source of foreign investments at some point of the 1990s and 2000s (Sieber 2006).[3]

This is a well-known story but if reduced to abstractions like GDP, investment flows, and growth rates, it remains confined to figures that neatly align with an inexorable logic of economic opportunities. The companies that invested in Central Eastern European countries appear as exchangeable elements of the grand narrative of growing wealth that caused and necessitated a drive toward internationalization. This leaves little analytical space for actors, their narratives and actions. It is economic functions that determine what will happen.

In the effort to make sense of what the fall of communism meant for Austria, a division of labor between institutions of economic analysis and business journalism can be observed. The former have mostly provided explanations that are heavy on quantitative data and light on actors. By contrast, business journalism and general interest media have cultivated a fascination with entrepreneurs as early movers who took their chances in the (former) socialist countries. Their reporting featured bold actors who reaped rich reward for jumping to opportunities that others missed out on. Inevitably, this had to include the possibility of failure because otherwise foreign direct investment would not constitute an adventure worth telling.

Stories about Austrian entrepreneurs going "East" aligned well with a move toward celebrating entrepreneurship that has been characteristic of neoliberalism. Beyond abstract macroeconomic ideas, neoliberalism needs colorful stories to be persuasive. Foreign direct investment as an entrepreneurial achievement fits the bill. It can easily be organized along

[1] Data from the Austrian National Bank, historical time series.

[2] Czech Republic, Slovakia, Hungary, Slovenia, Croatia, Poland, Romania. Data from the Austrian national bank.

[3] This includes investments by multinational companies that operated from Austria.

the patterns of the heroic journey: The protagonist leaves his native land, crosses the threshold into uncharted territory, encounters helpers, obstacles, and enemies, and achieves a transformation. Combining the narrative of the opening-up of the East with tales about entrepreneurship brings out particularly well the core tenets of the neoliberal cultural and political credo: the value of internationalization, entrepreneurial action as embodiment of individualism and heroism (Pilotta 2016; Anderson and Warren 2011).

The impersonal macroeconomic account and the individualized hero-worship are both highly conventionalized, but only the latter contains actors who have experiences and memories and can literally write history. In this respect, it is closer to the task that this chapter sets for itself. But it also has to find an epistemic stance that avoids mythologizing entrepreneurship, which business journalism is mostly oblivious to. The challenge lies in walking a fine line between falling for myths about entrepreneurship and recognizing that such narratives play a role in enabling actors to fashion a self willing and capable of performing what the cultural and social expectations of entrepreneurship demands. An obvious place where to look for guidance are management and organizational studies. Since the 2000s, they have engaged with the cultural turn, taking an interest in entrepreneurial discourse and narratives (Hansen 2012; Popp and Fellman 2017). However, they tend to err on the side of mythologization because their academic context is business schools. Their ultimate audience is people who want to absorb lessons about entrepreneurship that enable them to play the part—that is, to be the hero of the story (Kibler and Laine 2024).

The attention to narratives and ego-documents has to be balanced with an equally systematic and granular attention to how these narratives connect to socioeconomic relations and places of power. In the historical sciences, the closely related research strands of microhistory and historical anthropology can offer useful orientation (Trivellato 2015; Tanner 2017). Although they originally focused on the local and subaltern in contrast and opposition to central places of power, there is no intrinsic reason to avoid drawing inspiration from them for historical research into business and economic elites. A close look at distinct constellations or actor-networks brings into view the microphysics of power and seems a promising strategy for "reassembling the economic" (Lipartito 2016, 137). Microhistory has also been cast as the opposite of global history, which might seem a problem for this study insofar as the opening-up of the East represents a moment of accelerating globalization and connectedness. However, increasing numbers of scholars argue that this too is a misconception (Ghobrial 2019; De Vito 2019): historical research should always start from the specific, regardless of whether it wants to elucidate the social set-up of a village or transcontinental business networks (Trivellato 2012). Indeed, there are many promising examples of applying a microhistorical lens to business[4] and to its connections beyond the confines of one village or city. Francesca Trivellato explored the familial and commercial relations of Jewish merchants from Livorno in the early modern period (Trivellato 2012). Emma Rothschild similarly investigated the familial and business dealings of a Scottish family that profited from British imperialism and slave-holding plantations in the West Indies (Rothschild 2011). Christof Dejung's call for a socially embedded view of mercantile elites also owes a debt of inspiration to microhistorical approaches (Dejung 2024)—for instance, to Angelika Epple's study of the chocolate manufacturer Stollwerck conceived as a microhistory of globalization (Epple 2010).

3 Business and Memory

Analyzing how the leading actors at the Waldviertler Sparkasse and big Austrian banks communicated about business perspectives, brings into view different ways in which memory and business are connected. Companies are institutions that strive to create continuity. An inability to do so is interpreted as failure, with bankruptcy representing its most drastic form. Continuity is fundamental to memory, and conversely, memory is a guarantor of continuity. Therefore, management and organizational studies have turned to investigating organizational memory (Foroughi et al. 2020). A conspicuous element of organizational memory is corporate historical discourse, which can be accessed through sources such as company magazines, anniversary publications, marketing materials, and, in more recent times, websites—especially their "About Us"-sections (Gatti 2013).

While cultivating corporate memory is mainly a task for members of the organization, it can become an instrument of outreach toward potential customers and the wider public. As to an important degree consumer

[4] In management theory: Hargadon and Wadhwani 2023.

culture feeds on nostalgia, a brand's past can be turned into a valuable asset (Holt 2004). Therefore, history marketing has emerged as a field of activities that encompasses brand lands, exhibitions, and company museums (Schug 2013). Financial institutions might be more elusive because they sell services instead of tangible objects but, for example, presenting a bank as an old and venerable institution was an obvious way of inspiring trust. Management research treats the staging of history as a useful strategy to grant companies a competitive advantage. It aims to make the past a profitable part of cultural memory. Whether this effort employs the careful reconstruction of history or engages in unrestrained myth-making, is of only secondary concern (Suddaby et al. 2010).

Corporate memory forms part of what, in the 1980s, began to be discussed as company culture. The idea gained traction in reaction to the success of "Japan, Inc". Management discourses took a cultural turn, highlighting the advantages of a cohesive company culture (Deal and Kennedy 1982; Dellheim 1987; Matis and Stiefel 1987; Berghoff 1997). The concept of "company culture" is also contemporary with Pierre Nora's "sites of memory" (Nora 1984). Historians soon applied this notion to understand the role of companies as national champions, and it has equally found its way into management studies (Kühschelm and Pfoertner 2005; Currie 2019).

Both concepts can have the effect of highlighting community and shared memories while neglecting power differences among those who engage with corporate culture and its sites of memory. Although a company consists of a broad array of diverse actors, entrepreneurs and managers have resources at their disposal to shape corporate memory to a significant extent. It is they who, at Christmas parties and jubilees, celebrete and narrate what has been achieved. It is they who are interviewed by business journalists and the media more generally. While in interviews they relinquish some control to journalists, entrepreneurs also take matters into their own hands and write autobiographies, often promising insights into the business strategies that made them successful (Hulsink and Rauch 2021). Corporate storytelling has long since become an area of professionalized expertise (Thiessen 2019, 63–64), even at the regional level.

Prior to the financialization of the economy, banks already occupied a nodal position in national economies. They are perceived differently from companies in service and production. Banks are involved in processes that for centuries have been likened to blood circulating through the body, sustaining the life of the state(Kühschelm 2021, 286–287). Therefore, banks have themselves tended to identify their business progress with that of the state and the national economy. Smaller credit cooperatives and public savings banks have done the same with regard to their home regions. They act as custodians of cultural memory publishing anniversary publications that intertwine bank and town history. They give money for museums and exhibitions; they furnish public spaces with fountains and monuments.

This brings us to a discussion of the ways in which broad frames of reference that draw on a society's past are an important element of corporate culture. While anniversary publications obviously make such connections, they also appear in interviews that entrepreneurs give to business journalists about current affairs. Does such engagement with history matter for business decisions? One would think so. Economics itself has incorporated concepts of "bounded rationality", which describe decision-making processes more realistically than the idea of the *homo oeconomicus* (Morgan 2006; Dejung et al. 2014, 3–4).

The financial crisis of 2008 has further spurred a reassessment of presumptions of rationality, which also pertain to members of business elites who have privileged access to market information and hold degrees in economics. Arjun Appadurai (2015) analyzed derivatives—the financial instruments at the heart of the crisis—as resting on a chain of signs that obscures the eventual lack of a tangible referent. The role of calculation, mathematical formulae and models, then, is not—or not solely—that of instruments providing risk-assessment. They rather legitimize a practice of "banking on words". Performative force accrues to these empty signifiers because actors fill them with social "imaginiaries of profit" (Beckert 2016, 131–168). Finance may make this dynamic glaringly obvious, but it applies to entrepreneurial decision-making more generally. The concept of the entrepreneur has revolved around the role of a risk-taker ever since Richard Cantillon's writings from the eighteenth century. Joseph Schumpeter, twentieth century's most influential thinker on entrepreneurship, considered Cantillon's conceptualization "not infelicitous" because it focused on "direction and speculation" (Schumpeter 1965, 46). It is this combination that Schumpeter himself saw as the core of entrepreneurial action: on the one hand, it consists of having direction—and therefore the charisma to direct others; on the other, it means diverging from established routines, which inevitably contains a speculative element. "Creative destruction" is the narrative process in which an actor persuasively articulates what Jens Beckert calls "fictional expectations". They are based on "promissory stories" (Beckert 2016, 176–177), which convert uncertainty into a manageable risk—or something looking like that. Fictional expectations are embedded in "collective processes influenced by culture, history, and power relations" and form "imagined communities" (2016, 14). This is also where memory comes into play, individually and collectively.

It is the thesis of this chapter that references to the past and to the established role of companies in national and regional societies are more than adornments that distract from an ahistorical economic logic of profit. This implies insisting on the embeddedness of all economic action and actors. Here, social class, gender, rural or urban environment will prove relevant. Bankers are individuals who, in a non-metaphorical sense, have memories that shape their sense of belonging. Part of what they remember feeds into corporate memory, which also transcends them as individuals. When presented with the new situation in Central Eastern Europe, they regarded it as an opportunity—both because of what they remembered and because of what the institution, their professional environment, reminded them of.

The investigated case here concerns banking companies in the aftermath of 1989, at a critical juncture in Austrian and European history. However, the investigation cannot start there. In order to show the workings of memory as a social construction and make it a plausible explanation for why bankers chose to become early investors in a formerly socialist economy, it is necessary to take the long view.

4 Universal Banks and Savings Banks—Their History in Austria

The Austrian financial system of the late twentieth century had three major historical roots: the so-called universal banks, which were joint-stock companies; savings banks, which were financial instruments of associations or municipalities; and credit cooperatives, which served as institutionalized self-help for their members. Each of these sectors of the banking system took shape during the nineteenth century, had its own rules and limitations. In the 1970s and 1980s, savings banks, credit cooperatives, and joint-stock banks shed many of their differences. They have since operated in similar ways, participating in the global and globalizing trends of the internationalization of banking services and the financialization of the economy. Yet their histories and the memory these institutions kept of their histories still informed their approach to the "opening-up of the East". They also impacted how business journalism and the media in general framed investments in a region that was to become a "second home market" for Austrian banks.

In the mid-nineteenth century, European banking underwent a profound transformation (Cassis 2006, 42–43). In the Habsburg Monarchy, as in some other countries—among them principally Germany—universal banks emerged (Tilly 1998; Sandgruber 1995, 240–241). These institutions occupied the commanding heights of the economy and were closely entwined with state-building. Headquartered in Vienna, they were linked to the old elite of the aristocracy and the imperial house, but their supervisory boards and directors mostly formed part of an emerging social elite of members of the high bourgeoisie and top government officials. The most prominent example was the Creditanstalt, founded in 1855 under the auspices of Anselm Rothschild (März 1968). He was the eldest son of Salomon Rothschild, who as Vienna's most important private banker had underwritten the policies of Metternich. After the revolution of 1848, Anselm took over and grasped that even a fabulously rich and well-connected family had to adapt to remain competitive. This realization resonated with the ideas of Baron Karl von Bruck, who in 1855 became finance minister of the Habsburg Monarchy (Rumpler 2005; Brandt 2020a). He had been close to the Rothschilds since before the revolution, but more importantly, he propagated an economic policy that envisaged the Habsburg state as the leading power in the German-speaking lands. This would allow the Austrian Monarchy to dominate the non-German-speaking areas of East-Central and South Eastern Europe and to pursue imperialist designs in the Ottoman Middle East (Brandt 2020b; Stråth 2008, 178). Bruck was also enthusiastic about the joint-stock bank as an instrument capable of raising enough money to achieve such ambitious goals. And he wanted to keep out the brothers Pereire, whom he regarded as too closely connected with French interests.

After World War I, the banks' pretention to economic power ceased to match their diminished means, and the small Republic of Austria could not provide the political clout to back up their business policies (Weber 2016). This caused mounting troubles for the banking system. Some banks, like the Länderbank, were sold off to foreign investors, others disappeared in a series of mergers that inflated the position of the remaining bank, the Creditanstalt. The Great Depression exacerbated the unsolved problems, and in 1931 the Creditanstalt stood on the brink of bankruptcy. Its collapse threatened to take down world finance, but closer to home it was perceived as a potentially fatal blow for the Austrian economy. Much like in the crisis of 2008, fast-moving events together with the arcana of the financial business triggered panic reactions. Government officials had neither time nor capacity to think of any alternative to bailing out the most important Austrian bank. This meant nationalizing its debt, but, unlike the aftermath of 2008, it also led to long-standing state ownership. When in 1946 the Länderbank was also nationalized, state ownership of Austrian universal banks was complete.

The second branch of the Austrian banking system, savings banks, goes back to the early nineteenth century but expanded enormously in its latter half. Wealthy individuals founded institutes whose basic idea consisted of incentivizing people to lead a life of thrift and rewarding those who were able to do so. Savings banks were intented to help people from the lower classes and small burghers build up wealth. Technically, they were instruments of associations or municipalities. In both cases, their boards were formed by respected burghers active in their local communities. Although savings banks were not meant to turn out a profit for the individuals serving on their boards, local elites quickly recognized that these institutes could advance their business interests. Furthermore, lending money generated profits, which were used to support local associational life and to back municipal investments. Savings banks became vital tools for the infrastructural development of small towns that otherwise lacked easy access to credit (Fritz 1972; Dirninger 2012).

Whereas the Viennese joint stock banks represented state-building from above and were obviously linked to the imperial and imperialist pretensions of this state, saving banks were state-building on the local level. One might be tempted to describe them as state-building from below, but this would hide the fact that these local financial institutes were also run by social elites. While board members and directors did not wield power on the financial scale and with the leverage of their peers at the Creditanstalt, they were still powerful in local and regional contexts. However, there was undeniably an emancipatory side to the activities of savings banks: they empowered people by opening up secure ways of saving money and they enabled craftspeople to take out loans. They strengthened the autonomy of municipalities, thereby contributing to making the modern infrastructural state a polyvalent phenomenon—more than a one-way conduit of power from the center to the periphery.

The first Austrian savings bank was founded in Vienna in 1819 and established itself under the name "Erste Österreichische Sparkasse" (Rapp-Wimberger and Rapp 2019). Although its prominent place and pioneering role led to a heightened self-regard vis-à-vis the other savings banks, it was fundamentally just a regional institute, whose catchment area happened to be the capital city. This changed when, in the late 1970s, the laws that regulated the Austrian financial system abolished sectoral and regional protections. In 1982, the word "Bank" was added to the name of the Erste. It still was an institution that belonged to an association, which did not sit well with neoliberal concepts of private ownership. In the early 1990s, the Erste was converted into a joint-stock company. This allowed the bank to raise capital on the stock market to pursue expansionary policies more aggressively. In 1997, the Erste issued shares worth around EUR 500 million—the largest IPO on the Vienna Stock Exchange to date. That same year, the bank merged with the Girocredit, which sixty years earlier had been created to process payment transactions among savings banks and to hold their liquidity reserves. The Erste could now drive the concentration process among Austrian savings banks. In 1997, it also bought a Hungarian bank, starting its expansion to the "East". Among Austrian banks, it was a latecomer in the transition countries, but it caught up quickly.

The Waldviertler Sparkasse originated as one of the first savings banks that were founded in a small Austrian town. An innkeeper led the initiative in Waidhofen, which lay close to the border with Bohemia in a remote area of Lower Austria (Führer 1993). The authorities gave their approval, and in 1842 the savings bank began its operations. Over time, it expanded, albeit without dramatic changes to the character of its services. After World War II, spectacular economic growth began to transform the conditions of banking, and in the 1980s, liberalization increased the pressure on small financial institutions. Big Viennese banks could now freely open up branches in the provinces. This threat motivated local savings banks to seek partnerships. They could either join forces with other small institutes from their home region or integrate into corporations dominated from Vienna. The Sparkasse in Waidhofen pushed for regional integration under its leadership. It had some success with this policy and renamed itself "Waldviertler Sparkasse of 1842". It also incurred defeats at the hands of regional rivals and Viennese competitors. But at the turn of the 1990s, it had succeeded in gaining weight, and its directors quickly reacted to the downfall of communism. They first reached out to the neighboring communities on the Czech side of the border in 1989 and began to operate branch offices there in 1991. This move strengthened the bank's position enormously. From a small institute with 56 employees, it grew to 305 by 2003. More than half of them worked in the Czech Republic (Friedinger 2003).

By then the Erste had also set its sights on the Czech banking market. The Waldviertler Sparkasse and its director Werner Pohnitzer became a nuisance for the Viennese bank, which gained ever more control over regional savings banks. A joint liability scheme under its leadership was intended to insure small institutes against heightened risks in a liberalized market, but it also forced them to adhere to guidelines set by the Erste. As the Waldviertler Sparkasse jealously protected its autonomy, it stayed away from the scheme (Gewinn 2005). However, this increased its vulnerability to doubts about whether it had sufficient equity to back up its ambitious investment policies. In 2005, auditors criticized the bank for overstretching by financing a golf hotel. Viennese newspapers reported on a "hole in the balance sheet" (Domforth 2005); a bank-run ensued. The events led to Pohnitzer's retirement and the Waldviertler Sparkasse was integrated into the realm of the Erste. The fears about impending bankruptcy might actually have been overblown. Due to its position at the top of the whole sector, the Erste acted simultaneously as a competitor and a control organ (Komlosy 2010, 285). Pohnitzer suspected foul play and still does (Pohnitzer 2021, 200–206, 228–229, 245–251).

Werner Pohnitzer's social background and career path were emblematic of the social and cultural traditions that had defined the business of local savings banks. He came from the rural petty bourgeoisie, though not from the area of Waidhofen. He had been born in Southern Moravia to a German-speaking family. In 1945, when he was four years old, they were driven from their home and fled to Vienna. Eventually, they settled in a small village in Lower Austria near the Czech border. There they ran a tavern. Pohnitzer began studying medicine at the University but had to drop out for family reasons. He moved back to the Waldviertel and helped with the tavern. He married into a family from the social elite of the nearby town of Waidhofen, where his father-in-law had a small business. He suggested that Pohnitzer apply for a job at the local savings bank, on whose advisory board he served as a member (Pohnitzer 2021). Pohnitzer began working for the bank and, as he was ambitious and outgoing, he rose to an executive position. In the 1980s, he proved eager to take advantage of the opportunities that the liberalization of the Austrian market and the opening-up of the East seemed to offer. But he also took pains to present himself as an heir to the values of a rural middle class and a patriarchal tradition of regional power-broking. It was an exclusively male tradition. In 1992, the association behind the savings bank counted 102 members; among them, not a single woman (Führer and Hitz 1992, 197).

Pohnitzer's social profile contrasts starkly with that of Andreas Treichl, who led the Erste Bank from 1997 to 2020. Treichl presided over what had started as a local savings bank, yet his social background and ambitions had little to do with this tradition and much more in common with that of Viennese universal banks. Treichl was the scion of a family that, for generations, had occupied senior positions in Viennese banking. In the 1970s, his father Heinrich presided over the Creditanstalt. About his son's career, he noted approvingly that Andreas had "turned a well-behaved savings bank, which had operated within narrow limits, into a highly successful major Central European bank" (Treichl 2003, 347). It added to the prestige of Andreas Treichl that he was married to a journalist from an old aristocratic family. She edited a lifestyle magazine and organized the Viennese opera ball. One would be hard pressed to imagine anything more elite in Austria (Zehle 2008). In the post-war decades, leading positions in Austrian finance were relatively open to the advancement of managers from the middle and even working classes (Korom 2011, 153–154). Andreas Treichl, however, represented the high bourgeoisie that had dominated Viennese banking until the 1930s.

5 Universal Banking and Imperial Pretension

In the nineteenth century bankers at the Creditanstalt and the other big banks that followed its example were placed at the conjunction of bourgeois liberalism, German nationalism, and Habsburg loyalty that could morph into Austrian patriotism (Bruckmüller 2003; Komlosy 2015). They were open to an understanding of financial services that regarded them as a means of projecting power over foreign people within and beyond the boundaries of the Austrian or Habsburg state. Central Europe and its eastern and south-eastern hinterlands were regarded as "natural" territories of Austrian economic expansion. To achieve this goal, Austria had to seek German and Western support. Attaining it, however, would also heighten Austria's standing within the German nation and raise its profile as a Great Power. This combination of economic, political, and ideological goals has characterized Austrian—and especially Viennese—banking ever since. *Mitteleuropa* (Central Europe) remained a staple of elite thinking about its mission and rightful place beyond what where the Austrian core lands that in 1918 formed the small Austrian Republic (Brix 2011).

In 1988, Guido Schmidt-Chiari was nominated to the leadership position in the Creditanstalt. He occupied a position that was not yet called CEO but "general director". This designation situated him at the top of a bureaucratic organization closely tied to state administration, as befitted the corporatist setup of Austrian society. The so-called social partnership permeated the economic, social, and political fabric of the Austrian state. During the post-war era, this seemed an ideal arrangement for a small state (Katzenstein 1984), of which in the 1970s the Socialist Party appeared to become the natural party of government. Three times in a row, it obtained more than half of all votes in the elections for the national parliament. The old middle classes of the *Bürgertum*, private business, and their political representatives found themselves on the defensive. Schmidt-Chiari was cut from the same social cloth as the Treichl family, if more on the German nationalist side. He entered the service of the Creditanstalt, coincidentally on the same day as Heinrich Treichl, in whom he found a mentor (Schmidt-Chiari 2007, 125; Treichl 2003, 262, 314–315). As managers of a state-dominated bank they had to accomodate the prevailing powers, but at times they could not hide their resentment: Treichl despised the Social Democratic finance minister Hannes Androsch, who in 1981 succeeded him as general director of the Creditanstalt (Treichl 2003, 263, 298, 310–330). He perceived this as an insult to a bastion of the *Bürgertum*. Schmidt-Chiari's appointment restored the world back to order.

When Schmidt-Chiari died in 2016, an obituary called him the "grand seigneur of the Austrian banking scene" (Möchel 2016). About Heinrich Treichl, who only a few years earlier had passed away at the very old age of 101, an obituary read: "the last gentleman of money" (Rief 2014). They both represented the tradition of "gentlemanly capitalism" as social practice and as items of nostalgic memory. "Gentlemanly capitalism" is a notion coined to investigate the preponderance of finance in British imperialism. But its authors acknowledge their debt to concepts from the early twentieth century, chiefly Rudolf Hilferding's analysis of finance capitalism (Cain and Hopkins 2016, 40). Hilferding developed his ideas from what he witnessed in Vienna. As he knew its elite well, he also visited the salon of Heinrich Treichl's parents (Treichl 2003, 29). In post-1945 Austria, gentlemanly capitalism was a social profile and an ambition at odds with the social and economic reality of a banking system tailored to the needs of a small Keynesian welfare national state. But in the 1980s, the beginning neoliberal transformation breathed new life into the imperial vision that these holdovers from earlier times embodied and whom liberal and conservative media treated with great awe.

As Schmidt-Chiari took over the reins at the Creditanstalt, he was optimistic about his chances of gaining more autonomy vis-à-vis the state (Jones 1988). While in the early 1980s the concept of privatization had still been unpopular, huge losses in state-owned industries brought about a change of mind among the electorate and, above all, the governing elites (Müller 1988). It helped that the international environment was ever more conducive to enhancing the role of private business, of managers and entrepreneurs. The European Communities were on their way to achieving a single market and evolving into the European Union. In July 1989, Austria applied for membership. The surprising breakdown of the communist regimes added a new Eastern Europe dynamic because it was interpretated as definitive validation of the superiority of market-driven over planned economies. While the governments of the former socialist states hoped for a "return to Europe" (Weiner 2007, 62), Austrian elites saw their country newly placed at the continent's center. In both cases, elites were imagining a future that was also a partial "return to history". With respect to who would get there faster, Austrian elites not only thought that they had a head start, they also hoped to maintain it permanently. In the spring of 1990, Schmidt-Chiari showed himself confident that Austria—and thus the Creditanstalt—would be able to play the role of a bridge toward Eastern European countries. The new situation in Eastern Europe, he argued, would help Austria's application for membership in the European Community. However, he considered it implausible that the former socialist countries would themselves become members of the Community. Austria's position in the East–West-trade would remain safe for the foreseeable future (Handelsblatt 1990).

Well before the "annus mirabilis" of 1989, Austrian banks had already sought to expand their business once again into Central Eastern Europe. In 1976, the Creditanstalt established a foothold in Budapest; offices in

Prague and Warsaw followed in the 1980s. After the downfall of Communism, the Creditanstalt and the Länderbank quickly built up a network of branches in the former socialist countries (Richter and Stankovsky 1991, 66–67). Other Austrian banks—above all Raiffeisen-Zentralbank and many regional banks—also invested in the former socialist countries (Sulzer 2020).

In early 1991, Schmidt-Chiari shared his thoughts on the perspectives of Austrian banking in general—and of the Creditanstalt in particular—in lectures at the Vienna University of Economics and Business. The general director's reflections had an educational purpose: they should explain aspiring members of management and business elites what the place of Austria and Austrian banks would be in the future: He predicted that after its full integration into the European internal market Austria might even become more valuable as a "bridgehead" connected to Eastern Europe. But it also had to brace itself for "competition from Berlin" as "gateway to the East" (Schmidt-Chiari 1991, 4). The "neighboring countries that are historically so close to us" were developing into markets, which he deemed of great importance due to "the Austrian experiences, the Austrian mentality, our specific know-how". Given the prevalence of small and medium-sized enterprises and the structure of its economy, Austria could also serve as a template for the transition countries to follow (Schmidt-Chiari 1991, 14).

When again lecturing at the University in 1993, Schmidt-Chiari laid out a more developed international strategy of the bank he was leading. It rested on two pillars: on plans for "Europe", where the Creditanstalt could only aspire to playing the role of a regional mixed bank, and on a project for "Eastern Europe". Here Austrians enjoyed an advantage over their Western competitors. More concretely, Schmidt-Chiari spoke about a "specific knowledge of the 'terrain'". This gave his statement a slight flavor of colonialism. It insinuated an imagination of the former socialist societies as a space of nature waiting to be cultivated, which would create an "enlarged home market". The bank's presence in "Europe" and its investments in the reforming countries added up to a *Mitteleuropa*-strategy that would make the Creditanstalt into a "leading Central European Bank" (Schmidt-Chiari 1993, 23–28). According to his predecessor Heinrich Treichl, in the 1990s the Creditanstalt upheld "the old Austrian tradition in its mixture of domestic orientation—in the sense and area of the Danube Monarchy—and the natural foreign connections of the old major European banks that have existed for a century" (Treichl 2003, 281–282).

Fittingly, the Creditanstalt resided in a neoclassicist building in the center of Vienna. It had been erected in the last years before World War I, when Viennese universal banks were at the height of their power. It was a functional office building well suited to the administrative techniques of the early twentieth century but the historicist style anchored it in an imagined past (Zimmerl 2012). Its location placed it at the heart of the Habsburg State and its imperial self-fashioning, close to its administration and government as well as to the headquarters of the most important businesses. The building represented competitive signaling within a Viennese-centric world. By the 1980s, it had become a site of memory: as seat of the most renowned Austrian bank and as a prototypical building of the Ringstraße—the urban monument of a bygone era that fused the financial power of the bourgeoisie with the old wealth and privileges of the aristocracy (Hanisch 2005). Nineteenth-century Vienna then sparked renewed interest, both internationally and within Austria (Beller 2012). Especially for the old upper middle class, the *Bürgertum*, it was infused with a sense of loss waiting for an opportunity to restore former glories.

In an autobiographical text from the 2000s, Schmidt-Chiari mentions that he had a map of Austria-Hungary and its neighbors hung in the anteroom to his office. The map showed the branches the Creditanstalt had maintained at that time and the new subsidiaries that the bank had been opening since the 1990s. With obvious satisfaction, he added that the new network of branches had quickly become denser than in the Habsburg era (Schmidt-Chiari 2007, 134).[5] Memories of a lost Empire were thus linked to the hope of playing a prominent part in the enlarged European Union, whose own imperial features became particularly visible in connection with its enlargement toward the East (Zielonka 2015, 48–49).

[5] See also the article of a business journalist who remembers the map and its message: Frey 2024.

6 Regional Banking and the Promise of Embeddedness and Cooperation

The directors of the Waldviertler Sparkasse also imagined a role of leadership for their bank, albeit within a much smaller region. When explaining their banking philosophy, they highlighted how it differed from the approach they associated with the big Viennese banks. They invoked a tradition particular to public savings banks and used it to assert a claim to regional exclusivity aiming to prevent competition from Vienna on their home territory. In 1989, their argument for regional banking suddenly opened up chances for international expansion while staying close to home.

The Waldviertler Sparkasse and its core institute in Waidhofen had always defined itself as a protector of regional interests against capitalism written large. Its anniversary publication from 1992 reminded readers of the crisis of 1873, when the "Gründerzeit"-boom collapsed spectacularly (Führer and Hitz 1992, 11). Thanks to their statutes, saving banks could not participate in stock market speculation, which raised their profile as trustworthy institutions. However, parts of the local middle classes in Waidhofen had strayed from the regional circle of trust and lost about one million guilders invested with Viennese institutes. There was a moral to this story that not only the Waidhofener Sparkasse sought to convey to a regional audience: big banks do not care about you, whereas we do. In Vienna, they do not know you and your needs, but we do. This made preserving the autonomy of the local savings bank a goal to which both citizens and bank employees should subscribe.

An anniversary publication from 1983 warned that "the local roots of the savings banks in the Waldviertel region should not be lost through absorption into large centralized institutions in Vienna" (Neuwirth and Führer 1983). If, in the early 1920s, two major Viennese banks were prevented from opening branches in Waidhofen, this was understood as a success for the entire region. The anniversary publication from 1992 stressed that the banks had merely wanted to "soak up capital 'in the province' to bolster their own capital basis in the center Vienna" (Führer and Hitz 1992, 145). The passage reads like a vernacular version of dependency theory, insinuating a rapacious character of the transfer of resources from the periphery to the center. An argument can be made that since the nineteenth century, the Waldviertel—and especially its upper part, of which Waidhofen is the principal town—suffered from a process of peripherisation (Komlosy 2003). At any rate, complaints about mistreatment by the capital city formed an essential part of the region's identity. The complaints mostly formed a feedback loop with conservative and German-nationalist resentment but the pervasive feeling of having been left behind also fed into an entrepreneurial spirit that could take unexpected turns between catholic subsidiarity and anarchism, ecological commitment and heterodox left-wing ideas (Gunz 1995).

The functionaries of savings banks, who were often also members of the local municipal council, had to inscribe the beneficial role their bank had been playing for the town into the institute's memory and make it public knowledge. The impressive amount of anniversary publications dedicated to the savings bank of Waidhofen are testament to a continuous and systematic effort. This included gestures toward opposition against Vienna as the symbol of unfettered capitalism. However, it eschewed outright anticapitalism and rather aimed at reserving the role of the intermediary for regional actors. Despite all the advertising of regionally rooted services, the business of small-town savings banks never rested on an idyll of local self-sufficiency—not even in the nineteenth century. Savings had to be invested, which at that time meant either buying government bonds from the national bank or granting mortgage loans. In Waidhofen, borrowers always came from the wider region, including many clients from the southern parts of Bohemia and Moravia. An especially large share of loans was granted on real estate in Vienna. From both the lender's and the creditor's perspective, investing in a thriving real estate market was preferable to investing in a sleepy backwater. But this is also why savings banks from the provinces fueled the speculative housing market in Vienna (Feldbauer 1976, 61, 85, 90, 110).

One more aspect of the asymmetrical participation in markets beyond the local community deserves attention: From the perspective of a savings bank in the upper Waldviertel, putting money into houses in the metropolis of Vienna was as much a foreign investment—understood as venturing into a foreign place—as when, in the early 1990s, the institute began doing business beyond the Austrian state border. If this was new and adventurous for rather conservative institutions, it was not without precedent as the actors kept telling to themselves and to others. The expansion beyond the state border occupied an attractive spot between staying local and joining the neoliberal bandwagon.

It also held the promise that elites from the national center would see their provincial counterparts in a more appreciative light. "We have always been ridiculed", deputy director Eduard Führer pointed out when the Waldviertler Sparkasse received a banking license in the Czech Republic (Kurier 1993). In the company magazine, Pohnitzer explained to a regional audience that in spite of its small size—or more to the point: thanks to this size—his bank could win out against international competitors. They wanted to stick it to "opinion leaders and decision makers in Austria" that in the Waldviertel they were smarter and faster than they had been thought capable of (Vorteil 1993). National newspapers and business journalism indeed took note of the savings bank that had scored a surprising coup. It was not mere imagination that Pohnitzer could now talk back to "opinion leaders", find a hearing, and insert his story into the media discourse on the opening-up of the East.

The account Werner Pohnitzer gives today of his first contact with potential Czech partners shows him in the role of the entrepreneurial adventurer setting foot on hitherto unknown territory.[6] Thereby he fleshes out a conceptual metaphor that is often applied to stories of entrepreneurship and that is especially well suited to stories about foreign direct investments. With respect to the opening-up of the East, this metaphor features both in Austrian media of the early 1990s and in later narratives of entrepreneurs who look back on their achievements (Kühschelm 2017). It comes with connotations that evoke colonial contexts—sometimes openly, sometimes more obliquely.

In the case of the Waldviertler Sparkasse, the tale is interwoven with a narrative driven by the concept of cooperation. There is overlap because the start of a relationship means to venture into new territory—quite literally so when crossing a state border to look for business partners. According to his own tale, Pohnitzer drove to a nearby Czech town with little prior planning and went to the mayor's office. He did not know Czech (and would never learn to speak it), but an elderly man helped translate. So, he could explain to the mayor, who later became a friend, that he was the director of a savings bank that did a lot of good for its home community and that he wanted to develop the same kind of business in Czechia.

Pohnitzer's narrative stresses what he regards as the secret of the bank's success: its non-threatening appearance and that it made a fair business offer aimed at strengthening local communities. It is the narrative version

[6] Interviews with Werner Pohnitzer, conducted by Thomas Samhaber, 22 September 2021, and by Oliver Kühschelm, 19 September 2024.

of a line of communication that in the 1990s he evidently pursued in presentations to local dignitaries and businesspeople[7] as well as in press releases and contacts with regional media (Kaláb 1993). He told readers of the local paper of Dačice—a town of about 7000 inhabitants, roughly the same size as Waidhofen—that the most important thing about the "Waldviertler Sparkasse" was that it did not have foreign owners, that it was not even a joint-stock company. Therefore, it was neither influenced by foreign capital nor by political interests. It apparently did not matter that in Dačice the "Waldviertler Sparkasse" themselves were foreigners. What he wanted to communicate was that the bank was neither German nor big business in the way of the major Viennese banks. He drew both on the history of regional savings banks as a distinct kind of financial institution and on trust in longevity: the bank was "the second oldest in Lower Austria and the ninth oldest in the former Austrian-Hungarian Monarchy" (Kaláb 1993).

7 Crossing the Border and Reaching for the Horizon—Unmooring the Imagination

The Waldviertler Sparkasse invested in the Czech Republic years before the Erste Bank and it stressed cooperation between regions that were defined by their proximity to the state border. The idea of a border or frontier has a long history in the Waldviertel. The sparsely populated region is characterized by a sprinkling of small towns that were founded in medieval times to serve as the backbone of the colonization of a territory bordering Bohemia and the Czech lands (Knittler 2006). While in the nineteenth century the border was reduced to the administrative separation of two crownlands of the Habsburg Monarchy, the experience of remoteness from economic and political centers, as well as the political and cultural concept of a frontier region of the German nation, became important building blocks of the region's modern identity. The rivalry of German and Czech nationalism culminated in Nazi Germany's occupation of Bohemia and Moravia and the expulsion of its German-speaking population in the aftermath of World War II. Many of those who were driven out of Southern Bohemia and Moravia ended up living in the

[7] Notes from presentations in Jindřichův Hradec for members of the city council, 20 July 1993, and at the Chamber of Commerce, 28 July 1993; presentation to the municipal officials of Dačice, 12 August 1993. Private archive of Werner Pohnitzer.

border regions of Lower Austria. From 1948 to 1989, the fortified border became the epitome of what was called the "dead border" (Perzi and Haas 2012). It shaped an image of the Waldviertel as a heavily forested region destined to hemorrhaging people. It seemed itself a dead end. In the upper Waldviertel, 1989 did not feel like an "end of history". On the contrary, the stunning demise of the communist regime in Czechoslovakia opened up the possibility of a return to history from a place beyond time. This raised great hopes but also reactivated resentment against "the Czechs" (Engel 1990).

An essential part of the non-threatening persona that Pohnitzer crafted for the bank's expansion to the Czech Republic consisted of the way he handled the communicative and cultural memories of nationalist violence. He identified as "Sudetendeutscher" but tried to set himself apart from others of this memory community. In his autobiography he highlights that he has never been guided by nationalist resentment and his personal experience of expulsion from Southern Moravia in 1945. The prologue of his book begins with an aphorism that frames his biggest success as director of the Waldviertler Sparkasse as a historical achievement: "Getting a banking licence in the Czech Republic is one thing. Making peace with history is another. But it can only be done together" (Pohnitzer 2021, 7). Here Pohnitzer presents a version of the argument that economic cooperation ensures peace among former enemies. The argument has constantly been used with regard to the European Union and the benefits of neoliberal globalization. Although Pohnitzer's business history formed part of the latter, he also tried to carve out a regional niche of cooperation among (almost) equals. He imagined it as a counterweight to the imperialist drive that he and his colleagues associated with Viennese banks.

The Waldviertler Sparkasse presented itself as regional bank that transcended state borders and anticipated a Europe of regions. As the paper for an internal ideas session would have it in 1999: "We are the vitalisers of the region with the awareness that cooperation is our greatest energy reserve for the future. On both sides of our border… and some time later without it".[8] However, in the communication of the Waldviertler Sparkasse the border played an ambivalent role: on the one hand it had to disappear. When a savings book was introduced that allowed Austrians

[8] Draft for the exhibition "10 years of open borders", private archive of Werner Pohnitzer.

to save money in Czech Crowns and profit from higher interest rates in the Czech Republic, it was advertised as a means of "blowing up the borders" (Pohnitzer 2021, 176). On the other hand, to legitimize the saving's bank new cross-national market area, it was crucial to maintain the memory of the "Iron Curtain". The memory of the hardest conceivable version of a border lent urgency to the idea of economic cooperation in the present.

In a glowing portrait of Werner Pohnitzer and "his" bank, the "Wirtschaftswoche" explained in 1992 that if the Waldviertler Sparkasse opened new branches in Bohemia, it was only resuming activities from before World War II. The article went on quoting Pohnitzer: "We have 100 kilometers of border in our immediate catchment area, so we have to deal with that" (Jenny 1992, 45). In his autobiography, Pohnitzer himself remembered a conversation with deputy director Eduard Führer, a committed "lay historian" with a keen interest in the past of the bank and of Waidhofen. Führer asked his colleague to imagine a circle with Waidhofen at its center and to direct his attention to the upper, northern half of this circle, which lay in Czechoslovakia (Pohnitzer 2021, 255). In an oral history interview, Pohnitzer described the scene slightly differently: "We always sat together, Edi and me, and said: 'Look, that used to belong to us'".[9] He used an ambiguous expression: it can signify a communal as well as a possessive relation. Pohnitzer went on mentioning that Führer showed him documentation about the customers the bank had once had in Bohemian villages.

In 1993, director Pohnitzer stated that the bank did not have any interest in establishing a prestigious branch office in Prague (Der Standard 1993). The Waldviertler Sparkasse would stay strictly regional, offering a bottom-up contrast to the ambitions of big Austrian and Western banks. It would cater to customers in the fly-over land that the big players overlooked. But by 2000 the bank had an office in Prague and vaunted its international contacts. The border now became a metaphor freed from its constraints of the time-space of the Austrian-Czech border. A glossy brochure in German and English (but not Czech) was titled "The horizon is the only limit". The English word "limit" was used to translate the German word "Grenze" (border or limit).[10] The English translation

[9] Interview, 22.9.2024.

[10] Private archive of Werner Pohnitzer.

brings out clearer what the notion of a horizon implies: it is a moving line, fundamentally different from a border that separates one region from another. Pohnitzer's story about banking relied on a combination of spatial logic and historical plausibility. However, through upscaling it reached the point where the regional imaginary faded and a more abstract space of international business took form.

The representatives of big Viennese banks walked the same path in the opposite direction when they talked about Central Eastern Europe as their enlarged home market. Converting globalization into a regional affair of cultural affinities and a shared past was a comforting notion for both an Austrian audience and foreign investors. Both were to believe in the distinct capability of Viennese bankers to navigate the challenges of doing business in the (former) transition economies of Central Eastern Europe. In 2009, the global financial crisis turned into a threat for Austrian banks. Their "eastern exposure" was suddenly international news (Resch 2013, 212–213). The "New York Times" quoted Treichl with a reassuring message: "Look at our map and then look at the map of Austria in 1914". He added: "Every country we're in, we'd opened up savings banks 175 years ago" (Kulis 2009). While it was true that in the 1820s the Erste had opened branches in the provinces of the Habsburg Empire, they were soon reconfigured as independent savings banks (Natmessnig 2019, 54). The Erste did not have the past of a Viennese banking behemoth. That was rather the story of the Creditanstalt, which Andreas Treichl's father and his protégée Schmidt-Chiari had presided over. Treichl probably did not care about such details; in the midst of a crisis, he wanted to communicate that he and his bank were on top of the situation. Cultural memory is not history. The former serves the emotional and strategic needs of those who want to gain sure ground without the complexities of history interfering with this aim.

In a moment of crisis, the Erste Bank appealed to the reassuring notion of being at home in a specific region. It is what the Waldviertler Sparkasse had always been telling about itself: in a closed regional space, the bank knows its clients and they know their bank, so everyone can rely on the soundness of its business. The Waldviertler Sparkasse connected this claim to a story about cross-border cooperation. This held the promise of overcoming nationalist resentment that had permeated relations between Czechs and Austrian Germans in the border region. But while its imaginary of cooperation between peripheral regions differed from that of imperial pretension, it was not entirely innocent of ideas of dominance:

"Look, that used to belong to us." Furthermore, as the ambitions of the Waldviertler Sparkasse grew, its aspirations moved toward the expansionism of Viennese banks. It appealed to a Habsburg imaginary and equally strove to become the Austrian version of big finance, profiting from deregulation and globalization.

8 Conclusion

In the late 1980s, Austrian banks were feeling ever more pressure in a newly liberalized national market. They also had to face the prospect of even more competition if this market would become "European" following Austria's entry into the European Community. This was widely expected to happen within the next couple of years as indeed it did. The revolutions in Central Eastern Europe came as a godsend, both for big Viennese banks looking for what would make them special in an internationalized market and for regional banks that did business in areas bordering socialist countries. The banks sought to connect the neoliberal narrative of globalization and capitalist advancement with established national, regional, and business communities aiming to imbue their strategies with historical credibility. They combined ideas about internationalization and entrepreneurship with imaginaries of empire or cooperation. In one case this came with an expectation of control exerted from an imperial center; in the other, it relied on the experience of peripheral actors whose social and economic power had regional limits. There were differences of scale: The imperial imaginary moved billions, the imaginary of regional cooperation millions.

The Habsburg Empire had awarded itself the mission of civilizing the Slavic peoples. Connected to a German-nationalist outlook, this presumption survived the demise of the Habsburg state. The universal banks of Vienna played a leading part in the story of imperial pretension until it crashed in the Great Depression of the 1930s. But in the 1980s, big Austrian banks resorted to the cultural memory of what the Viennese banking place had been until 1918. Cultural and institutional continuities, the family history of some leading executives, headquarters in the city center and more generally the built environment of the former imperial capital established connections to a glorified past. All this impacted the perception of the possible and desirable and formed an elite habitus.

The tradition of regional savings banks was different and formed a set of practices and imaginaries that also had their bearing on how actors understood the chances on the Austrian and Central European market. A bank like the Waldviertler Sparkasse appealed to an imaginary of cooperation, which emphasized regional solidarity among people of good standing in the local community. It rested on a patriarchal, male-centered understanding of these communities. Their goals were fostering local infrastructure and enhancing the entrepreneurial perspectives of the local middle class: shopkeepers, manufacturers, and professionals.

The chapter has considered these two versions of how Austrian banks sought to profit from the transition in Central Eastern Europe. The investigated cases add layers of complexity to the ideal-typical distinction between imaginaries of imperial pretension and peripheral cooperation. These versions were not always mutually exclusive, and the differences often become muddled. This is all the more unsurprising as the Erste Bank had originally itself been a savings bank before it morphed into a major player in the mold of Viennese universal banks. In contrast, the Waldviertler Sparkasse continued to be a regional savings bank throughout the 1990s. But around 2000 it also tried to outgrow the limitations of this tradition.

However, the success of the Waldviertler Sparkasse in expanding to the Czech Republic was built on promoting itself as an alternative road to Western capitalism. It promised to open up a road to freedom associated with the idea of a market economy, without handing control to large corporations from abroad. A socialist command economy is generally thought of as being characterized by centralized decision making, which reduces local actors to recipients of orders from up on high. However, corporations are not necessarily different with respect to centralizing decision making. The Waldviertler Sparkasse propagated the empowerment of regional actors and offered itself as an antidote to making the transition from socialist planning to a market economy solely a story of large capital. This probably was an enticing perspective for provincial actors who aspired to broaden their role as regional power-brokers.

The opening-up of the East was about dramatic change in many respects. In the former socialist countries, allowing foreign capital to freely invest in ever more branches of the economy, was entirely new. Austrian economic and political elites had experience with receiving foreign investments, but they were less experienced when it came to carrying out investments abroad themselves. Increased capital flows were a highly visible symptom of the neoliberal transformation that shaped the end of the Cold War and the ensuing decades, when the former socialist countries turned themselves into catalysts of ever greater liberalization. Their persistence in neoliberal reforms surprised experts, and in some areas—such as the introduction of flat-tax schemes—they exceeded what international organizations and the European Union were demanding (Appel and Orenstein 2016). The broad population was introduced to a new social contract (Bartel 2022); the same happened in the West, and even in Austria this process started well before developments in the former communist states added to it, in what Philipp Ther has called a dynamic of co-transformation (Ther 2016).

Since the mid-1980s, the conservative Austrian People's Party—and above all its business league—had demanded with growing insistence that the state should rescind its hold on the economy. "Going East" and membership in the European Union increased the confidence of entrepreneurial and management elites. The environment of doing business changed, more gradually than in the transition economies, but also in the direction of giving them the upper hand over labor demands and a stronger position vis-à-vis political parties and the government (Dirninger 2017). They have increasingly felt empowered to shed the tenets of the social partnership that dominated the post-war decades.

Neoliberalism constituted a paradigmatic shift and demanded the unlearning of central elements of previous behavior. It might then seem that neither society at large nor business elites had much to gain from memory practices. Western elites have actually reacted with bewilderment to the widespread nostalgia for elements of the socialist past, which in Germany has been called "Ostalgie" (Weiner 2007, 95–116; Ghodsee and Orenstein 2021, 119–121). However, memory studies have long proposed treating memory not as a static inventory of elements but as a social process. From this perspective, the seeming paradox disappears and transforms into the task of elucidating the modes of construction that take shape in social interaction. In the investigated cases, bankers drew on organizational memory and employed references to the past in order to embark on an international expansion that was unprecedented in the Second Austrian Republic. Yet, this could be construed as returning to a happy state of affairs that had once existed or as a tradition of embedded banking now extended to neighboring regions.

The chapter has explored the role that cultural memory plays in the articulation of business strategies. Austrian banks that invested in the Czech Republic offer an example of the insights this approach can yield. The chapter can also be read as a step toward a social and cultural history of foreign direct investments, which catalyzed the neoliberal transformation of Europe. For any study of "economic memories" (Hilmar 2021), the 1980s and 1990s in Central Europe are a rewarding field of research. Paradigmatic shifts problematize an earlier set of practices and establish a new normal: this process generates narratives that obscure alternatives to accepting these changes.

References

Anderson, Alistair R., and Lorraine Warren. 2011. The Entrepreneur as Hero and Jester: Enacting the Entrepreneurial Discourse. *International Small Business Journal: Researching Entrepreneurship* 29 (6): 589–609. https://doi.org/10.1177/0266242611416417.

Appadurai, Arjun. 2015. *Banking on Words: The Failure of Language in the Age of Derivative Finance*. Chicago/London: University of Chicago Press. https://doi.org/10.7208/chicago/9780226318806.001.0001.

Appel, Hilary, and Mitchell A. Orenstein. 2016. Why Did Neoliberalism Triumph and Endure in the Post-Communist World? *Comparative Politics* 48 (3): 313–331. https://doi.org/10.5129/001041516818254419.

Bandelj, Nina. 2008. *From Communists to Foreign Capitalists: The Social Foundations of Foreign Direct Investment in Postsocialist Europe*. Princeton: Princeton University Press.

"Banken im Blickpunkt. Wie sicher sind die Banken?". 2005. *Gewinn*, No. 11 (November): 22.

Bartel, Fritz. 2022. *The Triumph of Broken Promises: The End of the Cold War and the Rise of Neoliberalism*. Harvard University Press. https://doi.org/10.4159/9780674275805.

Beckert, Jens. 2016. *Imagined Futures: Fictional Expectations and Capitalist Dynamics*. Cambridge, Mass.: Harvard University Press.

Beller, Steven. 2012. *Rethinking Vienna 1900*. Austrian History, Culture, and Society. New York: Berghahn Books.

Berghoff, Hartmut. 1997. Unternehmenskultur und Herrschaftstechnik: Industrieller Paternalismus: Hohner von 1857 bis 1918. *Geschichte und Gesellschaft* 23 (2): 167–204.

Brandt, Harm-Hinrich. 2020a. Die Wiener Rothschilds seit 1820 und die Gründung der Creditanstalt 1855. In *Austriaca. Abhandlungen zur Habsburgermonarchie im ›langen‹ 19. Jahrhundert*, ed. Matthias Stickler, 353–387. Vienna, Cologne, Weimar: Böhlau.

Brandt, Harm-Hinrich. 2020b. Von Bruck zu Naumann. »Mitteleuropa« in der Zeit der Paulskirche und des Ersten Weltkrieges. In *Austriaca. Abhandlungen zur Habsburgermonarchie im ›langen‹ 19. Jahrhundert*, ed. Matthias Stickler, 250–294. Vienna, Cologne, Weimar: Böhlau.

Brix, Emil. 2011. Austria and Central Europe. In *Global Austria: Austria's place in Europe and the World*, eds. Günter Bischof, Fritz Plasser, Anton Pelinka, and Alexander Smith, 200–211. New Orleans: UNO Press.

Bruckmüller, Ernst. 2003. *The Austrian Nation: Cultural Consciousness and Socio-Political Processes*. Riverside (Calif.): Ariadne.

Cain, P. J., and A. G. Hopkins. 2016. *British Imperialism: 1688–2015*, 3rd ed. London: Routledge. https://doi.org/10.4324/9781315677798.

Cassis, Youssef. 2006. *Capitals of Capital: A History of International Financial Centres, 1780–2005*. Cambridge: University Press.

Currie, Taylor Alexandra. 2019. Du Pont Turns 150: Corporate Culture as Public Culture. *Enterprise & Society* 20 (2): 445–474. https://doi.org/10.1017/eso.2018.59.

De Vito, Christian G. 2019. History Without Scale: The Micro-Spatial Perspective*. *Past & Present* 242 (Supplement_14): 348–372. https://doi.org/10.1093/pastj/gtz048.

Deal, Terrence, and Kennedy Allan. 1982. *Corporate Cultures. The Rites and Rituals of Corporate Life*. Reading, Mass.: Addison-Wesley.

Dejung, Christof. 2024. Mercantile Elites and the Making of Global Capitalism. *The Historical Journal* 67 (4): 748–768. https://doi.org/10.1017/S0018246X24000220.

Dejung, Christof, Monika Dommann, and Daniel Speich Chasse. 2014. Einleitung: Vom Suchen und Finden. In *Auf der Suche nach der Ökonomie. Historische Annäherungen*, eds. Christof Dejung, Monika Dommann, and Daniel Speich Chasse, 1–15. Tübingen: Mohr Siebeck.

Dellheim, Charles. 1987. The Creation of a Company Culture: Cadburys, 1861–1931. *American Historical Review* 92 (February): 13–44. https://doi.org/10.2307/1862781.

Der Standard. 1993. Finanzgeschäfte in Tschechien, June 23.

Dirninger, Christian. 2012. Institutioneller Wandel der Unternehmensführung bei den Sparkassen in Österreich vom frühen 19. bis in die Mitte des 20. Jahrhunderts. In *Unternehmensführung: State of the art und Entwicklungsperspektiven*, ed. Katharina Anna Kaltenbrunner and Sabine Urnik, 31–44. Munich: De Gruyter Oldenbourg.

Dirninger, Christian. 2017. *Austro-Keynesianismus: Zur wirtschaftspolitischen Rolle des Staates*. 2017. Aufl. Schriftenreihe des Forschungsinstituts für politisch-historische Studien der Dr. Wilfried-Haslauer-Bibliothek 59. Vienna, Cologne, Weimar: Böhlau. https://doi.org/10.7767/9783205205869.

Domforth, Christine. 2005. Sparkasse tief in der Krise. *Die Presse*, September 15.

Engel, Reinhard. 1990. Der kleine Anfang am Ende der Welt. *Trend* 3: 178–185.

Epple, Angelika. 2010. *Das Unternehmen Stollwerck: Eine Mikrogeschichte der Globalisierung*, Frankfurt am Main: Campus.

Feldbauer, Peter. 1976. *Stadtwachstum und Wohnungsnot. Determinanten unzureichender Wohnungsversorgung, Wien 1848 bis 1914*. Sozial- und wirtschaftshistorische Studien 9. Vienna: Verlag für Geschichte und Politik.

Foroughi, Hamid, Diego Coraiola, Jukka Rinamaki, Sébastien Mena, and William M. Foster. 2020. Organizational Memory Studies. *Organization Studies* 41 (12): 1725–1748. https://doi.org/10.1177/0170840620974338.

Frey, Eric. 2024. Wien, Hauptstadt des Ostens. *Der Standard*, September 19.

Friedinger, Daniela. 2003. Waldviertler Ost-Erweiterung. *Wirtschaftsblatt*, Dezember 4.

Fritz, Hedwig. 1972. *150 Jahre Sparkassen in Österreich*, vol. 1. Vienna: Hauptverband der österreichischen Sparkassen.

Führer, Eduard. 1993. Aufbruch des Bürgertums in einer Provinzstadt. *Die Niederösterreichische Wirtschaft* 4 (February): 32.

Führer, Eduard, and Harald Hitz. 1992. *Erfahrung, die der Zukunft dient: 150 Jahre Waldviertler Sparkasse von 1842; 1842–1992*. Waidhofen an der Thaya: Waldviertler Sparkasse von 1842.

Gatti, Maria Cristina. 2013. The Construction of Company Identity through Memory. 'Specialised' Metaphorical Meanings for Pastness on Italian Business Web Pages. *Textus* 26 (1): 69–79.

Ghobrial, John-Paul A. 2019. Introduction: Seeing the World like a Microhistorian*. *Past & Present* 242 (Supplement_14): 1–22. https://doi.org/10.1093/pastj/gtz046.

Ghodsee, Kristen Rogheh, and Mitchell A. Orenstein. 2021. *Taking Stock of Shock: Social Consequences of the 1989 Revolutions*. New York, NY: Oxford University Press.

Gunz, Josef. 1995. Überlebenszeichen. Regionale Initiativen zwischen Hoffnung und Resignation im nördlichen Waldviertel/Niederösterreich unter Berücksichtigung von Ostöffnung und EU-Beitritt. Endbericht einer Untersuchung von Studierenden der Soziologie. Linz: Univ. Linz.

Handelsblatt. 1990. Gespräch mit Guido Schmidt-Chiari. Mai 4.

Hanisch, Ernst. 2005. Die Wiener Ringstraße. Zwei Pole, zwei Muster der österreichischen Kultur. In *Memoria Austriae II. Bauten – Orte – Regionen*, ed. Emil Brix, Ernst Bruckmüller, and Hannes Stekl, 75–104. Vienna: Böhlau.

Hansen, Per H. 2012. Business History: A Cultural and Narrative Approach. *The Business History Review* 86 (4): 693–717.

Hargadon, Andrew B., and R. Daniel Wadhwani. 2023. Theorizing with Microhistory. *Academy of Management Review* 48 (4): 681–696. https://doi.org/10.5465/amr.2019.0176.

Hilmar, Till. 2021. "Economic Memories" of the Aftermath of the 1989 Revolutions in East Germany and the Czech Republic. *East European Politics and*

Societies: And Cultures 35 (1): 89–112. https://doi.org/10.1177/0888325420902248.

Holt, Douglas B. 2004. *How Brands Become Icons: The Principles of Cultural Branding*. Boston, Mass.: Harvard Business School Press.

Hulsink, Willem, and Andreas Rauch. 2021. About the Lives and Times of Extraordinary Entrepreneurs: The Methodological Contribution of Autobiographies to the Life Course Theory of Entrepreneurship. *Journal of Small Business Management* 59 (5): 913–945. https://doi.org/10.1080/00472778.2020.1865538.

Jenny, Stefan. 1992. Kleine Sparkasse, große Pläne. *WirtschaftsWoche*, August 6.

Jones, Rosamund. 1988. New Broom at Creditanstalt. *Euromoney* (June), 165 f.

Kaláb, J. 1993. Waldviertler Sparkasse von 1842 nabízí své služby v Dačicích. *Listy Jihozápadni Moravy*, August 27.

Katzenstein, Peter. 1984. *Corporatism and Change. Austria, Switzerland, and the Politics of Industry*. Ithaca, NY: Cornell Univ. Press.

Kibler, Ewald, and Lauri Laine. 2024. Counternarrating Entrepreneurship. *Business History* 66 (2): 437–454. https://doi.org/10.1080/00076791.2023.2177637.

Knittler, Herbert. ed. 2006. *Wirtschaftsgeschichte des Waldviertels*. Waidhofen an der Thaya: Waldviertler Heimatbund.

Komlosy, Andrea. 2003. *Grenze und ungleiche regionale Entwicklung*. Vienna: Promedia.

Komlosy, Andrea. 2010. Auswirkungen der Grenzöffnung 1989: Das Beispiel des Oberen Waldviertels. In *Der „Ostfaktor". Österreichs Wirtschaft und die Ostöffnung 1989 bis 2009*, ed. Dieter Stiefel, 247–292. Vienna, Cologne, Weimar: Böhlau.

Komlosy, Andrea. 2015. Imperial Cohesion, Nation-Building, and Regional Integration in the Habsburg Monarchy. In *Nationalizing Empires*, ed. Stefan Berger and Alexei Miller, 369–427. Budapest: CEU Press.

Korom, Philipp. 2011. Wirtschaftseliten im neuen Austrokapitalismus. Sozialprofil und Personalverflechtungen. PhD Thesis, Graz.

Kühschelm, Oliver. 2017. Contemporary History as Pre-history of the Present: Analysing the Austrian Media Discourse about Investment Opportunities in the East. *The Hungarian Historical Review* 6 (4): 81–111.

Kühschelm, Oliver. 2021. *Einkaufen als nationale Verpflichtung: zur Genealogie nationaler Ökonomien in Österreich und der Schweiz, 1920–1980*. Werbung – Konsum – Geschichte 3. Berlin: De Gruyter Oldenbourg.

Kühschelm, Oliver, and André Pfoertner. 2005. *Memoria Austriae III. Unternehmer, Firmen, Produkte*. eds. Emil Brix, Ernst Bruckmüller, and Hannes Stekl. Vienna: Böhlau.

Kulis, Nicholas. 2009. Goal of Unified Europe Falters Amid Downturn. *New York Times*, August 22.

Kurier. 1993. Tschechien: Sparkasse als erste Auslandsbank, July 29.

Lipartito, Kenneth. 2016. Reassembling the Economic: New Departures in Historical Materialism. *The American Historical Review* 121 (1): 101–139. https://doi.org/10.1093/ahr/121.1.101.

Marinova, Svetla Trifonova, and Marin Alexandrov Marinov, eds. 2003. *Foreign Direct Investment in Central and Eastern Europe*. Ashgate: Routledge.

März, Eduard. 1968. *Österreichische Industrie- und Bankpolitik in der Zeit Franz Josephs I. am Beispiel der k.k.priv. österreichischen Credit-Anstalt für Handel und Gewerbe*. Vienna: Europa-Verlag.

Matis, Herbert, and Dieter Stiefel. 1987. *Unternehmenskultur in Österreich. Ideal und Wirklichkeit; mit einer Analyse von 60 Fallstudien*. Vienna: Service Fachverl. and. Wirtschaftsuniv.

Möchel, Kid. 2016. Ex-Banker Guido Schmidt-Chiari gestorben. *Kurier*, August 22. https://kurier.at/wirtschaft/ex-banker-guido-schmidt-chiari-gestorben/217.062.191.

Morgan, Mary S. 2006. Economic Man as Model Man: Ideal Types, Idealization and Caricatures. *Journal of the History of Economic Thought* 28 (1): 1–27. https://doi.org/10.1080/10427710500509763.

Müller, Wolfgang. 1988. Privatising in a Corporatist Economy: The Politics of Privatisation in Austria. *West European Politics* 11 (4): 101–116. https://doi.org/10.1080/01402388808424712.

Natmessnig, Charlotte. 2019. Die Erste österreichische Spar-Casse. Die ersten 50 Jahre. In *Arbeite, Sammle, Vermehre – Erste Bank: seit 1819*, eds. Nadia Rapp-Wimberger and Christian Rapp, 48–61. Vienna: Brandstätter.

Neuwirth, Ernst, and Eduard Führer. 1983. *Eröffnung der neuen Hauptanstalt in Waidhofen an der Thaya*. Waidhofen an der Thaya: Waldviertler Sparkasse von 1842.

Nora, Pierre, ed. 1984. *Les Lieux de mémoire*, vol. 3. Gallimard.

Perzi, Niklas, and Hanns Haas, eds. 2012. *So nah, so fern: Menschen im Waldviertel und in Südböhmen 1945–1989*. Weitra: Verlag der Provinz.

Pilotta, Joseph J. 2016. The Entrepreneur as Hero? In *Neoliberalism, Economic Radicalism, and the Normalization of Violence*, eds. Vicente Berdayes and John W. Murphy, 37–52. Cham: Springer International Publishing. https://doi.org/10.1007/978-3-319-25169-1_4.

Pohnitzer, Werner. 2021. *Blüte & Frost. Wandel an der Grenze*. Waidhofen an der Thaya.

Popp, Andrew, and Susanna Fellman. 2017. Writing Business History: Creating Narratives. *Business History* 59 (8): 1242–1260. https://doi.org/10.1080/00076791.2016.1250742.

Rapp-Wimberger, Nadia, and Christian Rapp, eds. 2019. *Arbeite, sammle, vermehre – Erste Bank: seit 1819*. Vienna: Brandstätter.

Resch, Andreas. 2013. Austrian Foreign Trade and Austrian Companies' Economic Engagement in Eastern Europe. In *Austria's International Position after the End of the Cold War*, eds. Günter Bischof and Ferdinand Karlhofer, 198–223. Contemporary Austrian Studies 22. New Orleans: Uno Press/Innsbruck University Press.

Richter, Sándor., and Jan Stankovsky. 1991. *Die neue Rolle Österreichs im Ost-West-Handel*. Vienna: WIFO.

Rief, Norbert. 2014. Heinrich Treichl: Der letzte Gentleman des Geldes. *Die Presse*, November 5. https://www.diepresse.com/4586559/heinrich-treichl-der-letzte-gentleman-des-geldes.

Rothschild, Emma. 2011. *The Inner Life of Empires: An Eighteenth-Century History*. Princeton: Princeton University Press. https://doi.org/10.1515/9781400838165.

Rumpler, Helmut. 2005. Die Gründung der Credit Anstalt im Kontext der Neupositionierung von Österreichs Wirtschafts- und Außenhandelspolitik durch Karl Ludwig Freiherrn von Bruck. In *Bank Austria Creditanstalt. 150 Jahre österreichische Bankgeschichte im Zentrum Europas*, eds. Oliver Rathkolb, Theodor Venus, and Ulrike Zimmerl, 56–72. Vienna: Paul Zsolnay.

Sandgruber, Roman. 1995. *Ökonomie und Politik: Österreichische Wirtschaftsgeschichte vom Mittelalter bis zur Gegenwart*. Vienna: Ueberreuter.

Schmidt-Chiari, Guido. 1991. *Die österreichische Bankenwirtschaft in den neunziger Jahren*. Vienna: Creditanstalt.

Schmidt-Chiari, Guido. 1993. *Neue Märkte in Europa: Herausforderung für Österreichs Banken*. Vienna: Creditanstalt.

Schmidt-Chiari, Guido. 2007. Creditanstalt-Bankverein – Begegnungen und Erfahrungen. In *Österreichs Kreditwirtschaft. Von der Reichsmark über den Schilling zum Euro*, eds. Erwin Frasl, René Alfons Haiden, and Josef Taus, 125–144. Vienna, Graz: nwv.

Schug, Alexander. 2013. *History Marketing: Ein Leitfaden zum Umgang mit Geschichte in Unternehmen*. Bielefeld: Transcript.

Schumpeter, Joseph A. 1965. Economic Theory and Entrepreneurial History. In *Explorations in Enterprise*, eds. Hugh G. J. Aitken, 45–64. Cambridge, Mass.: Harvard University Press. https://www.degruyterbrill.com/document/doi/10.4159/harvard.9780674594470.c5/html.

Sieber, Susanne. 2006. Direktinvestitionen österreichischer Unternehmen in Ost-Mitteleuropa. *Monatsberichte des Österreichischen Institutes für Wirtschaftsforschung* 8: 613–626.

Stråth, Bo. 2008. Mitteleuropa: From List to Naumann. *European Journal of Social Theory* 11 (2): 171–183. https://doi.org/10.1177/1368431007087472.

Suddaby, Roy, William M. Foster, and Chris Quinn Trank. 2010. Rhetorical History as a Source of Competitive Advantage. In *The Globalization of Strategy Research*, eds. Joel Baum and Joseph Lampel, 147–173. Leeds: Emerald. https://www.emerald.com/insight/content/doi/10.1108/s0742-3322(2010)0000027009/full/html.

Sulzer, Friedrich. 2020. *Die Bedeutung der CESEE-Investments österreichischer Banken seit der Ostöffnung 1989 bis 2015*. PhD Thesis, Graz.

Tanner, Jakob. 2017. *Historische Anthropologie zur Einführung*, Hamburg: Junius.

Ther, Philipp. 2016. *Europe Since 1989: A History*. Princeton, Oxford: Princeton University Press.

Thiessen, Janis. 2019. The Narrative Turn, Corporate Storytelling, and Oral History: Canada's Petroleum Oral History Project and Truth and Reconciliation Commission Call to Action No. 92. *Enterprise & Society* 20 (1): 60–73.

Tilly, Richard. 1998. Universal Banking in Historical Perspective. *Journal of Institutional and Theoretical Economics (JITE)* 154 (1): 7–32.

Treichl, Heinrich. 2003. *Fast ein Jahrhundert. Erinnerungen*. Vienna: Zsolnay.

Trivellato, Francesca. 2012. *The Familiarity of Strangers: The Sephardic Diaspora, Livorno, and Cross-Cultural Trade in the Early Modern Period*. New Haven, CT: Yale Univ. Press.

Trivellato, Francesca. 2015. Microstoria/Microhistoire/Microhistory. *French Politics, Culture & Society* 33 (1): 122–134. https://doi.org/10.3167/fpcs.2015.330107.

Vorteil. 1993. *Die Zeitung der Waldviertler Sparkasse von 1842*, vol. 3.

Weber, Fritz. 2016. *Vor dem grossen Krach. Österreichs Banken der Zwischenkriegszeit am Beispiel der Credit-Anstalt für Handel und Gewerbe*. Vienna: Böhlau.

Weiner, Elaine. 2007. *Market Dreams: Gender, Class, and Capitalism in the Czech Republic*. Ann Arbor: University of Michigan Press.

Zehle, Sibylle. 2008. Die fabelhafte Welt der Treichls. *Manager Magazin*, April 25.

Zielonka, Jan. 2015. The Uses and Misuses of the Imperial Paradigm in the Study of European Integration. In *Revisiting the European Union as Empire*, eds. Hartmut Behr and Yannis Stivachtis, 45–58. Abingdon: Routledge.

Zimmerl, Ulrike. 2012. *Die Bank am Schottenring*. Vienna: Böhlau.

Economic Internationalization

Impact of the Memory of Kaikoku (Opening the Country to the World) on the Course of Industrialization in Early Meiji Japan

Naoki Odanaka

1 Introduction

This chapter analyzes the impact and influence that the memory of ***kaikoku*** (opening the country to the world) in the 1850s, forced by ***kurofune*** (black ships) and three subsequent treaties, exerted on the course of industrialization in early Meiji era. Here ***kurofune*** refers to the iron-armored battleships of the US Navy led by Commodore Matthew Perry (1794–1858) that came to Japan in 1853; Three treaties concerned are the Japan–US Treaty of Peace and Amity (1854), Anglo–Japanese Friendship Treaty (1854), and Treaty of Commerce and Navigation between Japan and Russia (1855); And the early Meiji era means the period from the Meiji restoration (1868) to the Sino–Japanese war (1894–1895). We use the comparative advantage theory formulated by David Ricardo (1772–1823) as an analytical tool, for it is commonly regarded as a basis of the standard economic development policy. As for the object of analysis, we take the arguments of major contemporary Japanese policymakers.

N. Odanaka (✉)
Department of Economics, Tohoku University, Sendai, Japan
e-mail: naokiodanaka@jcom.zaq.ne.jp

S. Berger and T. Fetzer (eds.), *Collective Memory of Economic Crises and Transformations*, Palgrave Macmillan Memory Studies,
https://doi.org/10.1007/978-3-032-09094-2_8

Concretely, we attempt to answer the following question: What characterized the economic policy adopted by early Meiji policymakers, and what was the impact of the memory of forced ***kaikoku*** on this characteristic? In order to do that, however, we have to make clear two following points, because the standard economics regards Ricardian comparative advantage theory as a fundamental basis of economic development strategy. The first is: Did the Japanese government adopt the comparative advantage theory as the basis of economic policy after the ***kaikoku*** and the Meiji restoration? And the second is: How did policymakers understand it? Did they accept it without changes from its origins in the UK, or did they modify it to suit their own country and situation? If the latter was the case, what led them to that modification? Was there an impact of the memory of forced ***kaikoku*** on their economic policy decision?

To address these questions, this chapter is structured as follows. In Sect. 2, we briefly discuss Ricardian comparative advantage theory and provide a general description of the characteristics of the early Meiji Japanese economic structure to understand which sectors or goods had a comparative advantage. In Sect. 3, we present and analyze representative arguments of early Meiji policymakers regarding the economic policy that Japan needed to adopt. In Sect. 4, we explore how these policymakers understood the comparative advantage theory and the Western civilization that created it, as well as the importance of the memory of forced ***kaikoku*** on this comprehension.

2 Comparative Advantage Theory and the Economic Structure of Early Meiji Japan

We begin by briefly presenting Ricardian comparative advantage theory (Krugman et al. 2015, chap. 3). Although it might seem strange to explain a well-known international trade theory as formulated by a famous classical economist, we begin here because, according to a famous economist, Paul Krugman, the theory is "a simple concept," but "experience shows that it is a surprisingly hard concept to understand (or accept)" (Krugman et al. 2015, 56).

The main implication of comparative advantage theory is simple: Each country (or any kind of economic unit) can maximize its wealth (or welfare or profit) by specializing in making goods that it can produce most efficiently, that is, those with comparative advantage, and export them in exchange for those for which it is at a comparative disadvantage.

Here we must address what "comparative advantage" means. Ricardian comparative advantage refers to the relative production efficiency of a good compared with other goods within a country. Consider the "two countries (*A*, *B*) and two goods (*m*, *n*)" model, where *m* is more productive than *n* in*A*. In this case, *m* has a comparative advantage over *n* in *A*, and *A* should specialize in producing *m*.

This theory becomes complicated when we introduce trade between *A* and *B*. Here, too, comparative advantage means higher productivity of a good in each country. Let us assume that the production cost (measured by person-hours) of *m* is 5 in *A* and 3 in *B*, whereas that of *n* is 8 in *A* and 2 in *B* (see Table 1). In this case, *m* has a comparative advantage in *A* and *n* in *B*. As *B* has an advantage over *A* in the production of both goods, because they are more efficiently produced there, trade seems impractical, as *m* and *n* produced in *A* are more costly and thus higher priced. This, however, is not what Ricardo argued.

The theory states that even if one country produces both goods more efficiently than the other does, increased wealth remains attainable for both. Assuming that *A* has 80 person-hours for producing *m* and *n*, and that *A* allocates 40 for producing *m* and 40 for *n*, *A* produces 8 units of *m* and 5 units of *n*. However, with the same person-hours, *A* could specialize in the production of *m* and produce 16 units. *A* could then export 6 units of *m* to *B* and import 9 units of *n* from *B*, because the production of *m* requires 3 person-hours per unit and that of *n* requires 2 person-hours; Thus, the value and price of *m* is 1.5 times that of *n*. Consequently, *A* would obtain 10 units of *m* and 9 of *n* using the same 80 person-hours. This means that even a country with lower productivity than other countries for all goods could still increase its wealth through international trade.

In sum, comparative advantage theory claims that, in a world of free trade, each country should specialize in manufacturing its most efficiently produced goods. A country can still increase its wealth by exporting

Table 1 Production costs (person-hours)

Country	*Good*	
	m	N
A	5	8
B	3	2

their efficiently produced goods and importing goods with comparative disadvantage.

Now let us look at Japanese economic structure during the early Meiji era in light of the comparative advantage theory. Before the Meiji Restoration, that is, in the late Tokugawa period, industrial policy was mainly implemented by the *han* (local domain) government. As a natural consequence of the Tokugawa government's *sakoku* (national seclusion) policy for over two centuries, each *han* encouraged the production of goods to be consumed within its territory, and promoted the production of specialty goods to be sold outside to increase wealth in *han* territory. Odaka (1988, 12) characterizes this policy as "mercantilist."

Many *hans* tried to encourage the brewing and textile industries toward the end of the Tokugawa era (Abe 1988, 69). When *sakoku* ended and Japan was forced to engage in international trade, the possible export goods were mainly products of these two industries, such as *sake* (Japanese rice wine), vinegar, soy sauce, and cotton (yarn and fabric) and silk (silkworm eggs, yarn, and fabric) products.

After *kaikoku*, Japan began primarily exporting silk products in exchange for cotton (Bernhofen and Brown 2004, 57). Early Meiji policymakers encouraged this international trade pattern (Saito 1992), which followed the comparative advantage theory (Bernhofen and Brown 2004, 62–64; Okazaki et al. 2006). As previously mentioned, this theory argues that goods with higher production efficiency rates should be exported and those with lower rates should be imported. Bernhofen and Brown (2004, 63) measured the comparative production efficiency rates of goods using their price rising rate after *kaikoku* (proxy variable of internal–external comparative price in the autarchy era) and found that goods with higher production efficiency, such as silk products, began being exported, and less production-efficient goods, starting with cotton products, were imported.

Comparative advantage theory was well suited to the late Tokugawa and early Meiji eras because the introduction of international trade brought an increase in wealth to Japan. Policymakers in the early Meiji government were impressed by the impact of international trade on their economy and the welfare of the people. According to Bernhofen and Brown (2005, 210), "at most the gain in real income was 8 to 9 percent of GDP." *Kaikoku* enhanced Japan's economy by making it possible to sell comparative advantage goods to foreign countries and buy comparative disadvantage goods from them.

In the mid-1870s, the situation began to change as the import of investment goods or heavy-industry products, which had occurred at a relatively low rate—in 1868–1875, estimate Bernhofen and Brown (2004, 57), machinery, instruments, and other goods accounted for little over 15% of imports, whereas cotton yarn and cloth accounted for over 30%—, became a subject of great attention for policymakers. The post-restoration era corresponded to the age of globalizing imperialism, when industrialization and modernization were regarded as crucial for every developing country or area to avoid colonization, for which these products were essential.

3 Economic Policy Debates in Early Meiji Japan

In this section, we analyze economic policy and the political debates over it in early Meiji era to determine whether the course of Japanese early-stage industrialization policy followed comparative advantage theory. If the Japanese government followed it, it would have adopted an economic policy that encouraged the production of comparative advantage goods and an international trade policy of exporting them and importing comparative disadvantage goods.

After the Meiji restoration, two factions emerged among Japanese policymakers, colliding with economic policy, industrial and international trade policies in particular (Ishizuka 1973, 3–8, 108–115, 292). The first faction—called *Kaimeiha* (Modernists) by Hiromichi Ishizuka, a Japanese historian, and led by Shigenobu Okuma (1838–1922) and Takayoshi Kido (1833–1877)—adopted an export-oriented policy that encouraged the growth of existing sectors, starting with agriculture and textile (especially silk) production, and the exportation of their products in exchange for trains, ships, or machinery (Kobayashi 1977, 72). The second faction—which Ishizuka called the *Minzokuha* (Nationalists) and contained Toshimichi Okubo (1830–1878), Tomomi Iwakura (1825–1883), Hirobumi Ito (1841–1909), and Masayoshi Matsukata (1835–1924) as leaders—adopted an import-substitution economic policy, which sought to introduce heavy-industry manufacturing technology, invite Western engineers and professors to Japan and hire them, and import machinery for reverse-engineering to develop heavy industries in Japan (Nakanishi 1982/1983/2003, 6–7, 265, 312).

The confrontation over the economic policies resulted in the so-called "governmental crisis of the 14th year of Meiji (1882)," wherein the

Minzokuha, led by Ito, expelled Okuma and his allies—the *Kaimeiha*—from government. The newly nominated Minister of Finance, Matsukata, began a radical austerity policy (*Matsukata Zaisei*), intended to collect and retain money for investment in domestic secondary industry, starting with locomotive and steamship manufacturing, and in tertiary industry—particularly, the shipping one (Harada 1972, 273).

Here, we explore the theoretical background of early Meiji policymakers' economic policy, particularly concerning industrialization and international trade. We begin by analyzing the policy discourses of the *Kaimeiha* and *Minzokuha* factions.

Two factions shared the economic policy characterized by the slogan "*fukoku* (enrich the country) *kyohei* (strengthen the army)" (Ishizuka 1973, 5–6; Ishii 2018, 325; Takeda 2019, 131). According to this view, Japan had opened its doors to foreign countries in the age of emergent imperialism, and the policymakers of the new Meiji government had to find a way to avoid colonization. Considering that the key to *fukoku kyohei* was the heavy industry that produced the machinery necessary for realizing the second purpose (*kyohei*), they encouraged the export of silk products and certain consumption goods, and, from the mid-1870s, the import of machinery and related technologies necessary for heavy industrialization in Japan.

This international trade pattern seems to follow the comparative advantage theory, but policymakers had a somewhat different goal for economic policy. Silk products were comparative advantage goods, whereas machinery was comparatively disadvantageous in Japan at the time. According to the Ricardian theory, specialization in the production of comparative advantage goods—that is, silk products—should increase the wealth of the nation. Policymakers, however, did not want the monoculturalization of silk products; They wanted to begin producing the comparatively disadvantaged heavy-industry products in Japan to realize not only *fukoku* but also *kyohei*. Although the *Kaimeiha* and *Minzokuha* clashed, resulting in a political purge with a huge historical impact, they shared a common purpose and economic theoretical framework: *Fukoku kyohei* and comparative advantage theory, respectively.

This political stance, shared by most Japanese policymakers, can be found in two policy documents: *Kobusho wo Mokeru no Mune* (Declaration of Establishing the Ministry of Industry), issued in 1870 and written by the leader of *Kaimeiha*, Okuma, and *Kaigai Chokubai no Kigyo wo*

Hiraku no Gi (Proposition of Establishing the National Exportation Company), written in 1876 by the leader of *Minzokuha*, Okubo.

In the former document, Okuma (1973) stated that the "world of iron" was spreading in Western countries, where the development of science and technology encouraged the production of iron goods, such as trains and ships, which were the foundation of national wealth and power:

> Western countries have developed through the invention of ironware and the progress of arts and engineering, which are the origins of development. Regarding our country, we have also developed ironware, but our technical level has not been high enough. In order to achieve development, wealth, and power, it is essential to promote industry. In Japan, railroads and communication devices are not widely used due to the opposition against them. This opposition, which does not understand their importance, considers them strange and unnecessary. If Japanese citizens understand that these tools are the foundation of the state's strength and the source of the people's wealth, they will accept and demand both... Communication devices can facilitate the movement of people and transportation of goods, bridging geographical gaps and connecting rural areas to the rest of the world. These devices are not only useful for individuals to communicate with each other, but also for the government to receive immediate information during emergencies... (Okuma 1973)

In the latter document, Okubo (1988b) claimed that the government had to encourage commerce and international trade to develop agriculture and industry and eliminate trade balance deficits:

> Industrialization should begin by promoting both agriculture and manufacturing industries. Commerce plays a crucial role in the success of industrialization. The distribution of these products to consumers is essential for their demand and consumption. To ensure success, it is important to encourage agriculture and industry in an appropriate manner. An appropriate way to encourage growth is by developing commerce and expanding the market. Since *kaikoku*, international trade has been dominated by foreign companies, as Japanese companies do not have the necessary knowledge and capital for international trade. Additionally, imports have exceeded exports recently, and we have to manage unlimited losses with limited national power. If this situation continues, our country will decline. Considering the current state of our country, we propose that Japanese merchants be granted the right to directly export domestically produced

> goods. This would eliminate the interference of foreign merchants and prevent the exportation of counterfeit or substandard products. Our country's specialties, such as silk yarn and tea, would gain a positive reputation. (Okubo 1988b)

Both *Kaimeiha* and *Minzokuha* thus encouraged the export of silk products, but there was a disagreement between them regarding which concrete policy line to adopt. *Kaimeiha*, who chose an exportation-oriented policy, intended to earn the necessary funds to import heavy-industry products and invest in heavy industrialization, with the purpose of developing that industry in a natural way. *Minzokuha*, who urged import substitution, intended to hasten the importation of heavy-industry products to be used as models for setting up factories, and the export of their products to achieve rapid heavy industrialization. In other words, *Kaimeiha* asserted the necessity of earning money first to invest in heavy industrialization, whereas *Minzokuha* advocated rapid heavy industrialization by any means (Sawai and Tanimoto 2016, 119).

4 "Movement" as a Key to Modernization

In this section, we address the following two questions. First, what were the characteristics of the economic policy implemented by early Meiji policymakers? In other words, which sectors were regarded as important for the rapid industrialization of Japan? Second, what was the origin of these characteristics? And did this origin have any relation with the memory of forced *kaikoku*?

Regarding the first question, we note that early Meiji policymakers emphasized the importance of trains and ships as heavy-industry products and that of railway and shipping as tertiary industries. The Ministry of Industry concentrated its efforts and funds on constructing railroads; In the early Meiji era, almost half of its budget was allocated to railroads, especially to construct the Tokyo–Yokohama and Kyoto–Kobe lines (Ishizuka 1973, 108–111). The government established public factories to function as test sites for new technologies and as models for private factories. In the 1880s, there were twice as many steamship construction factories as machine manufacturing factories in the public sector (Koyama 1972, 102–108).

The government also supported the tertiary railroad and shipping industries financially, legally, and administratively. It constructed railroads with public money, lent public land for railroads to private railway companies for free, sold public ships cheaply to private shipping companies, granted them a subsidy, and enacted the Shipping and Ship Building Encouragement Act (1896) (Umemura 1983, 239–240; Nishikawa and Abe 1990, 23–26; Sawai 1990, 215–218; Nakamura 1990, 24–26).

As for the second question, early Meiji policymakers regarded train and ship manufacturing and railway and shipping activities as important because they enhanced the "movement" of men, goods, and information. For policymakers, "movement" was the key to modernizing the nation. They tried to encourage "movement," because modernization was a precondition of *fukoku kyohei*, their main and ultimate objective (Yamamuro 1984, chap. II).

"Movement" was important for two reasons. First, it generated wealth. Consider the case of the Iwakura Mission. In 1871, three years after the Meiji restoration, the new government sent a mission to the US and Europe to negotiate the revision of treaties that the Tokugawa government had conducted, which were disadvantageous to Japan. The mission, led by Iwakura as the ambassador extraordinary and plenipotentiary, comprised the main policymakers of the Meiji government, including Kido, Okubo, and Ito. It lasted almost two years but could not succeed in revising the treaties. However, it was important for the modernization of Japan because it allowed policymakers to experience modernized Western society. As they realized the overwhelming inequality of wealth and power between Japan and Western countries, they decided to take the latter as a model, translated "modernization" into "Westernization," and tried to find a key to modernization in Western civilization.

According to the official report by the Secretary of Mission, Kunitake Kume (1839–1931), members of the Mission were greatly impressed by the importance of "movement," both of people, encouraged by their sociability, and of goods, realized by international trade in particular (Nishikawa 1995, 39). Western people were sociable and enjoyed going out and meeting friends, talking with neighbors, and so on. This sociability meant that people frequently gathered in public spaces, exchanged information, broadened their knowledge, and had more opportunities to acquire wealth. Western people also regarded international trade as an essential economic activity. Even farmers and artisans were interested in it, unlike in Japan. Further, Western countries processed raw materials provided by Eastern and Southern countries and sold the finished products back to them for high profits (Kume 1977–1982).

The second reason for "movement" being considered crucial for *fukoku kyohei* was the memory of *kaikoku* forced on Japan by *kurofune* and the three subsequent treaties. People were heavily impressed by *kurofune* and described them as "flying birds" (Kato 1988, 2), because, in the late Tokugawa era, Japanese ships were generally small wooden vessels. *Kurofune* thus were the symbol of the power of civilization and modernization, as they made "movement" more rapid and easier (Kato 1988, 51, 116).

The impact of this memory of forced *kaikoku* on the importance of "movement" was clearly expressed by Yukichi Fukuzawa (1835–1901), a Meiji intellectual who wrote many bestselling books that introduced Western civilization to a previously isolated Japanese audience and became the most influential ideologue of modernization in the Meiji era (Craig 2009; MacFarlane 2011). Fukuzawa realized that they were in the age of "movement" when international trade brought the "movement" of goods which would lead to the increase in wealth (Fukuzawa 1988, 257–258). Regarding the "movement" of men, he insisted that humans could make progress by moving physically to interact with others (Fukuzawa 2003, 375). According to him, the Tokugawa government decided to open the country, aware of the presence of and afraid of the power of *kurofune*, which was itself an innovation in the transportation-manufacturing industry (Fukuzawa 1962, 543). In his autobiography, Fukuzawa (1978, 31, 64) recalled that "When Perry came, the news that US battleships came spread among all the Japanese people, even those in the countryside," or that "the arrival of Perry had a great impact on the mind of the Japanese people." According to him, the memory of forced *kaikoku* indicated that Western progress was, above all, the result of the development of the transportation and transportation-manufacturing industries.

While Tokugawa government clung to the *sakoku* policy, American and European countries made astonishing progress, particularly with the invention of the steamboat. With this tool in hand, they transformed the global transportation network, navigating all over the world and forcing Japan to open its doors to the world. The opening of Japan was thus an inevitable event. It was natural that those accustomed to *sakoku* were astonished, and a confrontation occurred between supporters of *sakoku* and *kaikoku*. *Sakoku* supporters attacked European ships at Shimonoseki and Kagoshima, but Japanese antiquated weaponry and battleships could not compete with the advanced technology of Western countries. Following these events, Japanese intellectuals became aware of the situation and the dominant position held by the West. Japanese opinion changed drastically, realizing that opening doors to the world and communicating with the outside was advantageous. As the development of civilization was the purpose of human society, it was delightful to see today's Japan, which was the result of *kaikoku* and communication with foreign countries. The steam engine, telegram, postal service, printed materials, politics, literature, and more, all resulted from communication with foreign countries (Fukuzawa 2003, 370–373).

The memory of *kurofune* and forced *kaikoku*, held by Fukuzawa, was shared by both ordinary people and policymakers in early Meiji Japan.

Kana Himeno (2019) provides a comprehensive analysis of this memory among the former. According to her, *kurofune* was remembered as an intimidating threat to Japan that realized *kaikoku* against the will of the Japanese government. This memory was mainly reproduced by popular books, including school textbooks. For example, *Chuto Kokushi Kyokasho* (Secondary School Textbooks of Japanese History) published in 1897 wrote that "Perry declared that they were ready for war, and fear reached its peak in the Tokugawa government" (Himeno 2019, 34). *Shin Nihon Shi* (Japanese History New Version), written by a journalist Yosaburo Takekoshi (1865–1950) as a popular book in 1891 and becoming a bestseller, depicted that "*kurofune* were equipped with the threatening canons, and their arms were shining in the morning sun" (Himeno 2019, 33). After the Sino–Japanese War, however, the image of *kurofune* began to change from a threat to a benefactor who had given Japan a chance to modernize itself through *kaikoku*. This change reflected that of Japan's self-image from a tiny Eastern country, likely to be colonized, to a Westernized Eastern country seeking to become a colonizer.

Regarding the memory of forced *kaikoku* among policymakers, most of them remembered it, not as a crisis, but as a chance for modernization. For example, in 1899, Ito—the leading figure of government after the assassination of Okubo—as the Minister of Interior (1878–1880), four-time prime minister (1885–1888, 1892–1896, 1898, 1900–1901), and four-time president of *sumitsuin* (Privy Council, 1888–1889, 1891–1892, 1903–1905, 1909), still remembered the arrival of *kurofune*. He said that "at that time steamboats were coming and going in Europe and Atlantic Ocean. We had not seen them [until *kurofune* came—the author] by accident. Battleships were equipped with steam engine, and iron ships were already built there... I thus thought that we had to open the country to the world in order to encourage the national progress and to realize the enrichment of country and the strengthening of army" (Ito 2011, 273–274).

The memory of forced *kaikoku* impacted policymakers' stances on which economic policy to adopt. Consider three cases. First, in 1874, Okubo—the leading figure of the Meiji government from the restoration to his assassination (1878)—as *sangi* (government board member, 1868–1871, 1873–1878), Minister of Finance (1871–1873), and Minister of the Interior (1873–1878), insisted on taking the UK, one of the countries that forced Japan to open the country, as a model. The power of the UK seemed to him to prove the importance of the shipping industry, which would promote the movement of goods, economic development leading to the enrichment of people, and the strengthening of the state (Okubo 1988a). Second, in 1875, Okuma, then Minister of Finance, wrote that "if we use the state-owned ships properly, not only domestic shipping be promoted and domestic supply and demand be balanced, but also foreign countries will also cease despising Japan, international trade will be balanced, and economic development will begin… Encouraging shipping industry is very much important" (Okuma 1988, 28). Third, in 1879, Masana Maeda (1850–1921), high-ranking official of the Ministry of Finance and Okuma's right-hand man, proposed the introduction of a "direct trade system"—international trade by Japanese companies— based on the reason that "on the diplomatic level, that is to say, superficially, Japan is not despised by foreign countries as before, but in the field of international trade, our country is still exploited and heavily damaged" (Maeda 1988, 77).

In sum, the collective memory of forced *kaikoku* convinced policymakers that the "movement" of men, goods, or information was crucial to modernization and to *fukoku kyohei*, and thus contributed to their encouragement of transportation-related industries.

5 Conclusion

After examining the economic structure and policy of early Meiji Japan, policymakers' comprehension of comparative advantage theory, and the impact of the memory of forced *kaikoku* on their economic policy, we arrive at three conclusions.

First, the economic policy adopted by early Meiji policymakers generally followed comparative advantage theory. *Kaimeiha* urged adoption of an export-oriented policy that encouraged the growth of existing sectors, particularly silk production, and the export of their products in exchange for trains, ships, or machinery. *Minzokuha* advocated the import-substitution economic policy, which sought to introduce heavy-industry manufacturing technology and bring up that industry in Japan. Although these two policy lines clashed, bringing on a serious political crisis (1881), they shared comparative advantage theory. The difference lay in the concrete strategy they wished to pursue to give heavy industry a comparative advantage.

Second, early Meiji policymakers shared the belief that economic policy based on comparative advantage theory was an ambivalent tool for their ultimate purpose, *fukoku kyohei*. On the one hand, the theory, claiming that the production of comparative advantage goods by each country results in each nation's increased wealth, would contribute to *fukoku*. On the other hand, they realized that adopting an economic policy wholly based on that theory, leading Japan to the monoculturalization of silk goods, would not realize *kyohei*, which required heavy industrialization.

The goal of early Meiji policymakers was not the monoculturalization of existing comparative advantage goods, but heavy industrialization. However, this was a difficult task. New technologies were necessary to transform the economic structure, but Japanese heavy industry, especially machine manufacturing, did not expand during the early Meiji era. This phenomenon hastened the import of capital goods, which in turn hindered technological development (Ichikawa 1988, 235–236). Japanese heavy industry was about to enter this vicious cycle.

This situation was resolved by the recovery of customs autonomy in 1899. Subsequently, the government could use the customs policy to modify relative prices. Import customs on certain foods (sugar, flour), paper, woolen cloth, and machines rose gradually and functioned as a major protective policy (Miyajima 2004, 28–30).

Third, early Meiji policymakers, regarding "movement" as a key to *fukoku kyohei*, encouraged transportation-related industries. This policy, based on the knowledge of Western society, was also the product of the impact that the memory of forced *kaikoku* had on policymakers and Japanese people in general.

After the Sino–Japanese War, the Japanese government accelerated an industrial policy that encouraged the shipbuilding and shipping industries. This is usually said to be the result of the war (Miyajima 2004, 33), but we suggest that it also resulted from the persistent interest of policymakers in "movement," as a product of the memory of forced *kaikoku*.

As is shown in this chapter, Japan opened the country to the world when the later was entering an age of imperialism and colonization, a kind of globalization. Our findings suggest that the collective memory of globalization-related economic transformation has two characteristics.

First, such a transformation is memorized in two ways—as chance or as a crisis. In the case of early Meiji Japan, some ordinary people memorized forced *kaikoku* as a crisis, and other people and most policymakers remembered it as a chance.

Second, collective memory concerning globalization-related economic transformation contains a sense of hierarchy between the Self (Japan) and the Others (Western countries). The memory of forced *kaikoku* as a crisis was based on the judgment that Japan was inferior to the Western countries. Those memorizing forced *kaikoku* as a chance perceived Japan as relatively inferior to Western countries but believed that it was possible to catch up to them in the future. Over time, the event of *kaikoku* began to be remembered as an opportunity for Japan to realize equalization.

Acknowledgements This chapter is based on the research supported by JSPS KAKENHI (number of grant-in-aid 15K02925 and 19K01048).

References

Abe, Takeshi. 1988. Kinsei Nihon ni okeru Men Orimono Seisandaka [Output of cotton fabric in early-modern Japan]. In *Bakumatsu Meiji no Nihon Keizai* [Japanese Economy in the Late Tokugawa and Meiji Eras], ed. Y. Yamamoto and K. Odaka, 69–83. Tokyo: Nihon Keizai Shinbunsha.

Bernhofen, Daniel M., and John C. Brown. 2004. A direct test of the theory of comparative advantage. *Journal of Political Economy* 112 (1): 48–67.

Bernhofen, Daniel M., and John C. Brown. 2005. An empirical assessment of the comparative advantage gains from trade. *American Economic Review* 95 (1): 208–225.

Craig, Albert. 2009. *Civilization and Enlightenment*. Cambridge, MA: Harvard University Press.

Fukuzawa, Yukichi. 1962. Naichi Ryoko Nishi Sensei no Ron wo Bakusu [Criticism of Mr. Nishi's argument on inner trip by foreigners]. In *Fukuzawa Yukichi Zenshu* [Complete Works of Yukichi Fukuzawa], vol. 19, 542–551. Tokyo: Iwanami Shoten. Originally published in 1875.

Fukuzawa, Yukichi. 1978. *Fukuo Jiden* [Autobiography]. Tokyo: Iwanami Shoten. Originally published in 1899.

Fukuzawa, Yukichi. 1988. Boeki Rikkoku Ron [State building by international trade]. In *Keizai Koso* [Economic Ideas], ed. M. Nakamura, K. Ishii, and Y. Kasuga, 257–259. Tokyo: Iwanami Shoten. Originally published in 1884.

Fukuzawa, Yukichi. 2003. Hi Naichi Zakkyo Ron ni tsuite [On the non-mixed residence between the Japanese and foreigners]. In *Fukuzawa Yukichi Chosakushu* [Selected works of Yukichi Fukuzawa], vol. 8, 370–380. Tokyo: Keio Daigaku Shuppankai. Originally published in 1893.

Harada, Masataka. 1972. *Nihon no Kindaika to Keizai Seisaku* [Modernization and Economic Policy in Japan]. Tokyo: Toyo Keizai Shinposha.

Himeno, Kunisuke. 2019. Kurofune Gensetsu no Tanjo [The making of '*Kurofune*' discourse]. *Kokubun Kenkyu* [Kumamoto Kenritsu Daigaku Japanese Literature Studies] 64: 25–50.

Ichikawa, Takamasa. 1988. Yunyu Daitai Kogyoka no Katei to sono Ninaite [Process and carriers of the industrialization by import substitution]. In *Bakumatsu Meiji no Nihon Keizai* [Japanese Economy in the Late Tokugawa and Meiji Eras], ed. Y. Yamamoto and K. Odaka, 235–254. Tokyo: Nihon Keizai Shinbunsha.

Ishii, Kanji. 2018. *Meiji Ishin Shi* [History of Meiji Restoration]. Tokyo: Kodansha. Originally published in 1989.

Ishizuka, Hiromichi. 1973. *Nihon Shihonshugi Seiritsu Shi Kenkyu* [Studies on the history of the establishment of Japanese capitalism]. Tokyo: Yoshikawa Kobunkan.

Ito, Hirobumi. 2011. Chofu Kangeikai ni oite [Speech at the reception at Chofu]. In *Ito Hirobumi Enzetsu Shu* [Selected Speeches of Ito Hirobumi], ed. K. Takii. Tokyo: Kodansha. Originally given in 1899.

Kato, Yuzo. 1988. *Kurofune Ihen* [Black Ships Incident]. Tokyo: Iwanami Shoten.

Kobayashi, Masaaki. 1977. *Nihon no Kogyoka to Kangyo Haraisage* [Japanese Industrialization and 'Meiji Privatization']. Tokyo: Toyo Keizai Shinposha.

Koyama, Hirotake. 1972. *Nihon Gunji Kogyo no Shiteki Bunseki* [Historical Analysis of Japanese Military Industry]. Tokyo: Ochanomizu Shobo.

Krugman, Paul R., Maurice Obstfeld, and Marc J. Melitz. 2015. *International Economics*, 10th ed. Harlow: Pearson.1st ed., 1993.

Kume, Kunitake. 1977–1982. *Tokumei Zenken Taishi Beio Kairan Jikki* [Real Record of Visit to America and Europe by the Ambassador Extraordinary and Plenipotentiary]. Tokyo: Iwanami Shoten. Originally published in 1878.

MacFarlane, Alan. 2011. *Secrets of the Modern World: Yukichi Fukuzawa*. Milton Keynes: Nimble Books.

Maeda, Mitsuyo. 1988. Chokusetsu Boueki Iken Ippan [An Opinion upon the Direct Trade]. In *Keizai Koso* [Economic Ideas], ed. M. Nakamura, K. Ishii, and Y. Kasuga, 75–81. Tokyo: Iwanami Shoten. Originally written in 1879.

Miyajima, Hideki. 2004. *Sangyo Seisaku to Kigyo Touchi no Keizai Shi* [Economic History of Industrial Policy and Corporate Governance]. Tokyo: Yuhikaku.

Nakamura, Tamotsu. 1990. Macro Keizai to Sengo Keiei [Macro economy and post-Sino-Japanese-war economic policy]. In *Sangyoka no Jidai* [The Age of Industrialization], vol. 2, ed. S. Nishikawa and Y. Yamamoto, 1–36. Tokyo: Iwanami Shoten.

Nakanishi, Hiroshi. 1982/1983/2003. *Nihon Kindaika no Kiso Katei* [Fundamental Process of Japanese Modernization]. Tokyo: Tokyo Daigaku Shuppankai.

Nishikawa, Nagao. 1995. Asia to Sekai no Sai-Hakken [Re-discovery of Asia and the world]. In *Beio Kairan Jikki wo Yomu* [Reading 'Real Record of Visit to America and Europe'], ed. N. Nishikawa and H. Matsumiya, 371–401. Kyoto: Hohritsu Bunka Sha.

Nishikawa, Shunsaku, and Takeshi Abe. 1990. Gaisetsu [Overview]. In *Sangyoka no Jidai* [The Age of Industrialization], vol. 1, ed. S. Nishikawa and T. Abe, 1–80. Tokyo: Iwanami Shoten.

Odaka, Konosuke. 1988. Josho [Introduction]. In *Bakumatsu Meiji no Nihon Keizai* [Japanese Economy in the Late Tokugawa and Meiji Eras], ed. Y. Yamamoto and K. Odaka, 7–26. Tokyo: Nihon Keizai Shinbunsha.

Okazaki, Tetsuji, Esuke Taniyama, and Masaki Nakabayashi. 2006. Nihon ni okeru Kyodotai Kankei no Yakuwari [Role of community relation in Japan]. In *Shijo to Keizai Hatten* [Market and Economic Development], ed. Y. Sawada and T. Sonobe, 43–62. Tokyo: Toyo Keizai Shinposha.

Okubo, Toshimichi. 1988a. Syokusan Kogyo ni kansuru Kengi [Proposition of encouraging domestic industries]. In *Keizai Koso* [Economic Ideas], ed. M. Nakamura, K. Ishii, and Y. Kasuga, 16–19. Tokyo: Iwanami Shoten. Originally written in 1874.

Okubo, Toshimichi. 1988b. Kaigai Chokubai no Kigyo wo Hiraku no Gi [Proposition of establishing the national exportation company]. In *Keizai Koso* [Economic Ideas], ed. M. Nakamura, K. Ishii, and Y. Kasuga, 40–45. Tokyo: Iwanami Shoten. Originally written in 1876.

Okuma, Shigénobu. 1973. Kobusho wo Mokuru no Mune [Declaration establishing the Ministry of Industry]. In *Nihon Keizai Seisaku Shi Ron* [Studies on the History of Japanese Economic Policy], vol. 1, ed. Y. Ando, 28–29. Tokyo: Tokyo Daigaku Shuppankai. Originally written in 1870.

Okuma, Shigénobu. 1988. Shu'nyu Shisyutsu no Genryu wo Sumashi Rizai Kaikei no Konpon wo Taturu no Gi [Proposition of making clear the actual state of governmental budget and of establishing its principles]. In *Keizai*

Koso [Economic Ideas], ed. M. Nakamura, K. Ishii, and Y. Kasuga, 19–34. Tokyo: Iwanami Shoten. Originally written in 1875.

Saito, Osamu. 1992. Bakumatsu Ishin no Seiji Sanjutsu [Political arithmetic in the late Tokugawa and Meiji restoration eras]. In *Meiji Ishin no Kakushin to Renzoku* [Continuity and Change in Meiji Restoration], ed. Kindai Nihon Kenkyukai, 277–302. Tokyo: Yamakawa Shuppansha.

Sawai, Minoru. 1990. Kikai Kogyo [Machine industry]. In *Sangyoka no Jidai* [The Age of industrialization], vol. 1, ed. S. Nishikawa and T. Abe, 213–253. Tokyo: Iwanami Shoten.

Sawai, Minoru, and Masayuki Tanimoto. 2016. *Nihon Keizai Shi* [Japanese Economic History]. Tokyo: Yuhikaku.

Takeda, Haruhito. 2019. *Nihon Keizai Shi* [Japanese Economic History]. Tokyo: Yuhikaku.

Umemura, Maki. 1983. Matsukata Defure ka no Kangyo Seisaku [Industrial policy under the so-called Matsukata Deflation]. In *Matsukata Zaisei to Syokusan Kogyo Seisaku* [So-called Matsukata Fiscal Policy and the Industrial Policy], ed. M. Umemura and T. Nakamura, 239–263. Tokyo: Tokyo Daigaku Shuppankai.

Yamamuro, Shinichi. 1984. *Hosei Kanryo no Jidai* [The Age of Government Officials as Law Makers]. Tokyo: Bokutakusha.

Harking Back to the 'Golden Age' of National Economies: German Memory Narratives in Times of Economic Internationalization

Thomas Fetzer

1 Introduction

Golden age narratives are a well-established object of inquiry for memory studies scholars (Smith 1996; Mazur 2015). The study of such narratives is closely related to a broader field of analyses on political nostalgia discourses, which, in Svetlana Boym's evocative phrasing, revolve around a sense of 'homesickness' for bygone idealized times—a 'utopia oriented towards the past', powerfully nurtured by grievances about the present (Boym 2007).

Yet, golden age narratives are distinct in a number of respects: To begin with, their linkage to individual experience is of subordinate importance, as they put forward abstract and 'collectivized' portrayals of a lost 'paradise' highlighting properties such as prosperity, scientific and cultural achievement, or state power (see Mazur 2015, 231–235). The precise content of golden age narratives may of course change over time, and

T. Fetzer (✉)
Central European University, Vienna, Austria
e-mail: fetzert@ceu.edu

S. Berger and T. Fetzer (eds.), *Collective Memory of Economic Crises and Transformations*, Palgrave Macmillan Memory Studies,
https://doi.org/10.1007/978-3-032-09094-2_9

different groups may hold diverging versions of such narratives, which co-exist alongside each other in a particular society.

Moreover, while political nostalgia is rarely limited to pure escapism and has sometimes quite explicit future-oriented goals (see Atia and Davies 2010; Smith and Campbell 2017), golden age narratives are always co-defined by their political prescriptions. Their depictions of a lost past 'define an ideal, which is not so much to be resurrected [...] as to be recreated' (Smith 1996, 584). Relatedly, it is also constitutive of such narratives that they have a clear and agential account of how—and most importantly by whom—a golden age was destroyed or 'stolen', as well as a prescriptive agenda about how to reign in these adversarial forces in the future.

To date, scholarship on golden age narratives does not consider the economy as a salient realm of inquiry. While economic wealth, growth and prosperity are often mentioned as elements of golden ages, they are usually treated as generic background factors enabling what is seen as the symbolically more important processes, including territorial expansion, legal and political institution-building, or religious and cultural flourishing (see e.g., Smith 1996, 582–586). This is unsatisfactory for two main reasons.

First, conceptually, as recent work on the nationalism-economy nexus (see Berger and Fetzer 2019; Fetzer 2022) and the broader literature on cultural political economy (Best and Paterson 2010) suggest, the economy ought not to be reduced to a background condition—or an external cause—in ideational analysis. Economic thought, practices and policies are themselves continuously implicated in broader patterns of meaning making, and their analysis will therefore provide interesting insight about persistence and change of these cultural patterns. Narratives about past economic events and processes, while so far rarely systematically studied (see Kühschelm et al. 2012), are one important element in this regard.

Second, empirically, talk about a golden economic age abounds, particularly in relation to post-1945 Europe. On the one hand, this is discernible in the long-standing debate among economic historians seeking to understand the exceptionally strong growth performance of West European economies in the three decades after World War Two (Temin 2002). On the other hand, and of more relevance for the purpose of this paper, the empirical salience of golden age narratives is indirectly reflected in concerns, frequently voiced in academic and popular writing since the 1990s, that national economic traditions or 'models' were becoming endangered by relentless global market liberalization processes; in Europe, these concerns were further heightened by perceived encroachments upon these 'models' by supranational regulatory patterns. In a sense, the exponential growth of the 'varieties of capitalism' (Hall and Soskice 2001) literature since the 1990s was a response not least to such concerns, and the associated fear that economic Europeanization and globalization would entail an inexorable convergence dynamic toward the Anglo-Saxon model of capitalism. As academics and public pundits contemplated these questions, they sought to delineate the contours of nationally-specific institutions considered worthy of protection and support.

In this chapter, I probe whether these debates can be fruitfully analyzed in a memory studies perspective, which conceptualizes them as examples of golden age narratives. I use Germany as my case study—a country where post-1945 national identity has had a strong economic 'imprint' (see Müller 2005) and where debates about the existence and development of a national economic model—*Modell Deutschland*—have been particularly pronounced (see Berghahn and Vitols 2006). After a brief contextual section, the paper will map golden age discourses about the German national economy, distinguishing between three narratives that vary in their diagnosis of what constituted the core of the golden age of Germany's national economy (and how this core has been eroded), as well as in the associated political prescriptions. A final part briefly compares the German case to post-1945 Britain, which, while highlighting crucial differences in terms of chronology and themes, also points to the wider significance of economic golden age narratives.

2 National Identity and Political Economy in Post-1945 Germany

Understanding golden age narratives about Germany's economic model since the 1990s requires engagement with the complex patterns of national identity in post-1945 Germany, and the role of political economy in these identity patterns. The broader context is well-known: the catastrophic experiences of the National Socialism and World War Two, as well as the country's loss of political sovereignty and its territorial division constituted a sharp break with traditional political culture. National identity notions drawing on political and military power were thoroughly discredited, and a strong antimilitarist culture became embedded in postwar institutions, including a 'peace clause' in the FRG's constitution, while foreign policy came to be based on a 'civilian power' paradigm that focused on the promotion of peace and security through diplomacy (see Berger 1998). The break with pre-1945 German history was most acutely reflected in a successively emerging 'never again' memory culture that gave prominence to the commemoration of German World War Two crimes, especially the Holocaust, as the foundation of the new political identity of the Federal Republic (see Port 2023).

As Müller (2005) has highlighted, this transformation left a vacuum in relation to a more positive source of identification, and narratives concerned with the economy became an important element to 'fill' this vacuum. This was particularly reflected in the celebration of the 'economic miracle' of postwar reconstruction, a narrative that was later extended to more holistic notions of a German economic model. The strong economic imprint of post-1945 national identity was also discernible during the 1989/90 reunification process—not only did currency union precede political unification, but the overall yardstick to measure the subsequent success of unification strongly focused on the economic rebuilding of former East Germany (Müller 2005).

Just as such economically-centered identity notions reached their pinnacle in the 1990s, they were fundamentally challenged by wider transformations. The German economy entered a period of crisis, triggering anxious public debates about the future viability of the country's economic model. At the same time, accelerating economic internationalization put additional pressure on that model. It was against the backdrop of these challenges that narratives about a lost golden age started to emerge. In the following, I will sketch three distinct types of such narratives, focusing on their portrayals of *Modell Deutschland* and of the processes through which it is perceived to have been undermined, not least by processes of economic Europeanization and globalization.

3 The Deutschmark and the Golden Age of Stability Culture

The symbolic importance of the Deutschmark for post-1945 Germany is quite well-known and reflected in the inclusion of a relevant entry into German *lieux de memoire* volumes (see James 2001). On the level of everyday discourse and practice, its continuing salience is expressed in high levels of Deutschmark nostalgia in opinion polls and still stunningly widespread practices of shopping-related currency conversion. Taking advantage of this pattern, German supermarket and department store chains ran marketing campaigns listing products with EUR and DM prices still in the late 2010s, and at times even allowed customers to temporarily pay in Deutschmark (Siedenbiedel 2016).

In a longer historical perspective, this salience derived from the mythical association of the 1948 currency reform with a postwar 'zero hour', later 're-enacted' through the currency union preceding political reunification to mark the end of East German communism in 1990. At the same time, the Deutschmark became symbolically associated with monetary stability, as it was contrasted with the hyperinflation experiences of the interwar period. The *Bundesbank* with its overarching mandate of inflation containment and its independence from political interference was the institutional expression of this 'stability culture' (see Müller 2005, 149–154).

This is the backdrop against which the emergence of a monetary golden age narrative since the late 1990s needs to be considered. With its beginnings soon after the Euro transition, this narrative was in large part intellectually shaped by a group of German economists around key figures such as Wilhelm Hankel, Joachim Starbatty, Dirk Meyer, Bernd Lucke and Hans-Olaf Henkel, at various points seconded by political figures ranging from the Conservative Right (Peter Gauweiler) to the far Left (Oskar Lafontaine). The key theme—the alleged destruction of German monetary stability culture through the EU's supranational currency union—is easily discernible in the titles of general audience books of these protagonists—from 'Euro lie' (Hankel 2007) and 'Crime scene Euro' (Starbatty 2013), to 'Save our money – how the Euro fraud threatens our wealth' (Henkel 2010).

Differences in detail and emphasis notwithstanding, these narratives usually take the political debates about the Euro transition in the 1990s as their starting point, in particular with regard to the frequently repeated commitment of the then German government to make the Euro as stable as the Deutschmark. Indeed, the initial EMU design as set out in the 1992 Maastricht Treaty is seen—with some justification—as the transfer of the German stability culture to the EU level, chiefly expressed in the inflation-centered mandate of the European Central Bank (ECB) and the 'stability and growth pact' (SGP) committing EMU member states to a restrictive fiscal policy and a 'no-bail-out' clause (see Müller 2005, 161).

With EMU thus conceptualized as a promise to perpetuate the German monetary model, the subsequent development is then portrayed as a series of failures to live up to these promises. Initially focused on the dangers arising from the inclusion of Southern EU countries into EMU and the critique of the frequent non-compliance with SGP conditions, narratives significantly sharpened in the wake of the Greek debt crisis in the early 2010s, now chiefly concerned with how EMU rescue measures abandoned the 'no-bail-out' promise at the expense of German taxpayer interests. Subsequently, the focus further shifted to target the European Central Bank's new quantitative easing and state bond purchase programs, which were harshly criticized as hidden government funding through monetary policy and considered to illegitimately and dangerously exceed the ECB's mandate at the expense of its core task of inflation containment (Hankel 2007; Lucke 2019).

Monetary golden age narratives were not confined to these critiques, but also extensively addressed alternative policy options. Rather than simply advocating a straight return to the Deutschmark, these often sought to ensure a return to the cherished model of German stability culture in different ways; proposals included the re-introduction of national moneys as parallel currencies alongside the Euro, and the creation of a separate 'North European currency union' consisting of Germany and other 'stability-oriented' countries such as Netherlands, Finland or Austria (see Meyer 2012). However, none of these had any serious impact on political debates.

The political salience of monetary golden age narratives should nonetheless not be underestimated. On the one hand, radical critique of the EMU played a crucial role in the formation period of the newly emerging party *Alternative für Deutschland* (AfD), reflected not least in the fact that key figures such as Lucke or Henkel for a time held AfD leadership positions. Following the right-wing radicalization of the AfD in the wake of the 2015 migration crisis, most of its prominent economists left the party, and attempts to create substitute organizations ended in failure. Still, the critique of the Euro, inspired by the narrative of German stability culture, helped to put the AfD on the German party political landscape. With its emphasis on national and supranational elite betrayal it also established a key element of the populist political discourse, which AfD agendas continue to rely on to this day.

On the other hand, and still more significantly, the radical Euro critics also pushed German stability culture narratives through a series of legal cases brought to the German constitutional court, from a challenge to the SGP functioning in the late 1990s, to the legal questioning of Euro debt crisis management in the early 2010s and of the subsequent ECB state bond purchase program (see Beck 2014). While the court mostly rejected the substance of those challenges, its rulings nonetheless imposed significant constraints on German governments with regard to parliamentary rights and the scope for deviation from the stability-focused principles of initial EMU design. Indeed, in its latest 2020 ruling, the court not only questioned the constitutionality of the latest ECB bond purchase program, but also challenged the principle of the supremacy of EU law, causing a host of follow-up problems in relation to member-state acceptance of last-instance rulings by the European Court of Justice (Feld and Wieland 2021). The legacies of German monetary stability culture thus continue to be the source of major political debates about the governance of Europe's single currency.

4 The Golden Age of the Social Market Economy

While monetary stability culture narratives were rather narrow in terms of their analytical and political scope, a second golden age narrative concerned with Germany's 'social market economy' addressed a much wider set of issues and was also of a much more ambiguous and multi-faceted nature. The social market economy concept was originally developed by the so-called Freiburg ordo-liberal school, and it had mostly focused on the role of the state to ensure that markets were kept free from organized interests and power groups like cartels, in particular through competition policy and a stable regulatory framework (see Müller 2005). Over time, however, alternative interpretations emerged, which understood the 'social' in much more encompassing ways as the condition for German postwar capitalism's societal 'embeddedness' (Polanyi); these broader interpretations came to dominate political debates about the concept since the 1970s.

Such encompassing social market economy narratives—often also used synonymously with terms such as 'German capitalism', 'Germany Inc' or 'Rhenish capitalism' (Albert 1993)—came in a variety of forms associated with distinct, albeit not mutually exclusive, analytical approaches and political agendas. In particular, the 'social' could be conceptualized as a market-limiting and market-correcting realm akin to Esping-Andersen's (1990) de-commodification concept, which sees social policy's main task as making citizens' well-being less dependent on market outcomes. Alternatively, the 'social' could be interpreted more as a productive resource, which, rather than being juxtaposed to markets and economic efficiency, had a crucial function in providing the institutional foundations for economic growth and competitiveness (see Andersson 2004).

Golden age narratives related to the social market economy concept started to emerge in the 1990s when the German economy was exposed to the double challenge of reunification and accelerated European market integration, while economic globalization processes were frequently portrayed as an inexorable dynamic pushing national institutions toward convergence on global 'best practices'. This triggered debates about the sustainability of the German model, which temporarily culminated in the *Standort Deutschland* debate of the late 1990s (see Rehder 2003), but periodically recurred thereafter.

Against this backdrop, narratives about Germany's post-1945 economic model unfolded with the typical golden age ambiguity: The legacy of 'Rhenish capitalism' was defended as the 'endearing variant of real existing market economies', characterized by the reconciliation of a liberal economic order with an extensive welfare state and comparatively limited income inequality (Hassel 2006, 200), while, at the same time, this legacy was portrayed as an endangered species under threat from accelerated regional and global economic liberalization. This was reflected in publication titles like 'German capitalism: Does it exist? Can it survive?' (Streeck 1997), or 'German economic order – from role model to outdated?' (Beyer 2003).

Given their broad scope, narratives about the 'social market economy' or 'German capitalism' were multifaceted and came in numerous shades, which cannot be comprehensively reviewed here. For illustration purposes, I confine myself to two influential accounts by Werner Abelshauser and Wolfang Streeck, which reflect the above-mentioned distinction in the conceptualization of the 'social' as a market-correcting realm, or, alternatively, as a productive resource.

Abelshauser's perspective is that of an economic and business historian chiefly interested in the social and political embeddedness of German corporations. In this perspective, the German model is grounded in production structures designed to succeed in world markets for diversified quality products, requiring stable and cooperative relations with internal and external stakeholders, as well as a long-term entrepreneurial decision-making horizon. Accordingly, key elements of the model relate to supplier networks based on coordination, rather than arms-length competition, close and long-term company-bank linkages (rather than short-term financing through capital markets), an elaborate vocational training system to ensure the supply of skilled workforces, as well as worker participation schemes to address 'principal-agent' dilemmas through cooperative workplace relations (see Abelshauser 2001).

According to Abelshauser, accelerated contemporary globalization endangers precisely these pillars of the German production model, as its long-term and cooperative constitution is increasingly criticized as hampering firms' flexible adjustment and innovation capacities, questioning corporate governance structures, vocational training and industrial relations regimes alike. With particular emphasis on systemic competition from the American model of liberal capitalism, Abelshauser portrays the German production regime as being engaged in a continuous 'struggle of economic cultures'—with uncertain outcome (Abelshauser 2006).

Political scientist Wolfgang Streeck, on the other hand, conceptualizes the core elements of Germany's post-1945 economic order as the reflection of a broader, yet temporary social and political compromise between competing group and class interests, which tamed capitalism in a Polanyian counter-movement dynamic. In this perspective, firms are constrained by broader socio-economic institutions, and the potential of such institutions to become a productive resource is often driven by adjustment rather than choice. German industrial relations institutions, to take the clearest example, were based on a historical compromise between capital and organized labor, and German firms' competitive strength in diversified quality production was institutionally 'coerced' through the product and skill upgrading pressure exercised by the high-wage regime resulting from this capital-labor compromise in the 1970s and 1980s (see Streeck 1997, 2009).

Accordingly, the erosion of the German model since the 1990s is seen as driven by growing disquiet about the accumulating costs and obligations of the model for German capital, in particular following reunification. In this context, accelerated internationalization provided capital with new options for 'exit' to circumvent or altogether escape these constraints. At the same time, these new 'exit' options could also be used to put pressure on workers and trade unions through concession bargaining, as reflected in the numerous firm-level 'pacts for competitiveness' concluded since the late 1990s and early 2000s. 'For German firms, becoming more international [...] offered a promising way out of some of the increasingly uncomfortable constraints forced on them within Germany' (Streeck 2009, 197).

It is important to note that narratives about national socio-economic models, including the anxiety about their contemporary demise, are not something that is unique to post-1945 Germany—witness similar currents on the Left in Scandinavia (see Trägårdh 2002) or the UK (see below). Indeed, in comparative perspective, the political salience of 'Rhenish' capitalism memories may seem rather limited; the *Aufstehen* project for a new political movement, for example, co-founded by Wolfgang Streeck himself, attracted rather little resonance.

Yet, it would be a mistake to underestimate the impact of golden age narratives concerned with Germany's post-1945 social market economy model, as that impact, against the broader backdrop of the Europeanization of German collective identity, can also be discerned in the sustained attempts to 'upload' German concepts to the EU level, not least through the long-standing debates about the 'European social model' (see Fetzer 2018). The dynamic of this 'uploading' unfolds in complex ways. On the one hand, these legacies make German actors, especially those on the center-left, committed to create EU-level policies, which appear to replicate cherished national traditions. On the other hand, narratives of the European social model always carry a double meaning related to the role of EU institutions—as protecting social rights enshrined in member states, while simultaneously also promoting a new supranational regulatory framework. The balancing between these two objectives varies over time and across policy fields, yet always includes a dimension focusing on the purely defensive use of supranational frameworks to protect national practices (see Fetzer 2018). Thus, the political salience of German model narratives is expressed at once in the principled commitment to its re-imagination at the EU level, but also in the limitations placed upon the degree to which supranational regulation is deemed necessary to complement the national model.

5 The Golden Age of Productive Capital

A third golden age narrative related to Germany's national economy is rooted in ideologies of economic populism and 'producerism', positing a juxtaposition between a virtuous cross-class community of 'producers' and a group of exploitative 'parasites', chiefly made up of idle rentiers and financial capital, as well as the political elites supporting their interests (see Loeffler 2017). Typically, this juxtaposition also implies a national 'insider/outsider' dichotomy when 'parasitic elites' are associated with 'alien' actors or values—thus inserting nationalist *topoi* into populist ideology along the lines conceptualized by Rogers Brubaker (2020).

While producerism made deep inroads into progressive and labor movements in the United States since the early nineteenth century (see Breiner 2017), its political significance in Western Europe started to unfold only in the interwar period when it was appropriated by fascist and antisemitic ideologies (see Abromeit 2017). This was particularly evident in the German case where producerism played an important role in the rise of national socialism; Hitler's *Mein Kampf* specifically refers to Feder's propagandistic juxtaposition between 'productive' ('schaffendes') and 'speculative' ('raffendes') capital as a key foundation of NS ideology (see Loeffler 2017, 269–272).

The contemporary renaissance of producerism and its discursive association with golden age narratives of the national economy needs to be considered not only against the backdrop of the secular shift from industrial to digitalizing service economies, but also in light of 'financialization' as a core dynamic of accelerated globalization since the 1990s (Krippner 2005). In contrast to other world regions where these narratives became associated with a wide range of political forces across the Left–Right spectrum, producerism remained predominantly tied to the extreme Right in Western Europe (see Ivaldi and Mazzoleni 2019). In Germany, key protagonists are figures associated with the right-wing thinktank *Institut fur Staatspolitik* and the *Antaios* publishing group, as well as the weekly journal *Junge Freiheit*—all of which are more or less closely connected to the AfD (see Kellershohn et al. 2019).

To explore such far-right producerist narratives in more detail, it is useful to consider the writings of one of its key voices, the journalist and editor Jürgen Elsässer. Dubbed as the 'German Steven Bannon' (*Der Spiegel*) and with a political biography reminiscent of some early twentieth century fascists transitioning from the radical Left to the radical

Right, Elsässer became publicly notorious in 2009 through his call for a 'people's initiative against the dictatorship of finance capital'. In it, he postulates an economic war of international, Anglo-American finance capital against productive national economies in continental Europe and the BRICS countries, carried out chiefly by London and New-York based global banks and hedge funds, which, like a locust plague, descend on well-established productive firms through take-over and asset-stripping strategies (Elsässer 2009a).

This martial rhetoric is tied to a nostalgic golden age narrative about *Deutschland AG* with its close-knit corporate governance network, in which banks served, rather than dominated the 'real' value-producing economy. This model is portrayed as facing its demise, as continuous financial market liberalization measures have acted as a 'locust attraction program'. Domestic interest groups abetting these liberalization measures—not least the '*Anti-Deutsche Bank*'—are singled out for their betrayal of German traditions and their explicit agenda of 'de-Germanizing' the economic order of the Federal Republic (Elsässer 2009b, 65–73). Appealing to a coalition of workers, middle classes and industrial capital, far-right political agendas seek to remedy the demise of *Deutschland AG* through bank nationalizations and the re-imposition of national regulation of financial markets (see Elsässer 2009a)—radical programs that have so far found little political support. And yet, the influence of far-right narratives should nonetheless not be underestimated for two reasons.

On the one hand, the critique of financial globalization and the associated juxtaposition between 'productive' and 'unproductive' economic sectors has wider resonance in Germany, not least because it can be easily linked to traditional concepts of 'German quality work' and to the social market economy narrative outlined earlier. Indeed, the 'locust' metaphor was coined by then-SPD chairman Franz Müntefering in 2005. Further to the Left, prominent public figures like Sahra Wagenknecht advocate for a reform of the incorporation law that would protect 'productive property' (*Leistungseigentum*), while clamping down on property derived from financial market rents (see Wagenknecht 2021).

On the other hand, the German far-right makes conscious attempts to exploit this broader resonance to infiltrate the political mainstream through what lead ideologists like Götz Kubischek label a 'normalization patriotism' strategy (see Kellershohn et al. 2019). Elsässer and like-minded pundits regularly invoke Müntefering or former chancellor

Helmut Schmidt's verdict of 'predatory capitalism' to underpin their radical critique of financial globalization (see Elsässer 2009a, 18–19), while agendas for the transition from global capitalism to a production-centered market economy also seek to tap into environmentalist political resources. In turn, such strategies of mainstream infiltration can be seen as crucial elements in the strengthening of the position of the AfD in the contemporary German political system.

6 A Comparative Vignette: Post-1945 Britain

While it is beyond the scope of this contribution to engage in systematic cross-country comparisons, a brief vignette on post-1945 Britain provides interesting insights on how to place Germany in a wider European perspective. On the one hand, the British case likewise highlights the political salience of economic golden age narratives, including linkages to debates about international economic integration. On the other hand, however, given different historical legacies (devoid of the extreme German World War Two watershed) and post-1945 political dynamics, this salience found expression through very different themes and played out earlier and in two distinct periods separated by the transformation unleashed by Thatcherism during the 1980s.

The contrasting chronology is easily explained. While the postwar *Wirtschaftswunder* period forms the essential golden age backdrop against which the anxious debates of the 1990s and 2000s unfolded in Germany, there was no equivalent in the UK; indeed, by contrast, the 1960s and 1970s mark a peak in debates about the country's alleged economic decline. This was not because Britain did not participate in the wider European postwar economic growth dynamic, but because of the relative UK backsliding in comparison to the faster growing countries on the continent, not least West Germany (see Coates 1994). The strong emphasis on relative decline gave these debates their specific cultural significance, which later observers aptly captured through the notion of 'declinism' (Tomlinson 1996) and which, from a memory studies perspective, is best interpreted as tied to golden age narratives. On the one hand, there was the mythical vision of Britain as the industrial 'workshop of the world' whose preeminence was now perceived to have vanished; tellingly, much of the debate focused on the performance of the manufacturing sector, with the automobile industry frequently being singled out for particular scrutiny—if *Volkswagen* symbolically stood for West Germany's postwar rise, the fate of British Leyland, heir of the traditional Morris and Austin brands, encapsulated British decline (Whisler 1999). On the other hand, relative economic decline vis-à-vis continental Europe also fitted badly with the collective memory of Britain's 'finest hour' during World War Two, as quintessentially expressed by Thatcher prior to her 1979 election victory: 'I can't bear Britain in decline. I just can't. We who either defeated or rescued half Europe, who kept half Europe free, when otherwise it would be in chains. And look at us now' (Thatcher 1979).

Much like German debates in the 1990s and 2000s, earlier 'declinism' controversies in the UK featured multiple and often contrasting narratives about 'what had gone wrong'; influential interpretations ranged from diagnoses of a long-lasting productivity shortfall and the failure of Keynesian demand management policies, to more structural explanations that focused on a supposedly damaging tradition of 'adversarial pluralism' and the fragmentation of Britain's economic institutions, which had not had to undergo the radical shocks experienced in many continental European countries after 1945 (see Coates 1994; Kitson 2004). A particularly fierce controversy raged over the 'trade union question', as organized labor sought to defend its role as the age-proven 'social conscience' of British industrialization against attacks from business and the political Right that portrayed union militancy and strikes—frequently labeled as the 'British disease'—as the root cause of the UK's economic problems (see Fetzer 2012, chap. 3). Here, as elsewhere, these debates were directly connected to party political contestation, as Labour and Conservatives both deployed versions of 'declinism' to bolster their political agendas (Tomlinson 1996).

Britain's integration into the international economy played a crucial role for these debates on two levels. First, it constituted the backdrop for the political salience of the performance comparisons that gave credence to 'declinist' narratives; publicly debated 'benchmarking' between subsidiaries within single multinational firms illustrated such dynamics particularly well (Fetzer 2012, 60–64). Second, decline controversies were also connected to debates about Britain's membership in the European Common Market, which went on from the first failed accession bid in the early 1960s to the 1975 referendum. While most on the political Right successively came to see UK membership as a necessary alternative trading framework to reverse decline and compensate for the loss of empire, a thorough split ran through the Labour Party, as left factions recurrently adopted anti-accession agendas (Fetzer 2012, 56–57).

Thatcherism fundamentally transformed the overall terms of this debate. While the UK's growth performance in the 1980s and 1990s did not match that of the 1950s and was characterized by significant volatility, the relative decline vis-à-vis major continental economies was reversed, and core tenets of Thatcher's liberalization agenda were not challenged even during the 'New Labour' governments of the 2000s. In the process, the mainstream view of British post-1945 economic history significantly changed—today, diagnoses of decline are mostly confined to the troubled 1970s, which are demarcated from an earlier post-war growth period and a subsequent 'reboot' under neoliberal auspices (see e.g., Goodwin 2023).

However, this did not mean the end of political contestation, but rather shifted debates to new terrain, including refashioned golden age narratives. On the Left, the economic reset brought by the Thatcher governments from 1979 was charged to have introduced structural flaws into the UK's economic system through financialization and the increased influence of the City of London, as well as through the acceleration of deindustrialization that is held to have vastly increased regional and income inequalities; moreover, Thatcher's reforms are also identified with the weakening of the postwar welfare state (Dorey 2015). These assessments went hand in hand with a new emphasis on the early postwar golden age that had promoted a vision of prosperity and social cohesion. Such notions became especially pronounced in the post-Brexit period—Keir Starmer, Labour Party chairman since 2020, frequently invoked the boldness of the Labour government in rebuilding a battered United Kingdom on the basis of economic growth and a welfare state in the late 1940s (Merrick 2021).

On the Right, the main direction of the further development of Thatcher's legacy turned out to be her 1988 Bruges speech, in which she had argued against the vision of an 'ever closer' supranational Europe. Subsequently, this became a key reference in the debates about Britain's EU membership in the Conservative Party, which, in the new millennium, radicalized into the heated controversy about Brexit. In the process, there was a successive reversal of the positions adopted during the Common Market membership debate of the 1960s and 1970s: Those who clung to the traditional notion of Britain's EU membership as a crucial economic lifeline after empire slowly lost ground to a rival position that turned the argument on its head, asserting that the UK's economic potential was restricted through EU membership, and that the country should instead return to its nineteenth century role as the erstwhile (imperial) promoter of global trade and commerce—a twenty first century narrative harking back to a golden age of Britain as a 'free trade nation' (Trentmann 2008). Ever since the Brexit referendum campaign, this vision has been promoted not only by the Tory Right, but also by the rapidly growing right populist movements such as the UK Independence Party or, later, Reform UK, which, much as AfD in Germany, drew on economic memory narratives as part of their wider agendas of radical political transformation.

7 Conclusions

Academic debates on the relationship between collective memory narratives and internationalization/globalization mostly focus on whether cultural memory patterns are bound to erode due to convergence dynamics, and/or whether we can observe the emergence of a transnational, cosmopolitan memory framework (see Assmann 2010; de Cesari and Rigney 2014). Debates about golden age memory narratives very much conform to this paradigm. What I have sought to demonstrate here, however, is that internationalization can have the paradoxical effect of reigniting golden age narratives in precisely the realm where it is supposed to have its greatest convergence effect: the economy. At the same time, the chapter has also highlighted that such narratives are not mere nostalgia but can have significant political consequences.

Germany no doubt constitutes a peculiar case in this regard, not least because of the disappearance of large segments of pre-1945 cultural and political memory narratives and the associated potential for economic imaginaries to fill this 'memory void'. However, as the brief comparative reflections on post-1945 Britain demonstrate, there is no German exceptionalism here—even if UK patterns indicate that these memory dynamics always play out in country-specific ways and chronologies. Indeed, 'Golden Age' narratives with a strong economic dimension can be found far beyond Europe, as evident in 'Make America Great Again' Trumpism in the United States (Campbell 2018) or in 'Chinese Dream' imaginaries harking back to a past China-centred world order (Callahan 2013). Against this backdrop, it would be worthwhile for future research to systematically analyze similarities and differences of such narratives in a broader comparative perspective, as well as to explore transnational entanglements between them.

Acknowledgements I would like to thank James Dunne, Central European University, Doctoral School of Political Science, for extensive research support.

References

Abelshauser, Werner. 2001. Umbruch und Persistenz: Das deutsche Produktionsregime in historischer Perspektive. *Geschichte und Gesellschaft* 27 (4): 503–523.

Abelshauser, Werner. 2006. Der Rheinische Kapitalismus im Kampf der Wirtschaftskulturen. In *Gibt es einen deutschen Kapitalismus? Tradition und globale Perspektiven der sozialen Marktwirtschaft*, ed. Volker Berghahn and Sigurt Vitols, 186–199. Frankfurt/New York: Campus.

Abromeit, John. 2017. Transformations of producerist populism in Western Europe. In *Transformations of Populism in Europe and the Americas: History and Recent Tendencies*, ed. John Abromeit, et al., 231–264. London: Bloomsbury.

Albert, Michel. 1993. *Capitalism vs. Capitalism: How America's Obsession with Individual Achievement and Short-Term Profit Has Led It to the Brink of Collapse*. New York: Basic Books.

Andersson, Jenny. 2004. A productive social citizenship? Reflections on the concept of productive social policies in the European tradition. In *A European Social Citizenship? Preconditions for Future Policies from a Historical Perspective*, ed. Lars Magnusson and Bo Stråth, 69–88. Brussels: Peter Lang.

Assmann, Jan. 2010. Globalization, universalism, and the erosion of cultural memory. In *Memory in a Global Age: Discourses, Practices and Trajectories*, ed. Aleida Assmann and Sebastian Conrad, 121–129. Basingstoke: Palgrave Macmillan.

Atia, Nadia, and Jeremy Davies. 2010. Nostalgia and the shapes of history. *Memory Studies* 3 (3): 181–186.

Beck, Gunnar. 2014. The Court of Justice, the Bundesverfassungsgericht and legal reasoning during the Euro crisis: The rule of law as a fair-weather phenomenon. *European Public Law* 20 (3): 539–566.

Berger, Thomas. 1998. *Cultures of Antimilitarism: National Security in Germany and Japan*. Baltimore: Johns Hopkins University Press.

Berger, Stefan, and Thomas Fetzer, eds. 2019. *Nationalism and the Economy: Explorations into a Neglected Relationship*. Budapest: Central European University Press.

Berghahn, Volker, and Sigurt Vitols, eds. 2006. *Gibt es einen deutschen Kapitalismus? Tradition und globale Perspektiven der sozialen Marktwirtschaft*. Frankfurt/New York: Campus.

Best, Jacqueline, and Matthew Paterson. 2010. Introduction: Understanding cultural political economy. In *Cultural Political Economy*, ed. Jacqueline Best and Matthew Paterson, 1–25. London/New York: Routledge.

Beyer, Jürgen., ed. 2003. *Vom Zukunfts- zum Auslaufmodell? Die deutsche Wirtschaftsordnung im Wandel*. Wiesbaden: Westdeutscher Verlag.

Boym, Svetlana. 2007. Nostalgia and its discontents. *Hedgehog Review* 9(2).

Breiner, Peter. 2017. 'Ideologies of economic populism in America and their subversion by the Right'. In *Transformations of populism in Europe and the Americas: History and recent tendencies*, ed. John Abromeit et al. 308–329. London: Bloomsbury.

Brubaker, Rogers. 2020. Populism and nationalism. *Nations and Nationalism* 26 (1): 44–66.

Callahan, William A. 2013. *China Dreams: Twenty Visions for the Future*. Oxford: Oxford University Press.

Campbell, John. 2018. *American Discontent: The Rise of Donald Trump and the Decline of the Golden Age*. Oxford: Oxford University Press.

Coates, David. 1994. *The Question of UK Decline: The Economy, State and Society*. London: Harvester-Wheatsheaf.

De Cesari, Chiara, and Ann Rigney. 2014. Introduction. In *Transnational Memory: Circulation, Articulation, Scales*, ed. Chiara de Cesari and Ann Rigney, 1–21. Berlin: De Gruyter.

Dorey, Pete. 2015. A farewell to alms: Thatcherism's legacy of inequality. *British Politics* 10 (1): 79–98.

Elsässer, Jürgen. 2009a. *Gegen Finanzdiktatur: Die Volksinitiative – Grundsätze, Konzepte, Ziele*. Berlin: Compact.

Elsässer, Jürgen. 2009b. *Nationalstaat und Globalisierung. Als Linker vor der Preußischen Gesellschaft*. Waltrop: Manuscriptum.

Esping-Andersen, Gøsta. 1990. *The Three Worlds of Welfare Capitalism*. Oxford: Polity.

Feld, Lars P., and Volker Wieland. 2021. 'The German Federal Constitutional Court Ruling and the European Central Bank's Strategy'. *Journal of Financial Regulation* 7 (2): 217–253.

Fetzer, Thomas. 2012. *Paradoxes of Internationalization: British and German Trade Unions at Ford and General Motors 1967–2000*. Manchester: Manchester University Press.

Fetzer, Thomas. 2018. Die Gewerkschaften und die Debatte über das europäische Sozialmodell. In *Zwischen Institutionalisierung und Abwehrkampf: Internationale Gewerkschaftspolitik im Prozess der europäischen*

Integration, ed. Johannes Kiess and Martin Seliger, 85–102. Frankfurt/Main: Campus.

Fetzer, Thomas. 2022. Beyond "economic nationalism": Towards a new research agenda for the study of nationalism in political economy. *Journal of International Relations and Development* 35: 235–259.

Goodwin, James. 2023. *Values, Voice and Virtue: The New British Politics*. London: Penguin.

Hall, Peter, and David Soskice, eds. 2001. *Varieties of Capitalism: The Institutional Foundations of Comparative Advantage*. Oxford: Oxford University Press.

Hankel, Wilhelm. 2007. *Die Euro-Lüge ... und andere volkswirtschaftliche Märchen*. Vienna: Signum.

Hassel, Anke. 2006. Die Schwächen des deutschen Kapitalismus. In *Gibt es einen deutschen Kapitalismus?*, eds. Volker Berghahn and Sigurt Vitols, 200–214. Frankfurt/New York: Campus.

Henkel, Hans-Olaf. 2010. *Rettet unser Geld: Wie der Euro-Betrug unseren Wohlstand gefährdet*. Munich: Heyne Verlag.

Ivaldi, Gilles, and Oscar Mazzoleni. 2019. Economic populism and producerism: European right-wing parties in transatlantic perspective. *Populism* 2 (1): 1–28.

James, Harold. 2001. Die D-Mark. In *Deutsche Erinnerungsorte*, vol. 2, ed. Etienne Francois and Hagen Schulze, 145–155. Munich: Beck.

Kellershohn, Helmut, et al., eds. 2019. *Zwischen Neoliberalismus und völkischem Antikapitalismus: Sozial- und wirtschaftspolitische Konzepte und Debatten innerhalb der AfD und der neuen Rechten*. Münster: Unrast Verlag.

Kitson, Michael. 2004. Failure followed by success or success followed by failure? A re-examination of british economic growth since 1949. In *The Cambridge Economic History of Modern Britain*, vol. 3, ed. Roderick Floud and Paul Johnson, 145–167. Cambridge: Cambridge University Press.

Krippner, Greta. 2005. The financialization of the American economy. *Socio-Economic Review* 3 (2): 173–208.

Kühschelm, Oliver, et al. 2012. *Konsum und Nation: Zur Geschichte nationalisierender Inszenierungen in der Produktkommunikation*. Bielefeld: transcript.

Loeffler, Mark. 2017. Populists and parasites: On producerist reason. In *Transformations of Populism in Europe and the Americas*, ed. John Abromeit, et al., 265–294. London: Bloomsbury.

Lucke, Bernd. 2019. *Systemausfall: Europa, Deutschland und die AfD – Warum wir von Krise zu Krise taumeln und wie wir den Problemstau lösen*. Munich: Finanzbuch Verlag.

Mazur, Liudmila. 2015. Golden age mythology and the nostalgia of catastrophes in post-Soviet Russia. *Canadian Slavonic Papers* 57 (3–4): 213–238.

Merrick, Rob. 2021. Keir Starmer to vow to be as bold as Labour in 1945, amid rising criticism of his leadership. *The Independent*, 17 February. https://www.independent.co.uk/news/uk/politics/keir-starmer-labour-attlee-covid-b1803524.html. Last accessed on 22 July 2025.

Meyer, Dirk. 2012. *Euro-Krise: Austritt als Lösung?* Münster: LIT Verlag.

Müller, Klaus. 2005. Nationalist undercurrents in German economic liberalism. In *Economic Nationalism in a Globalizing World*, ed. Eric Helleiner and Andreas Pickel, 141–163. Ithaca: Cornell University Press.

Port, Andrew. 2023. *Never Again: Germans and Genocide After the Holocaust*. Cambridge, MA: Belknap Press.

Rehder, Britta. 2003. *Betriebliche Bündnisse für Arbeit in Deutschland: Mitbestimmung und Flächentarifvertrag im Wandel*. Frankfurt/M.: Campus.

Siedenbiedel, Christian. 2016. 'Eine Kiste Bier für zwanzig D-Mark', Frankfurter Allgemeine Zeitung, 5 January 2016. https://www.faz.net/aktuell/finanzen/pro-finanzen/geld-ausgeben/bei-kaufland-kann-man-seit-jahresbeginn-mit-d-mark-zahlen-13998852.html

Smith, Anthony D. 1996. The LSE Centennial Lecture: The resurgence of nationalism? Myth and memory in the renewal of nations. *British Journal of Sociology* 47 (4): 575–598.

Smith, Laurajane, and Gary Campbell. 2017. Nostalgia for the future: Memory, nostalgia and the politics of class. *International Journal of Heritage Studies* 23 (7): 612–627.

Starbatty, Joachim. 2013. *Tatort Euro: Bürger, schützt das Recht, die Demokratie und eure Vermögen*. Munich: Europa Verlag.

Streeck, Wolfgang. 1997. German capitalism: Does it exist? Can it survive? *New Political Economy* 2 (2): 237–256.

Streeck, Wolfgang. 2009. *Re-forming Capitalism: Institutional Change in the German Political Economy*. Oxford: Oxford University Press.

Temin, Peter. 2002. The golden age of European growth reconsidered. *European Review of Economic History* 6 (1): 3–22.

Thatcher, Margaret. 1979. TV interview for BBC Campaign '79. Margaret Thatcher Foundation. https://www.margaretthatcher.org/document/103864.

Tomlinson, Jim. 1996. Inventing 'decline': The falling behind of the British economy in the postwar years. *The Economic History Review* 49 (4): 731–757.

Trägårdh, Lars. 2002. Sweden and the EU: Welfare state nationalism and the spectre of "Europe." In *European Integration and National Identity: The Challenge of the Nordic States*, ed. Lene Hansen and Ole Wæver, 130–181. London/New York: Routledge.

Trentmann, Frank. 2008. *Free Trade Nation: Commerce, Consumption and Civil Society in Modern Britain*. Oxford: Oxford University Press.

Wagenknecht, Sahra. 2021. *Die Selbstgerechten: Mein Gegenprogramm – für Gemeinsinn und Zusammenhalt*. Frankfurt/New York: Campus.

Whisler, Timothy R. 1999. *The British Motor Industry 1945–1994: A Case Study of Industrial Decline*. Oxford: Oxford University Press.

Conclusions: Mapping the Economy/Memory Nexus—Themes and Future Agendas

Stefan Berger and Thomas Fetzer

When we look at the sum total of the previous eight substantive chapters of this volume, with our lead questions in mind that we put to all our contributors, what then emerges in this volume about the economy/memory nexus that stood at the heart of all the contributions assembled here? First, we will reflect on who were the carriers of memory narratives in the case studies discussed here. Which actors and institutions have we identified as key ones in the economy/memory nexus? And how do their memory narratives help the political management of economic transformations? How do they acquire political salience? Secondly, drawing on the chapters of this volume, we will examine when and how economic crises and transformations produce memory narratives. Which power relationships underpin economic memory narratives? How prominent was the

S. Berger (✉)
Institute for Social Movements, Ruhr University Bochum, Bochum, Germany
e-mail: stefan.berger@ruhr-uni-bochum.de

T. Fetzer
Central European University, Vienna, Austria
e-mail: fetzert@ceu.edu

S. Berger and T. Fetzer (eds.), *Collective Memory of Economic Crises and Transformations*, Palgrave Macmillan Memory Studies,
https://doi.org/10.1007/978-3-032-09094-2_10

construction of earlier crises as lessons from which to learn in the present, in order to forge a better future? Thirdly, and finally, we will offer some thoughts on which concepts of memory are usefully employed in the analysis of the economy/memory nexus. In the last part of the conclusions, we will then proceed to reflect on the implications of our findings for the future of studies seeking to explore the economy/memory nexus. Here we identify some of the potentially fruitful themes and areas in which more research is needed.

1 Who Are the Carriers of Economic Memory Narratives?

It is striking to note the variety of key actors and institutions engaged in producing memories on economic events and processes. They range from journalists, charity representatives, economists and nation-builders to intellectuals, academics, artists, film-makers, novelists and creative writers, politicians, entrepreneurs, industrialists, bankers, trade unionists, representatives of religions, preservationists and other heritage actors, social movements and a whole host of civil society actors. All of these actors had a strong local base, but they were also often regional and national figures and institutions, and in some cases transnational ones, like (neo) imperial or European (EU) ones. Overwhelmingly they were presentist in orientation. In other words, they sought to mobilize the past, in order to legitimate their vision of the future in contemporary debates about the relationship between past, present and future. As Kühschelm argues in his chapter, 'returning to history' was an important motivating thought for bankers in Austria to invest in East-Central and South-Eastern Europe after the collapse of communism, as memories of the Habsburg empire were mobilized to envision a transnational future for banking in the region. He also highlights the importance of personal (transnational) memory in wider collective memory discourses, as his main memory actor, Pohnitzer, comes from an expellee family in Southern Moravia that had to settle in Austria after the Second World War. An economic rationale that partly preceded the collapse of communism, namely to enlarge the Austrian home market for banking, merged here with the personal desire to recover lost homelands and contribute to a peaceful reconstitution of violent memory landscapes dominating the memory of the first half of the twentieth century. However, with larger economic players, like Austria's Erste Bank of Vienna, also involved in this game of expansion, history and memory became mere branding exercises, where memory served primarily as a resource to frame corporate historical discourses meant to justify greater business profits. Vodotyka's chapter shows, in a similar vein, how a new capitalist order in post-independence Ukraine is making use of a benign paternalist memory of Ukrainian entrepreneurs before the incorporation of the country into the Soviet Union.

Other memory narratives discussed in this volume celebrate industrial modernity in places as diverse as the Ukraine, Poland, Germany and Britain. It found expression in concrete memorials (some of them even 'knighted' as UNESCO world heritage) and, more widely, in impressive memorial landscapes often celebrating industrial pasts. However, given the legacies of industrial modernity for the Anthropocene, these memorial landscapes sometimes also carry an ambiguity which turns memorials of pride into memorials of shame reminding their visitors of the destruction of ecological biospheres that accompanied industrialization. Similarly, the memorial languages around hunger crises appeal to a shameful past but also one on which diverse forms of 'victimhood nationalism' could be erected (Lim 2025), i.e., a form of nationalism that is based on remembering the (national) victims of past struggles for an independent nation state. In some respects, a 'crisis' could also always be remembered as an 'opportunity'. In all of the preceding chapters we have seen how diverse political ambitions were justified by their promoters by looking toward memory and how they invariably used the past in order to legitimate their present political programmes. Heritage as memorial landscapes has therefore been deeply intertwined with the search for 'practical pasts' (White 2014) which were used to justify future ambitions. The vilification of 'enforced' industrialization in post-communist Armenia and Lithuania as well as the importance of economic golden age narratives in post-reunification Germany for the strong economic self-identification of Germans are good examples for the construction of such 'practical pasts'. Thus, to stick with the latter example discussed in Fetzer's chapter, Deutschmark nostalgia was linked to monetary stability and tied to Euroscepticism in the memory landscapes of post-Euro Germany. Memories of the social market economy were tied to visions of the social embeddedness of capitalism and justified an anti-globalization discourse on the center left. Memories of the golden age of 'productive capital' were juxtaposed to finance capitalism as lecherous thus indicating a preference for the future development of capitalism. Comparing the German economic memory landscapes with the British ones, Fetzer also highlights how debates surrounding Britain as sick man of Europe in the 1970s could be contrasted to a previous proud memory of Britain having been the workshop of the world in the industrial revolution feeding directly into anti-EU sentiments which argued that the latter restricted British economic potential—an important argument in the successful Brexit referendum of 2016.

2 When and How Do Economic Crises and Transformations Produce Memory Narratives?

Long-term economic processes like economic decline, or sudden events, such as the Wall Street crash, or Black Monday, are both capable of generating powerful memory narratives. The economic opening up of Eastern Europe after 1990 and its accompanying entrepreneurial adventurism was based on specific memory landscapes of communism and itself produced memoryscapes that influenced reactions toward the specific ways in which such 'opening' to capitalism was accomplished. There are also what we might term existentialist events, such as hunger crises, which have become powerful collective memoryscapes, be it for particular social classes, or specific nation states. We can also see in many of the chapters collected in this volume how the memory of economic crises and transformations competes and interacts with alternative pasts, social, political and cultural that can be re-enforcing economic memoryscapes but can also constitute an alternative to them. Thus, the recovery of national memory in post-Communist states often meant forgetting about industrial pasts. In the memory politics of the Federal Republic of Germany, the memory of the hunger years after 1945 as part and parcel of a memory of victimhood in Germany was overshadowed from the 1980s onwards by the memory of German perpetratorship which continues to stand in considerable tension with a memory of victimhood, especially as the latter is often exploited by the far right (Niven 2006). In Japan, the strong connection between economic modernization and imperial ambitions before 1945 had to be recast in the post-Second-World-War memory landscape so as to fit with the new Cold War Order.

In the Cold War, economic memoryscapes were closely bound up with capitalism and communism respectively and their diverse attempts to justify their respective power relationships. In the liberal-democratic capitalist west the power of capital produced memory landscapes justifying its economic and political order and putting immense resources behind these efforts, as they were continuously challenged by anti-capitalist groups seeking to forge alternative futures out of a critical memory of capitalist pasts. Where capitalism developed under dictatorships, these oppositional memory activists could only operate underground or in exile. Under communism, the 'dictatorship of the proletariat'—meaning the dictatorship of the alleged party of the proletariat—produced memory landscapes based on an idealized struggle of the working class against their 'oppressors' resulting in the coming of communism. Given that these memoryscapes tended to be far less convincing than the capitalist ones, opposition also arose here but was duly repressed and could only exist underground or in exile. The left–right dichotomies that underpinned the Cold War and much of nineteenth and twentieth century history in the global north thus became problematic, as the growth orientation of both communism and capitalism and its willingness to operate under dictatorships increasingly looked alike, while those in favor of an embedded liberal-democratic capitalism or a democratic communism looked in vain for ways to overcome the thinking in Cold War bloc logics. Especially in Western Europe an embedded capitalism in the sense of Karl Polanyi (1944) emerged after the end of the Cold War, and the memory landscapes produced by the European Union have, at different times to a greater or lesser extent, been closely aligned to attempts to justify an embedded capitalism in contrast to a more market-radical capitalism as well as in contrast to state communism and the kind of turbo-capitalist communism that has been emerging in China over the last fifty years. However, the memoryscapes developed to underpin the vision of various alternative third ways to the logics of both capitalism and communism remain understudied to date.

The power relationships underpinning economic memory narratives crucially involve state power, as states held manifold financial, institutional and organizational resources to influence memoryscapes, not just in the legitimation and delegitimation of capitalism, but also in the fostering of nationalism. Thus, it is no surprise that the nation state figures prominently in the economy/memory nexus that the contributions to this volume investigate. The memory of economic crises, systemic economic transformations, and deindustrialization are all intimately connected with national memory landscapes. However, many of the chapters assembled here also stress that powerful national memoryscapes invariably interacted with a transnational memory, as economic crises, systemic economic transformation, deindustrialization and the transformation of national economies took place in a transnational and often global frame that invariably impacted on the national. It is nevertheless intriguing how this international dimension was often nationalized in a way that the transnational disappeared behind the foregrounding of the national dimensions and, to this day, needs to be recovered by memory scholars (De Cesari and Rigney 2014).

Another pattern that emerges strongly from the pages of this volume has to do with the strong link of the economy/memory nexus with attempts to learn lessons from economic crises, be they stock market crashes, hunger crises or deindustrialization crises. This mantra of the need to learn lessons relates strongly to the contemporary politicization of memory landscapes that we already observed above. Thus, the rust belt of the United States has become one of the most powerful reference points for those memoryscapes seeking alternative ways out of deindustrialization than the market-radical one that produced the rust belt in the first instance. In much of post-communist Eastern Europe communism has become the negative foil against which alternative economic memoryscapes are being developed and often packed once again in national garb. The developing memory of entrepreneurship in Ukraine as counter-memory to the Soviet vilification of industrialists is a good example of this, as is the ruthless forgetting of industrial pasts in both Lithuania and Armenia. Going further back in time, memories of the forced opening of Japan to the West formed a key memory site for the modernization and westernization of Japan. The development of Japan's heavy industry, in particular, formed the precondition for the powerful build-up of its industrial infrastructure and its army allowing the country against the odds to avoid colonization by the West—a fate that its once far mightier neighbor China could not entirely avoid.

3 Which Concepts of Memory in Order to Study Economic Memory Narratives?

Looking at the various concepts of memory that are being employed by the different authors in this volume we can observe a wide range of them. The contrast between an active, 'hot' memory and an archive memory is usefully applied, when it comes to discussing why some economic events and processes have been remembered so well, while others continue to be silenced (Assmann 2008a). The useful distinction between a 'communicative memory' of those living human beings who can still remember events that occurred during their lifetime, and a 'cultural memory' in the form of museums, monuments, novels and many other tangible and intangible forms of cultural heritage that talk of things which occurred in the more distant past (Assmann 2008b) is also applied frequently to the memory/economy nexus. Furthermore, several of the preceding chapters have made good use of the idea of the 'fluidity of memory' and of 'travelling memory' often referenced back to Astrid Erll's work (Erll 2014). Some contributions relate memory to diverse narrative patterns (Wertsch 2002), and to concepts of multi-directional memory associated with the work of Michael Rothberg, who emphasized how memorial discourses and practices of different memorial landscapes travel across space and time (Rothberg 2009).

Conceptually, memory studies went from a strong emphasis on national memory that underpinned the multitude of national realms of memory projects from the 1980s onwards (Berger and Seiffert 2014) to emphasizing the importance of transnational memory landscapes (De Cesari and Rigney 2014). Aleida Assmann has argued that memory scholars ignore the national memory concepts at their own peril (Assmann 2011). This tension between the national and the transnational memoryscapes is also visible in the chapters assembled here. Rigney's work on mediation and mobilization underlines, however, that any simple return to national frames of memory will not do justice to the manifold transnational entanglements that constitute different spatial memoryscapes (Erll et al. 2024).

Furthermore, there is much evidence here of 'memory activism'—a concept championed and popularized by Yifat Gutman and Jenny Wüstenberg (Gutman and Wüstenberg 2023). It emphasizes the agency of those involved in constructing memoryscapes. These, in turn, are invariably the basis of contested memory landscapes. Much of that contestation is about the political relevance of particular memories. Here the concept of 'agonistic memory', originally championed by Anna Cento Bull and Hans Lauge Hansen (Bull and Hansen 2016), comes to the fore as a means to repoliticize memory discourses and contribute to the re-legitimation of voices previously excluded from either antagonistic or cosmopolitan memory discourses. Ideas of mnemonic pluralism fit well here as do 'invention of tradition' approaches that have had such a strong impact on nationalism studies (Hobsbawm and Ranger 1992). Insofar as many economy-related processes are slow in registering historical change, investigations into the economy/memory nexus can also make good use of the concept of 'slow memory' (Wüstenberg 2023). Finally, several of the contributions in this volume also highlight, how useful the concept of 'nostalgia' can be in understanding the 'memory/economy' nexus (Boym 2001). There are, of course, a great variety of concepts coming out of memory studies that are potentially relevant. Overall, the chapters in this volume collectively underline how diverse concepts coming from memory studies can be usefully applied to the memory/economy nexus. Its study can be framed through these concepts which also help to understand the empirical evidence assembled through the interpretation of cultural memory or the creation of new archives of oral history manifesting the existence of powerful 'communicative' forms of memory.

4 Outlook

Taken together, the contributions to this volume thus speak to the salience of the economic realm for the study of collective memory through a variety of different perspectives and approaches, and they also point to the importance of economic memory in terms of its impact on subsequent political agendas and public policies. As such, our volume clearly demonstrates the fruitfulness of economy-focused collective memory research and provides a mapping of this emerging field of studies. As befits such an initial exploration, our volume also highlights the conceptual and empirical potential to inspire more in-depth research in the future, and this concluding chapter thus ends with a series of reflections on such a future research agenda, building on themes developed in individual chapters, as well as pointing to other issues not squarely tackled by our contributors.

In one way or another, all case studies explored in this volume invite further research that places them in a wider comparative and transnational context. This is perhaps most obvious in the case of memory narratives of cyclical crises—while the chapters by Corporaal, and by Cassis and Telesca, explore the memory of famines and of financial crises mostly through a European/transatlantic lens, they are pieces to be integrated into a global perspective that addresses comparisons across world regions, as well as the analysis of transnational mnemonic entanglements (on famine memory see e.g., de Waal 2024). The same is true for Odanaka's study of Japanese nineteenth century economic victimization narratives, which could be compared to other cases such as China or India (Chatterjee Miller 2013), and the 'Golden Age' narratives explored by Fetzer; the latter, as evident in 'Make America Great Again' Trumpism in the United States (Campbell 2018) or 'Chinese Dream' narratives harking back to a past China-centered world order (Callahan 2013), address a theme that resonates far beyond contemporary Germany and Europe.

From a very different perspective, the collective memory of individual entrepreneurship, explored in the contributions by Vodotyka and Kühschelm, also provides great potential for further research, not least, as highlighted in both chapters, because of the frequent intersection between local, national and transnational memory levels. For example, a study of memory narratives of well-known global business tycoons like Henry Ford, building on available work on specific countries (Barndt 2007; Eifert 2009), would provide an exemplary case to examine dynamics of transnational 'travelling memory' (Erll 2011) across borders. Similar questions could be asked in relation to various socially responsible entrepreneurs—from Robert Bosch to Anita Roddick (Jones 2023)—or the memory of legendary events and places associated with innovative entrepreneurship (see Lippmann and Aldrich 2016). Moving away from business leaders, but still addressing the level of individual personalities, it would also be worthwhile to study the 'travelling memory' of famous economic thinkers; the German economist Friedrich List whose economic nationalist concepts spread across several continents (Suesse 2023), would be a case in point.

Beyond themes addressed by contributors to this volume, a range of further avenues for future research exist, of which the analysis of transnational economic networks and institutions merits particular attention. This can build on scattered earlier work on the mythical significance of the 1944 Bretton Woods agreements (James 2011) and on the memory politics of the Gold Standard (Kessler 2009), as well as on scholarship concerned with liberal economic elite networks (Bilderberg Group, Mont Pelerin Society) and their 'pilgrimage' places, such as the World Economic Forum in Davos (Garsten and Sörbom 2018). Moreover, such a research agenda should include the collective memory of anti-(or alter-) globalization movements (e.g., Daphi 2017) and their *lieux de mémoire*, such as the 1999 World Trade Organization meeting in Seattle (Brecher and Moodliar 2020).

In a more regional European perspective, one is struck by the marginal importance attributed to the economic realm in the current European

Union memory debates (e.g., Sierp 2023), notwithstanding the crucial linkage between economic and broader political goals, associated with mnemonic lessons from past war and conflict, which had characterized the history of European integration since the launch of the Coal and Steel Community in the early 1950s. Future researchers await not just the task to 'bring the economy back in', but, perhaps still more importantly, to explore the dynamics through which this mnemonic marginalization of the economy occurred, from the culture-dominated focus of the contemporary 'memory boom', to generational change (Verovsek 2014) and EU leaders' own role (e.g., Jacques Delors' mantra that 'one cannot fall in love with a Single Market'). Particular attention ought to be paid to the mnemonic dimension of monetary integration, not least because, as indicated by research on diverging collective memories of the debt crisis of the early 2010s (Arnemann et al. 2021), the European common currency has now become a significant mnemonic 'vector' in its own right.

Although not directly addressed in contributions to this volume, further work on economic redress for past injustices and human rights abuses will also constitute an important part of future research agendas. As briefly highlighted in the introduction, such work can build on an already significant body of scholarship addressing the theme of economic redress in relation to a variety of historical and regional contexts—from the debates about compensation for victims of Nazi and World War Two crimes, to the role of economic redress in processes of coming to terms with the dark legacies of slavery and colonialism (Barkan 2001; Araujo 2020; Filipkovski and Wawrzyniak 2023). Future work should go still further in the transnational analysis of how redress and reparations debates have (or have not) 'travelled' from one context to another; in this endeavor, more attention should be paid to non-Western cases of redress debates. Moreover, scholars concerned with the relationship between collective memory and economic redress have an important contribution to make to ongoing legal and international relations controversies connected to notions of global redistributive justice (Young 2006; Lu 2018): Can and should past injustices be partially remedied through global institutions, for example through reforms of the global governance of trade and migration (e.g., Goldstone 2024)?

Here, again, the relevance of the study of the relationship between collective memory and the economy stands out in stark terms. We hope this book has set out an agenda that will inspire much further research to deepen our understanding of this relationship.

References

Araujo, L. 2020. *Slavery in the Age of Memory: Engaging the Past*. London: Bloomsbury.

Arnemann, Laura, Kai Konrad, and Niklas Potrafke. 2021. Collective memories on the 2010 European debt crisis. *European Union Politics* 22 (4): 762–784.

Assmann, Aleida. 2008a. Canon and archive. In *Cultural Memory Studies. An International and Interdisciplinary Handbook*, ed. Astrid Erll and Ansgar Nünning, 97–107. Berlin: De Gruyter.

Assmann, Jan. 2008b. Communicative and cultural memory. In *Cultural Memory Studies. An International and Interdisciplinary Handbook*, ed. Astrid Erll and Ansgar Nünning, 109–118. Berlin: De Gruyter.

Assmann, Aleida. 2011. *Der lange Schatten der Vergangenheit. Erinnerungskultur und Geschichtspolitik*. Munich: C.H. Beck.

Barkan, Elazar. 2001. *The Guilt of Nations: Restitution and Negotiating Historical Injustices*. Baltimore: Johns Hopkins University Press.

Barndt, Kerstin. 2007. Fordist nostalgia: History and experience at the Henry Ford. *Rethinking History: The Journal of Theory and Practice* 11 (3): 379–410.

Berger, S., and J. Seiffert, eds. 2014. *Erinnerungsorte: Chancen, Grenzen und Perspektiven eines Erfolgskonzeptes in den Kulturwissenschaften*. Essen: Klartext.

Boym, S. 2001. *The Future of Nostalgia*. New York: Basic Books.

Brecher, Jeremy, and Suren Moodliar. 2020. Seattle 1999: Creating a Two-Sided Batttle. *Socialism and Democracy* 34 (1): 228–241.

Bull, Anna Cento, and Hans Lauge Hansen. 2016. On Agonistic Memory. *Memory Studies* 9 (4): 390–404.

Callahan, William A. 2013. *China Dreams: Twenty Visions for the Future*. Oxford: Oxford University Press.

Campbell, John. 2018. *American Discontent: The Rise of Donald Trump and the Decline of the Golden Age*. Oxford: Oxford University Press.

Chatterjee Miller, Masnjari. 2013. *Wronged by Empire: Post-imperial Ideology and Foreign Policy in India and China*. Stanford: Stanford University Press.

Daphi, Priska. 2017. *Becoming a Movement: Identity, Narrative and Memory in the European Global Justice Movement*. London: Rowman and Littlefield.

De Cesari, Chiara, and Ann Rigney, eds. 2014. *Transnational Memory: Circulation, Articulation, Scales*. New York: De Gruyter.

De Waal, Alex. 2024. Memory and the social meanings of famine. *Third World Quarterly* 24 (2): 439–443.

Eifert, Christiane. 2009. Antisemit und Autokönig. Henry Fords Autobiographie und ihre deutsche Rezeption in den 1920er Jahren. *Zeithistorische Forschungen/Studies in Contemporary History* 6: 209–229.

Erll, Astrid. 2011. Travelling memory. *Parallax* 17 (4): 4–18.

Erll, Astrid. 2014. From 'District Six' to District 9 and back: The plurimedial production of travelling schemata. In *Transnational Memory: Circulation, Articulation, Scales*, ed. Chiara de Cesari and Ann Rigney, 29–50. Berlin: De Gruyter.

Erll, Astrid, Susanne Knittel, and Jenny Wüstenberg, eds. 2024. *Dynamics, Mediation, Mobilization: Doing Memory Studies with Ann Rigney*. New York: De Gruyter.

Filipkovski, Piotr, and Joanna Wawrzyniak. 2023. Redress economies. In *The Routledge Handbook on Memory Activism*, ed. Yifat Gutman and Jenny Wüstenberg. New York: Routledge.

Garsten, Christina, and Adrienne Sörbom, eds. 2018. *Discreet Power: How the World Economic Forum Shapes Market Agendas*. Stanford: Stanford University Press.

Goldstone, Zara. 2024. Migration as reparation for colonialism. *Res Publica* 30: 763–781.

Gutman, Y., and J. Wüstenberg, eds. 2023. *The Routledge Handbook of Memory Activism*. London: Routledge.

Hobsbawm, Eric, and Terence Ranger, eds. 1992. *The Invention of Tradition*. Cambridge: Cambridge University Press.

James, Harold. 2011. The multiple contexts of Bretton Woods. *Past & Present* 210 (6): 290–308.

Jones, Geoffrey. 2023. *Deeply Responsible Business: A Global History of Value-Driven Leadership*. Cambridge, MA: Harvard University Press.

Kessler, Oliver. 2009. Finance as transnational space and the memory of the gold standard. In *Transnational Spaces: Agents, Structures, Encounters*, ed. Matthias Albert, et al., 185–211. Frankfurt: Campus.

Lim, Jie-Hyun. 2025. *Victimhood Nationalism: History and Memory in a Global Age*. New York: Columbia University Press.

Lippmann, Stephen, and Howard E. Aldrich. 2016. A rolling stone gathers momentum: Generational units, collective memory, and entrepreneurship. *Academy of Management Review* 41 (4): 658–675.

Lu, Catherine. 2018. Responsibility, structural injustice, and structural transformation. *Ethics & Global Politics* 11 (1): 42–57.

Niven, Bill, ed. 2006. *Germans as Victims. Remembering the Past in Contemporary Germany*. Basingstoke: Palgrave MacMillan.

Polanyi, Karl. 1944. *The Great Transformation: The Political and Economic Origins of Our Time*. New York: Farrar and Reinhardt.

Rothberg, Michael. 2009. *Multi-directional Memory: Remembering the Holocaust in the Age of Decolonization*. Stanford: Stanford University Press.

Sierp, Aline. 2023. Europeanising memory: The European Union's politics of memory. In *Handbook on the Politics of Memory*, ed. Maria Mälksoo, 81–94. Cheltenham: Edward Elgar.

Suesse, Marvin. 2023. *The Nationalist Dilemma: A Global History of Economic Nationalism 1776-present*. Cambridge: Cambridge University Press.
Verovsek, Peter. 2014. Memory and the Euro-crisis of leadership: The effects of generational change in Germany and the EU. *Constellations* 21 (2): 239–248.
Wertsch, James. 2002. *Voices of Collective Remembering*. Cambridge: Cambridge University Press.
White, Hayden. 2014. *The Practical Past*. Evanston/Illinois: Northwestern University Press.
Wüstenberg, Jenny. 2023. Towards a slow memory studies. In *Critical Memory Studies: New Approaches*, ed. Brett A. Kaplan, 87–109. London: Bloomsbury.
Young, Iris Marion. 2006. Responsibility and global justice: A social connection model. *Social Philosophy and Policy* 23 (1): 102–130.

Kolibri 360 GmbH
Ferdinand-Jühlke-Straße 7
99095 Erfurt, Deutschland
produktsicherheit@kolibri360.de